REVELATION RIDDLE

REVELATION RIDDLE

David Pawson

Anchor Recordings

Copyright © 2025 David Pawson Ministry CIO

The right of David Pawson to be identified as author of this Work has been asserted by him in accordance with the Copyright, Designs and Patents Act 1988.

This edition published in Great Britain in 2025 by Anchor which is a trading name of David Pawson Publishing Ltd, Synegis House, 21 Crockhamwell Road, Woodley, Reading RG5 3LE.

No part of this publication may be reproduced or transmitted in any form or by any means, electronic or mechanical, including photocopy, recording or any information storage and retrieval system, without prior permission in writing from the publisher. Nor be otherwise circulated in any form of binding or cover other than that in which it is published and without a similar condition being imposed on the subsequent purchaser.

Unless otherwise indicated, Scripture quotations taken from the Holy Bible, New International Version copyright © 1973, 1978, 1984, By International Bible Society and the New King James Version®. Copyright © 1982 by Thomas Nelson. Used by permission. All rights reserved

For more of David Pawson's teaching, please visit www.davidpawson.org

For further information email contact@davidpawson.net

ISBN 978-1-917360-23-4

Printed by Ingram Spark

Contents

1:	How Was it Written?	7
2:	Why Was it Written?	37
3:	This is Your Life	61
4:	How Has the Book Been Interpreted?	85
5:	Big Trouble	105
6:	Will Christians Escape by Secret Rapture?	135
7:	Hallelujah Chorus	157
8:	Will Christ Ever Reign on Earth?	185
9:	Happily Ever After	211
10:	Can Believers Lose Their Inheritance?	237

Chapter 1

HOW WAS IT WRITTEN?

We are going to study the strangest book in the New Testament, and you can divide Christians very neatly into two groups. There is one group of Christians that you cannot get into the book of Revelation, and another group that you cannot get out of the book of Revelation. It seems you are either frightened by it or fanatical about it, and I want to try and strike the balance. But I am sharing these insights because I believe it is probably the most important book in the New Testament for the Church to be studying right now for the very practical purpose for which it was written, and we shall come to that.

It is a very different book from every other book in the New Testament; that puts many people off. It is also a difficult book for many when they first read it. How many Christians have read it through at some time in their Christian life? If you have not done so, may I urge you to do so? It will enable you to get the most out of the present book. The book of Revelation is full of bizarre symbols and frightening predictions. Many people, having read it through, close it up and do not go back to it. Yet I want to show you how important it is. Opinion about this book has varied enormously, and I want to look at human opinion about it, then the devil's opinion about it, then God's opinion about it.

Human opinion is divided between very negative comments and very positive comments. Here are some of the negative ones. Somebody has said that in the book of Revelation, there are as many riddles as there are words. That is enough to put anybody off. Another person said, "It either finds you mad or it leaves you mad." We will see which one it does after reaching the end of this study. Somebody else said, "It's a haphazard accumulation of weird symbols." So, people have gone on making very negative comments. One of the unfortunate things is that the Protestant Reformers, 350 years ago, had a very poor opinion of this book of the New Testament and came to the conclusion that it should not be there at all.

Martin Luther said, "It is neither apostolic nor prophetic." He said, "Everyone thinks of this book whatever his own spirit suggests." In other words, people read into the book whatever they want to find there rather than reading out of the book what is already there. He said, "There are many nobler books to be retained." He said, "My spirit cannot acquiesce in this book." So, for Martin Luther, this book was not part of God's Word. I am afraid that John Calvin held the same opinion. He wrote commentaries on every book of the New Testament apart from this one. So, Calvin preached the whole New Testament with the exception of this book, and he never wrote on it. Another prominent reformer of those days was a man called Ulrich Zwingli and he simply said, "It is not a book of the Bible," and so he did not treat it as part of God's Word either.

The difficulty is that most Protestant churches in Europe, and the missionary societies which are spun from them have inherited this suspicion about this book and this tendency not to look at it and not to preach it and not to study it, and so it is against that rather negative background that we are looking at it. But it is important to note that when the canon, as we call it, of Scripture, the complete standard of God's Word, was finally agreed in the Church, Revelation was a part of it, and it is part of God's Word to us.

The positive comments are quite marvellous. One man said, "It's the only masterpiece of pure art in the whole New Testament." It is a book of art; it is a book of music; it is a book of pictures; it is a very artsy book. If you do not appreciate art, then that could be a handicap in understanding this book because it very much appeals to sight and sound. Another person said, "It is beautiful beyond description." Somebody else said, "It's infinitely worthwhile wrestling with it until it yields its blessings to you." What a contrast between the negative and the positive comments I have just given you!

Let us look at Satan's opinion of this book, and I know what he thinks of it. He hates it. He really does, because there is more about Satan in this book than in any other book in the Bible; it is a revelation of the devil as well as the revelation of Jesus Christ. He hates being shown up for what he is, and, above all, he hates being in the opening chapters of the Bible and the closing chapters of the Bible. He hates the first few pages and the last few pages in this book. Because in the first few pages, we are told how he got hold of this world and how he got his way in, and in the last few pages, we are told how he is going to be kicked out of the world, and he does not want you to know either; he just wants you to remain ignorant of his devices.

Indeed, years ago, I made a tape on Revelation 20 in which there was a seven-minute section where I described the downfall of Satan, and that tape has been interfered with more than any other tape we have sent out. It has gone out in perfect condition, and by the time it has got to the recipient, it has been interfered with electronically, either by being wiped out or another voice has come on it, or something has spoiled that section where I describe Satan's downfall.

So, I just want you to bear this in mind. Pray that Satan will not get a hold of us while we study this book, because he has a direct interest in confusing you. He wants to persuade you that it is so complicated that you will never understand it. He wants you to treat it as myth or as legend, as he wants you to treat Genesis as myth or legend. So, we are in a spiritual battlefield when we study this book. It is all about the battle between Satan and God. It reveals his awful character and his frustration and anger at the very end of history when he knows his days are numbered.

What is God's opinion of this book? Now, this is very different. God takes this book very seriously. It is the only book in the whole Bible to which God has attached a special blessing and a special curse. Well, that makes it very significant to God, and therefore to us. The special blessing he has put on this book is for anyone who reads the book aloud. I underline the word "aloud". Now, you may read it aloud to someone else, or you may read it aloud to yourself, but it is a book to be read aloud.

Of course, originally addressed to the seven churches of Asia, it would have been read aloud to those churches, and God says, "Blessed is he who reads this book aloud." It is a great thing to read the Bible aloud, even to yourself, and not just to let your eyes go along the lines, because you tend then to pay more attention to how you read, and your voice will change, and your emotions will change as you read it aloud.

What, then, is the curse that God has put on this book? Well, the curse is on anyone who tampers with it. It is right at the end of the book, and it says, and if anyone takes away anything from this book, God will take away his place in the new Heaven and in the new earth and from the tree of life. That is pretty serious. It means that anybody who takes away from this book could lose their future salvation. That is a strong curse. Just before that, it says, "If anyone adds to these things, God will add to him all the trouble and plagues and disasters mentioned in the book to that person."

Now, that is pretty serious. It means we must take the whole book as it is and not try and cut it up or cut things out of it or put our own things into it, and that makes me tremble at teaching this book. I must not take anything from it; I must not add anything to it of mine; I must help you to understand the book as it is. That is a solemn responsibility. If you are going to teach it to others, you will be passing on what you learn in the present book, and therefore, you must treat this with seriousness, with respect, with reverence and awe.

Now, it is different from all of the other books in the New Testament in many ways. In content, as we shall see, it covers things that no other book covers, but also in its origin, and I want to begin with that. How did it come to be written? It has the strangest history behind it. Let us start with the writer. He says, "I, John", and he does not say anything more about himself than that; "I, John". Therefore, we must assume straight away that he is a man well enough known throughout the churches just to call himself John. He does not say John this or John that or John the other, just "I, John", and he assumes that everyone who reads this book will know perfectly well which John it is.

Of course, there were many Johns, even in the New Testament, but there is one John who qualifies, obviously, and that is the beloved disciple who was closest to Jesus, from whom we already have four other books in the New Testament. We have the Gospel of John and we have the three letters of John. Yet this book is so different that scholars have argued that it cannot have been written by the same person. They have tried to find some other John, somewhere else, who was also well known. From a rather obscure reference in a letter written by a bishop of the first century called Ignatius, they have said there was an elder in the early church in Ephesus called John, and it must be him. So, you will find in some of the Bible commentaries and handbooks this theory that it was not the Apostle John who wrote this book.

I believe it was, but I want to give you an explanation as to why it is so different from his Gospel and from his letters. It is not totally different. The vocabulary is the same. For example, there are only two books in the New Testament that call Jesus the Logos or the Word of God. One is John's Gospel and the other is the book of Revelation, and there are a number of other things like that which the two have in common. Words like "witness", "glory", and "life" are characteristic of John's Gospel and the book of Revelation.

The grammar is very similar, but the differences are also there.

I have told you about the difference in content already. John here is writing about things that he never wrote about in his Gospel or in his letters. Moreover, the style is quite different. John's Gospel and his letters are written with very good grammar, good Greek—for they were written in Greek—and the style is very good. But in this book, the grammar is very bad, and it is a little difficult to understand why the same man could write so badly in this book when he wrote so well in the other books he wrote. That is another thing that makes the scholars say, "It can't have been the same man," and so they postulate another John, John the Elder, instead of John the Apostle.

There is very slender evidence for this other John, and I believe the scholars have seized on that stray reference to try and explain away the difference. But I can explain it in another way. Every other book that John wrote, he intended to write, decided to write, and thought about what to write before he wrote it. Therefore, in other books, there is a strong impression of his character, of his temperament, of his outlook, of his experience. John, as a person comes through the other books, but he does not come through this book as a person because he did not decide to write it. He did not say, I must write to the seven churches of Asia; I must write a book to them; I must write about the future to them. He did not decide that at all.

Quite suddenly, one morning, John had a series of words and pictures from God, and in visual and verbal form, he saw things and he heard things that he had never seen or heard before. He was told to write them down while he saw them and while he heard them. It was as if someone sent you to the cinema and said, "Write down whatever you see on the screen, whatever you hear the actor saying." You would be scribbling as fast as you could, and I guarantee you would not be producing very good grammar in your notes if you were trying to keep up, and to write down everything that you heard said. You would be scribbling it down, and later you would look at it and say, "Did I write that?" Now, if

I asked you to write a paper for me then you would think about it and you would write it properly, but writing things down at the time you see or hear them, that makes it more difficult and your style goes, your handwriting probably changes, and it is more scribbly than it would be if you were writing a letter to me.

Well, that is what happened to John, and one of the key words in the book of Revelation is "Write". "What you see, write in a book"; "Write the things which you have seen"—write, write, write,—and it occurs so often that you get a picture of poor John, sort of with his mouth open and his eyes out on stalks while he sees these astonishing things in the future that are going to happen and God has to prompt him—You're not writing John! Write it down, I'm not just showing you I want you to tell other people about what you've seen. He is told to write it down "for these words are trustworthy and true". Write it down, write it down, write it down!

In fact, if I put a ring around each "Write", it would be six times on the first page. The poor chap is overwhelmed with visions and voices because the revelation came to him in two forms; it came to his eyes and it came to his ears, and so he keeps using the verbs, "I saw" and "I heard". All he did was write down as quickly as he could what he heard. When you consider that the whole thing came in just an hour or two, you can imagine he needed healing for his wrists at the end. But he was writing down as fast as he could, and it is no wonder that his grammar went to pieces, and I am sure that his writing was hopeless, but he got it down.

That raises a question: Having made all his notes, why didn't he write it out properly afterwards? Well, if you had just been told of the consequences of altering or taking away from it, then you would not have dared to alter the notes either. So, we have it in this rather unfinished form. There are whole sentences that never finish. There are sentences without verbs in them and you just have to translate it as best you can.

This means that this is probably the only book in the New

Testament that was, in a sense, dictated by God. With all the other books, God inspired the writers to think about what they wrote, and God used their personalities to impress on what they wrote; the character of Paul, the character of Peter, and it comes out in their books. The character of John does not come out in this book because it is virtually being dictated to him by God. There is only one other part of the Bible that has the same hallmarks as coming from God, and that is Genesis chapter 1; all the rest show signs of a human sort and human intention.

Now you see, for example, when he wrote a letter, Paul did not use his own handwriting because of his eyesight; he always wrote in huge letters. So, he always got somebody else to write for him, and he would dictate a letter to the equivalent of a shorthand typist; they called them amanuenses in those days— letter writers. So, Paul would say to Silas, "Silas, I want to write to someone. Take this letter down for me," and he would dictate it. He dictated Romans, for example, to a secretary called Tertius.

So, Paul would dictate the letters to a secretary who wrote them down, and Paul might put his signature at the end. Or he might say, as he did in Galatians, "I'm writing this last bit in my own hand. Look what large letters I write with." So, everything else was dictated by a human being to a human being, but when you get to Revelation, John was simply the amanuensis, he was the secretary who was just writing down what he saw and heard as best he could, and that is how we got it.

Now, to me, that explains everything about the difference in style and content and grammar—everything that is different in the book of Revelation. There is no need to find another John. This is John doing something he had never done before. It is John seeing visions and hearing voices and trying to write down as quickly as he could what he saw and heard. Notice the words: "I saw"; "I heard"; "I saw"; "I heard". John says right from the first chapter, "I heard a loud voice behind me and I turned to see who was speaking to me and I saw." He hears things, he sees things, and he writes them down, and, of course, that makes the book quite different from every other.

So, who is the author of this book? Not John. Well then, who gave him the visions and the voices? The answer is angels did. But then you ask the question, "Who gave the angels what they gave John?" The answer is the Holy Spirit gave it to the angels to give to John. Then you ask, "Well, who gave it to the Holy Spirit to give to the angels to give to John?" The answer is Jesus himself gave it to the Spirit, who gave it to the angels, who gave it to John. Then you ask, "Well, who gave it to Jesus?" You finally get back to the real author. In the first few verses, it says, "This is the revelation of Jesus Christ, which God gave him". So actually, the author of this book is God himself, and therefore, to understand it, we have to get into the mind of the author.

Now, with other books in the New Testament, you try to get into the mind of Peter or Paul or John. But with this book that is of no use. Getting into the mind of John is not going to help us; we have got to get right back to the ultimate source. What was in the mind of God that he should show all this to Jesus, that Jesus would show it all to the Spirit, that the Spirit should show it all to the angels, that the angels should show it all to John? Now, because John realised that it was God who was behind it all, he made a mistake twice of worshipping the angel who was giving it to him. He was so impressed with the fact that all this was coming from God that he mistook the angel for God, and twice the angel had to say, "Don't worship me, I'm just a servant like you are."

So, it shows how unusual the whole origin of this book really was. It is called "The Revelation of Jesus Christ", but it is the revelation of Jesus which God gave him and which is being shown through angels to John. Now, we are not used to angels, so we do not think of them much. But every time we worship God, the angels are there, and it rather looks as if every church in Asia had an angel looking after it. It rather looks as if angels not only told John what to write, but then took what was written and delivered it to the churches, because John was in prison at this time. He was in prison on an island called Patmos, which was the Robben Island or the Alcatraz of those days, where political prisoners were completely shut off from people. So, he had no means of delivering the letters he wrote to the seven churches. Therefore, the letters are addressed to the angels of that church. Well, it could be that there is an angel in your church.

Does it strike you that there is an angel looking after your church, wherever it is? Well, this book is full of angels; it is full of supernatural things, and that again makes it a bit strange to us. So that is the real reason why it is very different from the other books. Its origin is directly in God, and it is God who reveals things that Jesus then reveals, that the Holy Spirit then reveals, that the angels reveal, that John writes down. So, it is a rather lengthy process, and we have the end product in a man's feverish scribbling of what he heard and saw.

Now, the result of all that is a very special kind of literature. We all know what letters are, and we know what history books are. The Bible is full of different kinds of books. It is not one book, the Bible, it is many books. The word "bible" is actually the word *biblia*, which is a plural word, and it means library. So, this is not a book. It is a library of books, and there are different kinds of books. There are poetry books and books of proverbs, and there are song books, and there are history books, and there are prophecy books, and there are apocalyptic books. That is the kind of literature we are dealing with, apocalyptic. In fact, the very first word in this book that we are studying is *apokalupsis,* from which we get our word apocalyptic.

Now, in the world's use of that word, it means doom and disaster, but in the Bible's use of the word, it does not mean that. It may include doom and disaster—in fact it will—but that is not what the word means. But I see it in the newspapers now a lot, and when they say, "There's an apocalyptic event happening," they mean there is a pretty big crisis or disaster. Hollywood is using the word "apocalypse" now in the titles of their films, but they mean the end of the world sort of thing.

It does cover that, but it is not what it means. It means to draw the curtain aside and reveal what is beyond; to show you things that you could not see until the curtain was drawn aside. It is a wonderful word. It means to go beyond the veil and to see things that you have not seen before, and especially apocalyptic books reveal what human beings cannot see for themselves. One of the biggest things we cannot see as human beings is the future. So apocalyptic books invariably draw the veil aside from the future and show us what is going to happen in the world. Now, nobody else can do that; they might guess, but they cannot do it.

There is another dimension that we cannot see. We cannot see what is happening up in heaven. We can see what is happening down on earth, but we cannot see either what is happening up in heaven or what is happening in the future. Now, apocalyptic books draw the curtain back from both of those two dimensions: the dimension in space where we can only see what is happening down here and not up there, and the dimension in time where we can only see what is happening in the past and the present, but we cannot see the future.

Apocalyptic history covers a very much larger field than normal history books.

In diagram 1 *(see page 18)*, there are two circles with one smaller circle inside the larger circle. Let us take the smaller circle first. That circle includes the earth and all that happens down here. It includes everything that has happened from the past through to the present. All human history books are limited to that smaller circle. Every book that has ever been written, every book in the history section of a library, even a university library, can only cover what has happened from the past to the present and what has happened down here on earth, because the rest has been invisible to us. We cannot see what is happening up in heaven, and we cannot see what is happening in the future.

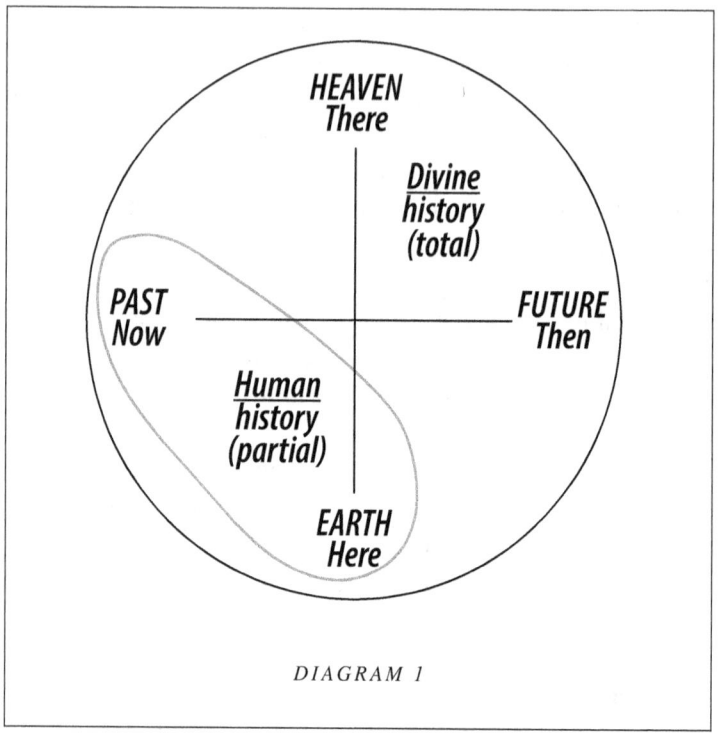

DIAGRAM 1

But God can see all that. God knows the future as well as the past; he knows the end from the beginning. God knows what is happening up in heaven as well as down here. Therefore, when God writes a history book, he writes on a much larger scale than any historian could ever write. He includes the future as well as the present and the past, and he includes what happens up in heaven as well as what happens down on earth. He knows how all these things relate to each other. In other words, things can happen in heaven which affect what is happening on earth. I give you one example from Revelation chapter 12, where it begins by saying, "And there was war in heaven," and the battle was between two angels: a good one and a bad one. The good one was Michael, and the bad one was Satan, for he is simply an angel who is in rebellion against God. That battle is won by Michael, and Satan is thrown out of heaven and thrown down to earth, and is so mad at losing the battle that he wreaks havoc down here on earth.

Now you see, what it is saying is that behind the scenes, the real cause of many crises on earth is actually something happening in the heavenly places; principalities and powers are up there, and we suffer the overspill of what they do. Now, I do not know whether you have ever been in a television studio, but it is remarkable. You see far more than you see on the screen at home, and you realise how much is going on behind the scenes.

For example, when I was last in a television studio, I noticed that there was a man who held up a notice saying, "Applause", and another man was miming clapping, and everybody clapped. Or it was "Laugh" or "Shout" or the sound "Oh." All this was going on, and the cameraman was moving around. All sorts of things were happening in the studio that were not on the screen, and people watching the screen did not realise all that was happening behind the scenes to make that programme. Now, apocalypses draw back the curtain and help you to see what is causing it all and that what is happening down here is the result of what is happening up there.

Likewise, we can see in apocalyptic history the end product of what is happening now. We can see what is going to be the result of what is happening in our world now, and we can see where it is heading, and we can see why it is heading in that direction. We see the present in a different light when we know how it is going to end, and we can read back into the present and the past from the future, as we can read down into earth from heaven. Now, all this stretches your mind, of course, we are not used to reading history books like this. But you see, the book of Revelation covers the whole because it is divine history and divine history is historic, and it is in story form, but it gives you the end of the story.

Actually, the whole Bible is a romantic story. It is the story of God's search for a bride for his Son, and it ends like all good romances, and they get married and live happily ever after. I am quoting the book of Revelation right at the end. The Bible ends with a wedding, and Jesus gets married right at the end. Without the book of Revelation, you would not know how the courtship ended; you would not know if it ended happily or not. But we do know because God is telling us the whole story.

Now, although it is what we call "apocalyptic literature", that does not mean that it is totally different from every other kind of literature; it just means that we have extra dimensions. It is interesting that God in this book is repeatedly described as the God who is and who was and who is to come. Jesus is described as "the First and the Last," One who descended and One who ascended. So, between them, God and Jesus cover this whole picture. Jesus is the one who descended from heaven and ascended there again, so he knows all that story. He is also the First and the Last, so he knows all that story. So, Jesus knows all the dimensions of history and so does God, because God is the God who is and who was and who is to come, so that they can together reveal to us the whole of human history. That is why the Bible is a revelation of the whole of history from the beginning of our universe to the very end of it, and no other historian can write such a history; but here we have in the book of Revelation the end.

But it is not totally different. For example, the whole book is in the form of a letter, a letter addressed to the seven churches of Asia. Now, within the big letter, there are seven smaller ones. The big letter is addressed to seven churches, so there are seven smaller letters.

In the map of western Turkey *(see page 21)*, you see the Black Sea, the Bosphorus Strait, and the Aegean Sea. Then, off the western coast of Turkey are these little islands. This area was called Asia in the days of which we talk. Now, we think of Asia as the big continent with, further on, India and China, but this is called Asia. And there is the little island of Patmos. The whole book is in the form of a letter to seven churches that are on a circular road, and no doubt John had been preaching in all the

How Was it Written?

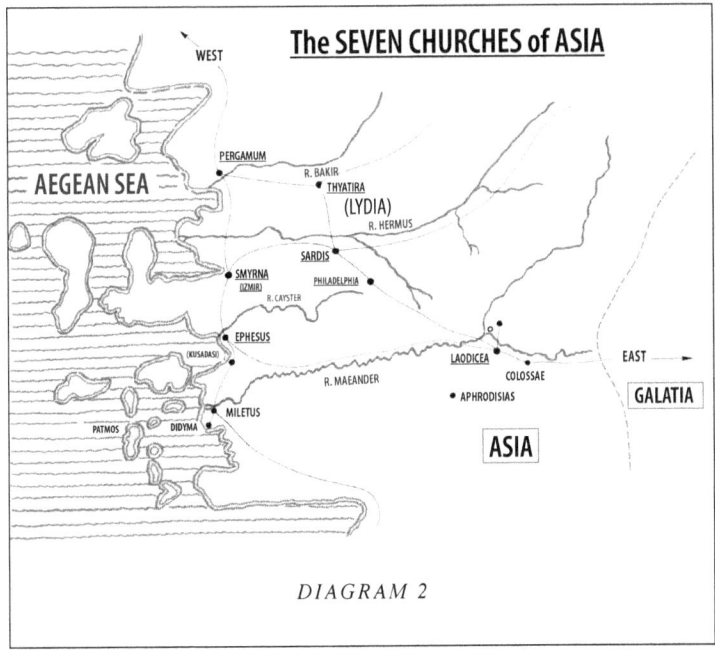

DIAGRAM 2

churches and would have walked around them from one to the other. Interestingly, they are always addressed in the right order, starting at Ephesus, where John lived with Mary, the mother of Jesus. You can actually see both their graves there to this day. John took Mary to live there in Ephesus, and Ephesus, Smyrna, Pergamum, Thyatira, Sardis, Philadelphia, and Laodicea are the seven churches to which he writes. Within the big letter are seven smaller letters.

So, it has something in common with the epistles of Paul, Peter and John. They are letters here, but it is as a whole called a prophecy, and altogether five times, mainly in the prologue and the epilogue at the beginning and end, it is called "This prophecy", and it is like many other books of prophecy in the Bible, but it is primarily in this apocalyptic history that it exists. It is an apocalyptic book as well as a letter and a prophecy.

If you are describing things to people that they cannot

understand, that they are not familiar with, how do you do it? You have to use symbols, you have to use pictures, and these symbols have to be something that people already understand. Whenever you describe something that a person has no experience of, you say, "Well, it's like this," and you use "this" as something they are already familiar with. That is how Jesus taught, "The kingdom of heaven is like this", it's like a woman looking for a lost coin. That is something that they knew. Now, of course, he is not actually describing the kingdom of heaven; he is using a symbol, or what we call an analogy: "It's like this."

So, for example, when we have the revelation of the New Jerusalem, it is like these precious jewels or the New Jerusalem is like a bride adorned for the wedding. It does not say the New Jerusalem is the bride, but like a bride adorned for her wedding. So, when you are describing the future and when you are describing heaven, you have to use symbols of earthly experience that people already have. It is the only way you can do it. I was thinking the other day about how I would describe for my grandfather satellite telephones or television— something so far beyond his experience. I would have to try and find something that he knew and I could say it was like that. It is the only way you can describe the unknown.

Therefore, apocalyptic literature is full of symbolism, and that again throws people a little bit, because clearly, you cannot take symbols literally. If you do, you get into problems. One of the questions that people debate is should you take the book of Revelation literally or symbolically? Well, the answer is nobody can take it all literally or all symbolically—nobody does. Some of it is literal, but a lot of it is symbolical, and I have never met anybody who took it all literally. It is full of symbols, and therefore, you have to be fairly careful about interpreting it. You must be sure that you understand the meaning of the symbol.

So, one of the problems with the book of Revelation is explaining the symbolism. The symbolism is not just in objects or pictures, it is also in numbers, and each number symbolises something. I am sure that you are aware that the number seven symbolises perfection or completion. It is a round number. For the same reason, the number six means to fall short of perfection and the number 666 means to fall very short of perfection.

We are going to have to unravel the symbols. There are four groups of symbols in the book of Revelation that we deal with. It is a mistake to treat them all literally; it is equally a mistake to treat them all allegorically and press the details too far. The first group of symbols are the obvious symbols; there are some symbols in the book of Revelation so obvious that nobody argues about them, and we start with those. For example, it says, "The lake of fire". That is a funny sort of symbol, isn't it? It literally is a sea on fire. Have you ever seen a sea on fire? Not unless there has been an oil spillage. An oil spillage could do it, but it literally says a sea on fire. Now, all of us know that that is a symbol of hell. Nobody argues about that because it is an obvious symbol.

Then there is the symbol of the Great White Throne. Well, we all know that is the throne of judgment, and nobody argues about that. It says that books are opened on the Day of Judgment. We all know what the books are a symbol of. God has kept a record of everything we have done and said and thought and felt. We know those books have a red cover and in gold lettering on the cover, "This is your life." But it is a symbol. Well, there are the obvious symbols.

Then, the second group of symbols consists of those that are explained in the book of Revelation. So, for example, in the first chapter, we are told about seven stars and seven lampstands and seven spirits, or seven lamps. What do these mean? We are told; it is explained. The seven stars are the angels, and the seven lampstands are the seven churches of Asia. So, we do not have any problem with those symbols because they are explained.

Then there is a lot of incense in the book—clouds from burning incense. What is that a symbol of? We are told that when you see the picture of the smoke of incense going up, that represents the prayers of the saints going up; it is a symbol of prayer. So, we know what that means because it is explained for us. Then there is a horrible prostitute at the end of the book, a whore, a harlot, a scarlet woman, and it is explained that she is a symbol of a city called Babylon. Again, there is no problem with it. Then there is a dragon—a large serpent—which keeps popping its head up. What does that symbol mean? There is no argument; it says that the dragon, that serpent, is the devil. What I am trying to tell you is do not be put off by all the symbolism because some of the symbols are obvious and many are explained.

There is a third group of symbols that are paralleled somewhere else in the Bible where they are explained. Although the book of Revelation does not explain them, you will find an explanation of them; for example, in the book of Daniel or in the book of Ezekiel or in the book of Jeremiah or Isaiah or Zechariah or even the Psalms. Many of the symbols in the book of Revelation come from the rest of the Bible.

The tree of life comes straight from Genesis and you know what it means. It bears fruit that, if eaten, enables you to live forever. It is a symbol of eternal life. You will find the explanation of the Morning Star in the Old Testament. We also read about the rod of iron and the four horsemen. In one chapter of Revelation, there are four horses. The first is white, the second is red, the third is black, and the fourth is pale green. What does that mean? Well, read Ezekiel and you will find out that the white stands for military conquest, the red, bloodshed, the black, famine, and the pale green, disease. We find all those four things in parts of the world right now, and those four horses are charging through eastern Europe at the moment. Do you see? It makes sense. Do not be put off by the symbolism. It is picture language.

Now, this leaves just a few symbols that we do not understand. I wish I did. What does the white stone mean? I have to tell you that I do not know, and until I get it, I will not be able to tell you.

I was in a Christian meeting where there was a white stone on everybody's chair before the meeting began, and we were told to pick it up and meditate upon it. I did, and all I could think of was a white stone because I do not know what it means where Jesus says that he will give a white stone to "him who overcomes". I do not think it is a marble headstone, but that white stone means something. I can guess, but I do not know.

There are one or two others, but not many. For example, I do not know the full meaning of the number 666. I will know when a man comes with that number. It could mean his name in code. If you take the letters of Nero Caesar and turn them into numbers, it comes to a total of 666, which is very interesting. I do not know if that is the meaning or not. If you take the Roman numerals "I", one, plus, "V," five, plus "X," ten, plus "L" 50, plus "C" 100, plus "D", 500, what does that come to? Six hundred and sixty-six. So, is this a reference to the Roman Empire? We do not know. I will say more about it when we get to that part of the book of Revelation.

What I am trying to tell you is there are many symbols that are very obvious in meaning; there are a lot of symbols that are explained in the book of Revelation; there are a lot of symbols that are explained elsewhere in the Bible; there are only a few that we are still puzzled about. So do not let the symbolism put you off, as we can handle most of them quite easily. So, apocalyptic unveils what is above and ahead, neither of which human eyes can see by themselves; only if God draws the veil back can we see what is above in heaven and what is ahead in the future, and, of course, this is supernatural.

Therefore, it is concerned with the ultimate outcome of the battle between good and evil. But good and evil do not exist by themselves; they only exist in people. So, it is the outcome of the battle between God and Satan. So, apocalyptic tells us how the future is going to shape up. Apocalyptic always has tremendous confidence that nothing is out of God's control, and therefore always in apocalyptic history, somewhere you will find a picture of God on his throne in perfect control of the situation, and therefore, it is a peaceful scene.

God actually does not struggle with Satan. Satan has to ask God's permission before he can do anything. We struggle with Satan, but God does not. God is on the throne. You get that picture in Revelation chapter 4, where John sees God sitting on the throne in perfect peace with a glassy sea in front of him and a rainbow over him. It is a picture of great peace and it is telling you that even though the worst may happen down here, it is not shaking God up there. God is still in total control.

A little girl went home from Sunday school singing, "God is still on the phone; God is still on the phone." That is the truth, but it is not what the Bible is trying to say. God is still on the throne is the truth, and Jesus is by his side, and between them, they have total control of everything. So even though apocalyptic history reveals disasters and catastrophes on a world scale, it is always the case that against this background, God is not affected. God is not worried. God is not surprised. God is not taken aback. God sits on his throne, and he is working out his purpose, and what he has decided will happen.

Now, that leads us to ask, what is the shape of future history? I want to show you the different patterns of history that you will find in different history books *(see diagram on page 27)*. There are what we call philosophies of history that you will find in other history books. Where is history going? Is it going anywhere? Is it going to get better or worse? Will it just get better and then worse, and then better and then worse? This is the big question when you read the newspapers, when you listen to television news; you ask what is going to happen? Are parts of Africa going to get better or worse? Is Europe going to get better or worse? Where is history going? Is there any discernible pattern in history?

The ancient Greeks believed in what we call the *cyclic* view of

How Was it Written?

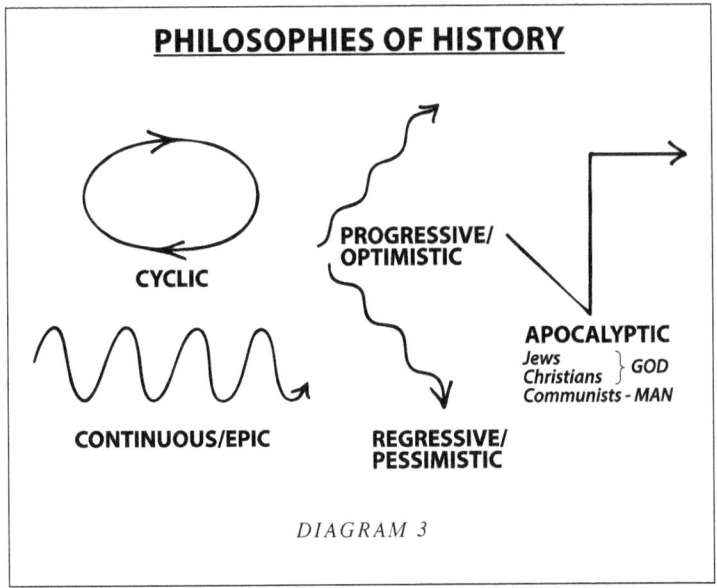

DIAGRAM 3

history. This is the view that history goes round in circles. Have you ever heard the phrase "history repeats itself"? That is Greek thinking. It is not biblical thinking, it is the way the Greeks thought and the way most people think today, that life is a roundabout; you just go round and round and you get off at the same place. It sometimes gets better and it sometimes gets worse, but it is just going around in circles. Or as one modern poet has put it, "History repeats itself; it has to, no one listens." Not a bad little poem called "Blank Verse".

Then there is the *epic* or *rhythmic* view of history, that history just goes on getting better or worse, but it does not repeat itself. The same situation never occurs again, so it is always changing and getting better and worse, and it just goes on up and down, up and down; war and peace, war and peace, inflation, recession. We are on a rollercoaster ride—not a roundabout, but a rollercoaster. It does not go back on itself, so the past never happens again; things never happen in quite the same way again, and they just go up and down.

Then there is the *optimistic* view of history, and this was the philosophy of history that introduced the twentieth century. At the beginning of the century, people said, "progress" was going to be the word that characterised the century. As one English prime minister put it in the year 1900, "Up and up and up and on and on and on." Well, that sounds a bit more stirring than "Back to Basics"! But anyway, that was his call, "Up and up and on and on," history was an escalator and the twentieth century was going to be the best century of all, and two world wars just completely destroyed the optimistic view of history.

In the 21st century, I think the word on most people's lips is "survival". Not progress, but survival. Will we survive the 21st century? The *pessimistic* view of history is very common today and is leading people to eat, drink, and be merry for tomorrow we die. There are forecasts already that human life will become impossible by the year 2040. They say that given the present population growth, limited food resources and fuel reserves, and even the shortage of fresh, clean water, the crossover point of all this is forecast to come in 2040.

The forecast of the Massachusetts Institute of Technology is that by 2040, life will become impossible on earth. It is no wonder, then, that people say we must have it now, grab everything we can now, because the world is just going to get worse and worse and worse until somebody presses the wrong button and we fade away. With air pollution and with the oceans getting polluted, life cannot go on. That is the most common view in the 21st century. We have got problems.

Now, none of those views is the Bible view. The apocalyptic view of history, which has been revealed to us by God, is this: that history is going to get progressively worse until it reaches rock bottom and then it will suddenly get better and stay good.

Now, if you see the apocalyptic line in diagram 3, the line is going down and then suddenly right up and then straight along, that is the apocalyptic view of history, and this, of course, is why it has found its way into popular usage, even in Hollywood. They see only the first bit of it; they do not see the next bit, the sudden improvement.

This apocalyptic view of the future, that things are going to get worse but will suddenly get better, is shared by Communists, Jews, and Christians. They all share the apocalyptic view of history, and they all got it from the same source, because it is essentially the Jewish view of history, and it is essentially the view that the prophets had revealed to them by God the Holy Spirit. The Bible's view of the future is consistently that things are going to get much worse and then suddenly better. So, the Jews talked about this present evil age (a down line) and the age to come (a high line).

The Communists, of course, got it from Karl Marx, who was a Jew. The Communist believes that the struggle between the bourgeoisie and the proletariat will get worse and worse and worse until suddenly the revolution will take place and then you will get a classless, crimeless society. Well, communism is now in eclipse; it has proven not to be the truth, and it is dying everywhere. But the apocalyptic view of history is shared by Jews and Christians. The difference between the three is what they believe will happen that will suddenly reverse the situation.

The communist believes that man will cause that reversal and by revolution. The Jew believes that God will intervene in history and bring about his kingdom on earth. But the Christian believes the change will come when Jesus comes back to earth, and that is the outline of history as you see it in the book of Revelation. Things get progressively worse, disasters increase in intensity until the very worst happens, and then, quite suddenly, you almost come out of the clouds and into the sunshine and everything is beautiful.

What is it that happens to cause the downward line suddenly to jump up? The answer is in chapter 19: Jesus gets back. That is why the return of Jesus Christ is the heart of the Christian hope.

I have no hope whatever that any earthly politician can solve our problems. I tell you, the present government does not know what to do. They do not know, and that includes the opposition. They do not know either and I think the country realises that the politicians do not know what to do to stop the crime, to make Britain a safer place, to stop fraud. They do not know. The answer is we have no hope except in Jesus and he knows what to do.

Who knows what to do about the current conflict zones in the world? We do not know, but the Bible says that Jesus, when he comes, will settle the disputes among the nations and will do it with justice. You cannot have peace without justice, and that occurs in chapter 19, the sudden reversal. From chapter 19, the whole situation gets better. So, we are beginning to get a feel for the whole book. I am not going to get into any particular parts of the book until the next chapter, though.

Now, in all this, the book of Revelation does not stand alone. For example, there are 400 allusions to the Old Testament in this book. That is almost one for every verse; 400 allusions, but not a single quotation from the Old Testament. I hope you know the difference between an allusion and a quotation. A quotation would be a sentence or a verse from the Old Testament quoted in full. There is not a single one, and yet the mind behind this book is steeped in the Old Testament and there are allusions, languages, phrases, words that are used which come straight out of the Old Testament, and in particular from three books: Ezekiel, Daniel, and Zechariah.

One of the reasons Christians do not understand the book of Revelation is that they do not know their Old Testament well enough and therefore they miss these allusions—400 of them—and that is why you need to know your whole Bible. If you want to understand Revelation, then study the Old Testament. But there are also allusions to what we call the intertestamental period. You probably know that between the last book of the Old Testament, Malachi, and the first book of the New there is a gap of 400 years, between Malachi and Matthew. There are no books in our Bible from those years.

Now, books were written, and in Roman Catholic Bibles, you will find those books in the Bible. Why are they not in yours? Well, they are very interesting books about what happened in those 400 years, but they are not the Word of God. There is one phrase that is missing from those books, which occurs nearly 4,000 times in the Old Testament (3,808, if you want the exact figure). You can check me out on that. The phrase is, "Thus says the Lord", and that is missing from all the books between the Old and the New Testament. For 400 years, God had nothing to say to his people. That is a long time for God to be mute, to be silent.

While the books were written about what happened to the people of God, to the Jews, God did not speak to them for 400 years. That is why they are not in our Bible, but that does not mean that there was nothing true in those books and the book of Revelation does refer and does have allusions to some of the books that were written in between. I just threw that in. But of course, the book of Revelation does not stand alone in the New Testament, and there are other books and parts of books in the New Testament that help you to understand this one.

For example, there is one chapter in the first three Gospels that is so close to the book of Revelation, and it is a discourse from the lips of Jesus, and since Jesus gave us the book of Revelation, it is not a surprise that he gave a condensed version of it in his lifetime. The chapters are Matthew 24, Mark 13, and Luke 21. In a sense, they all report the same sermon of Jesus given to his disciples on the Mount of Olives, and they are a condensed version of the book of Revelation, and if you read them and then read the book of Revelation, Revelation is Jesus expanding on what he had already told the disciples. It is as simple as that.

There are one or two other parts of the New Testament that have a lot in common with Revelation: the second letter of Peter, the second letter to the Thessalonians, and the little letter of Jude.

Jesus had three brothers and Jude was the youngest, and he wrote a letter. Again, if you want to understand Revelation, read those, there is an awful lot in common between them.

Let me finish this chapter by underlining that here we have in this book a Revelation of Jesus Christ. Now, does that mean a revelation about him or a revelation from him? Scholars argue as to whether it means a new revelation about him or a new revelation from him about something else. I can only say I think the answer must be both; I cannot come down on one side or the other. Certainly, we have in this book an unveiling of Jesus, a Jesus you do not find anywhere else in the New Testament, a Jesus who is different from the Jesus of the Gospels.

For one thing, for example, his hair is snow white in this book. You certainly do not get that impression from the Gospels. If he was typically Jewish, then his hair would have been dark brown, almost black, but here we have Jesus whose hair is white as snow. That tells you that the Jesus we are meeting here is a little different from the Jesus we are used to in the Gospels, but that is only a little hint. The Jesus we meet here is a Jesus to fear if you are not living a righteous life. It is an awesome picture of Jesus, a frightening picture of Jesus to most people, and I am afraid, therefore, that it is a Jesus that they never think about, they never hear about, and preachers never preach about. When John first sees Jesus in chapter 1, he faints, falls as if dead. He is so shocked.

Now remember, this is the man who was closest to Jesus during his life. The man who used to lean on Jesus' breast at meals, the man who whispered things in his ear, the man whom Jesus loved, and now he sees Jesus in such a different light that he faints. He sees Jesus with blazing eyes, eyes that are blazing with anger. He sees Jesus covered in light. He sees Jesus with brass feet, brazen feet. It is a different Jesus. He is overawed, overwhelmed by this Jesus, and yet he had actually leaned on him when Jesus was on earth.

Jesus says the same thing that he said all through his life to people: "Don't be afraid." It is one of Jesus' favourite sayings. Do you know, in your Bible it says, "Don't be afraid" 366 times? That is one for each day of the year including a leap year. It is one of Jesus' favourite sayings but John was afraid of him. He is later presented as a lion, and not just a Narnia kind of lion, if you have read *The Lion, the Witch, and the Wardrobe* by C S Lewis, but a fierce lion and also as a ram.

Now, I wish the word "lamb" had never got into your Bible. When Jesus is described as the Lamb of God, invariably in pictures or stained glass, you see a little white cuddly thing, a few weeks old. You think, "How nice, a lamb." But you see, the lamb that was sacrificed for sin was always one year old and a one year old lamb is not a nice cuddly thing, it has big horns. It is fully grown. It is equivalent to a 30 year old man in human terms. Therefore, I do not call Jesus the Lamb of God. I call him the Ram of God. You would not like to be shut up in a room with a one year old ram with seven horns, because that is how he is described here. It is a very strong picture. I have heard many preachers say that Jesus is the Lion and the Lamb; no, he is the Lion and the Ram. Neither is a soft gentle picture. They are both very strong pictures, aggressive pictures and that is how he is presented here. It is not gentle Jesus, meek and mild.

This is a Jesus who fights and a Jesus who kills. He kills millions before this book closes. He himself kills them. That is a side of Jesus that people rarely think about. It is the angry side of Jesus, which only appeared five times during his life on earth; when they would not let him bless the children, or when they did not want him to heal the man with a withered hand on the Sabbath, or when he found money changers in his Father's house and then he was so angry. But this book is so full of his anger.

At one point, it says that when people see Jesus' face and his blazing eyes of anger, they will actually pray to the mountains, "Fall on us". They cannot bear to look at him. They will pray for an earthquake to swallow them up rather than look at Jesus' angry eyes. This is a different dimension of Jesus. It is the apocalyptic Jesus, and this time, he does not ride on a donkey; he rides on a white horse. That is very significant. To ride on a donkey is to come in peace. To ride on a horse is to come in war. He comes with blood-stained robes and a sword, because here we have Jesus coming the second time on earth, not to be a Saviour, but to be a Judge.

Could I put it like this? In the Gospels, Jesus is the Prophet; in the Epistles, he is the Priest, but here he is the King and the Judge, the King of Kings and the Lord of lords. Yet it is the same Jesus because the ram still bears the nail prints, and it looks as though it has been slain. So, it is the same Jesus who died on the cross; it is the same loving Jesus who healed the sick and cast out demons and raised the dead, who fed the 5,000 and stilled the storm. It is the same Jesus who now comes to do something totally different, and because of this, in the book of Revelation, he is given many new titles.

And with this, I close. Throughout history, the more important a person is, the more titles they have. How many names and titles do you think Jesus has? The answer is 250. Nobody in the entire history of the world has ever had so many names and titles, and if you want a nice little exercise, if I were setting an exam for you, I would say, "Write out the 250 names and titles of Jesus." The average Christian can get to about 35, but there are 250 and many of them are in this last book in the Bible.

Here are some of them: I am the Alpha and the Omega, the Beginning and the End. Here are some others: the Amen, the Faithful and True Witness, the ruler of God's creation, the Lion of the Tribe of Judah, the Root of David, the King of kings and Lord of lords, the Bright Morning Star. Do you know what that is, by the way, the Bright Morning Star? Have you ever been up early enough to see the stars disappear? They all go out, but there is always one left, low down, near the horizon.

That is the bright morning star, and when all others have

faded, there is one still shining and Jesus calls himself the Bright Morning Star. So, when all the pop stars and all the film stars have gone, there will still be one star shining. That is what it means. It is a lovely title, isn't it? The Bright Morning Star, the only star that will still be shining in the morning after the night of darkness has gone.

So, it is a different book, it is a different Jesus, and it helps to fill out the picture. People who do not know the book of Revelation will have an unbalanced and distorted view of Jesus. They will have a nicer view of Jesus, one that does not strike terror into the hearts of people, but that is not the Jesus the world is going to see when he comes back. He is not coming back as a little baby. He is coming back riding a horse to deal with all those who have ruined God's wonderful world. That is how he is coming back. The book of Revelation is about his return to planet Earth.

We will end this chapter here. I have tried to answer the question, "How was this book written?" But in the next chapter, I want to deal with an even more important question: Why was it written? What is the point of it? What is the message of it for us today? Why was it written?

Chapter 2

WHY WAS IT WRITTEN?

In this second chapter, I want to tackle the question, "Why was the book of Revelation written?" This is, in fact, the key that will unlock every part of it for you.

PHOTOGRAPH 1

The island of Patmos is a very small island, but right on the top of it, above a cave, they have built a monastery, the Monastery of Saint John the Theologian. If you go there today, you will see this monastery towering over the little island, but it was here that John was put in prison. He says this was for two crimes: "for the Word of God and for the testimony of Jesus Christ". That is why he was there, totally cut off from his people. An old man, lonely in a sense, because all the other disciples by this time had been killed, and he was the only one who lived to old age and who died a natural death. God kept him until he died.

Now, the first thing I want to say is that Revelation was written for ordinary people—that is terribly important. It was not written for scholars, or professors, or students. It was written for very ordinary believers in the seven churches of Asia. It is scholars who have made it complicated. That is why you need to read it as a very ordinary person. It says in the Gospels that the common people heard Jesus gladly.

That is not just a tribute to Jesus, it is a tribute to the common people. I find you can fool professors very easily, and you can fool students very easily. Just dress it up in the right philosophical language, and they think you are brilliant, but you cannot fool the man in the street. The man in the street just says the emperor has no clothes, and that is the beginning and the end of it. It is very important that we apply common sense and the rules of common speech to our reading of the book of Revelation, meaning that if you take it in its plainest, simplest meaning, you are likely to be right.

Here are two quotations from scholars, which I find interesting. Here is the first: "It is one of the misfortunes of our expertise-oriented culture that when anything seems difficult, it is sent off to the university to be figured out." I am afraid that has happened to the book of Revelation—they have not figured it out. Or here is a quotation from way back in 1884, by a German scholar called Reuss:

> We boldly affirm that the study of this book of Revelation would present absolutely no possibility of error if the inconceivable, often ridiculous, prejudice of theologians in all ages had not so trammelled it and made it bristle with difficulties that most readers shrink from it in alarm. Apart from these preconceptions, the Revelation would be the most simple, the most transparent book that prophet ever penned.

Why Was it Written?

That is quite a quotation coming from a professor, but that is what he said. There were some theological students in America, and they had attended lectures on apocalyptic literature, and they were thoroughly confused, so they decided to go and have a game of basketball in the campus gymnasium. While they played basketball, they noticed that the janitor, the man who looked after the building, was waiting to lock up. He was a simple man sitting at the edge of the court while they played, waiting for them to finish.

They noticed he was reading his Bible, so they went over to him. They said, "Good to see you reading your Bible." He said, "Oh yes, I'm always reading my Bible." They said, "What part of it are you reading?" He said, "Oh, the book of Revelation." The students said, "You don't understand that, do you?" He said, "Of course I do." They said, "Well, what's the message of the book?" He said, "Simple, Jesus wins."

Now, that man was coming to the book with a simple mind, and he was reading it and letting it speak to his simple mind. That is by far the best way to tackle this book. However, there is one important qualification to what I just said. That is, it was written for ordinary readers 2,000 years ago and 2,000 miles away in a very different situation to us. We have, therefore, to try and get inside their situation and understand what it would have meant to the ordinary reader or hearer back then. Then we can begin to apply it to ourselves today.

For example, it was very clear that it was written to Christians who were suffering. If you are not suffering as a Christian, then the book, in a sense, is closed to you. Wherever Christians are suffering, the book of Revelation makes sense. That is why it is the most popular book among Chinese Christians. They are being tortured with electric cattle prods to deny Jesus, and they love the book of Revelation; it keeps them going. The one key that unlocks this book is to suffer for Jesus. Some of us do not possess that key, and so we make such a meal of it that we make it more complicated than it really is.

So, it is written for people in the first century and in that particular part of the world. It was written on the island of Patmos for ordinary believers in those seven churches in what is today western Turkey. That is the first key to understanding it—it was written for ordinary people in a very ordinary situation.

The next thing I want to say is this: it was written for Christians. Not one word of it is for unbelievers, but then I hope you realise that all but two of the New Testament books were written for Christians. The only two books written for unbelievers are Luke and Mark. Every other book in the Bible, including John, including Matthew, is addressed to believers or disciples. That is very important, because if we are not careful, we throw a book that is written for Christians at unbelievers and wonder why it does not work.

For example, it is very dangerous to give the Sermon on the Mount in Matthew to an unbeliever because they would immediately assume that being a Christian is doing good, which it is not. The Sermon on the Mount is addressed to sons of the kingdom who are already in the kingdom of heaven on earth. John is written to those who already believe that they may go on believing. By the way, there is one other book that is written for an unbeliever, and that is Acts, but it is just volume two of Dr Luke's work.

Every letter was written to believers, and above all, we must emphasise that Revelation is written to Christians. Therefore, when it warns people what kind of behaviour would cause them to finish up in the lake of fire, it is speaking to believers. It is not a warning to unbelievers. It is a warning to believers of the kind of thing that can lead a believer to finish up in the wrong place.

The next thing I want to say is the most important. It is written for a very practical purpose. It is not written to satisfy our curiosity about the future. It is not a kind of Old Moore's Almanack with a detailed forecast of the end of the world. If you approach it that way, you will have real difficulty working out the order of events. The order is far from clear, and that tells me that the important thing is not the order of the events but the fact that they are going to happen.

This book was written not to tell us about the future, but to get us ready for the future—that is the practical purpose. It is not so we can work out what time it is on God's clock and somehow be in the know and know how near we are to the very end, as if we can have secret knowledge. It is written so that we may be ready for whatever is going to happen. Here is a little bit of good news: nothing worse will happen in our world than what you read in this book. That is a comfort in a sense, isn't it? After you have studied this book, you know the very worst. Actually, I think there is comfort in knowing the worst. It is better than not knowing, it really is.

When it was discovered that my wife was within weeks of her grave with cancer the doctor told me the worst. Funnily enough, the worst was that he was going to have to cut half her face off. I would rather she were in heaven with a whole face than here with half of one; that is just being personal, but he said even then it may be too late. Then he said to take her home and prepare her for it. On the way home, she said, "David, tell me the whole truth." I shared it with her, and from that day, she had total peace.

The outcome is that the Lord had mercy on us and removed the whole thing. Now, many years on, she tells people, "I won't die of that, I'll die of something else, because the Lord has healed it." So, he had mercy on us. She wanted to know the worst, and when she did, she was at peace; she was ready. Jesus, in his mercy, has told us the worst that can happen in our world, so we know the worst. That is a comfort to me—I can be ready for it.

Now, the people in the world out there, the unbelievers, they do not know the worst that is going to happen. They fear the unknown, but we can be ready for what we know is coming. That is the whole purpose of the book—to help believers be ready for everything that is yet to come. That is a very practical purpose. Now, certainly there are many predictions in this book; there are many events that are forecast. As I have told you, the order of events is far from clear, but the events are clear enough, and we know the worst that can happen.

I do not know whether you know just how much the Bible has to say about the future. Twenty-seven per cent of the verses of the Bible have a prediction about the future in them. Altogether 734 separate events are forecast in the Bible—734. Some are predicted only once, one is predicted up to 300 times, but 734 separate events. How many of those have happened yet? The answer is 593. Approximately 81 per cent of them have come true. Well, I am prepared to believe the rest will come true. The score is pretty good.

That is not 81 per cent accurate; it is a 100 per cent accurate because most of the other things that it predicts are about the end of the world, and that has not happened yet, or we would not be here. So, actually, there are only about 17 things that are yet to happen before Jesus returns according to the New Testament—out of 734, that is not many, is it? There are only a few more things to happen before Jesus gets back. But in the book of Revelation itself, there are 56 events predicted—56. That is something like two out of every three verses in the book of Revelation contain a predicted event about the future. So, it is a very concentrated number of predictions.

Why are all these things revealed to us? The answer is not so that we can be "in the know" about the future, but so that we can influence the present by drawing on our knowledge of the future. We are the people of tomorrow; we live today because we belong to tomorrow. It is the future that should govern your behaviour every day. It is what is going to happen that should decide what you do now. Of course, that happens in ordinary life.

Let us suppose that you had a nice house, but you were thinking of improving it, fitting a new bathroom, building a new kitchen

Why Was it Written?

in it, and decorating it. Then you heard they were going to pull it down to make way for a motorway in two year's time. Would you still go ahead with your new bathroom and your new kitchen? Highly unlikely—the future would influence the present, wouldn't it? What you know is going to happen influences you now. That is why Peter says in 2 Peter 3:11–12, "Since everything will be destroyed in this way, what kind of people ought you to be? You ought to live holy and godly lives as you look forward to the day of God and speed its coming. That day will bring about the destruction of the heavens by fire, and the elements will melt in the heat."

What sort of life should you be living if everything in this world is going to disappear? It affects your thinking. There are people who look after their homes so well, as if they are going to live in them forever, and they are only going to be a few years in them. You see, if you know what is going to happen, it affects how you live in the present. Jesus only revealed to us what we need to know about the future so we can live right in the present. That is the whole emphasis; the Bible is not there to satisfy curiosity.

Right in the middle of the book of Revelation, in chapter 14:12, is this verse, "Here is the patience of the saints; here are those who keep the commandments of God and the faith of Jesus." Now, in that one verse, you have got the key that unlocks the whole book. The aim of the whole book is to help people to remain faithful to Jesus. Why, therefore, should that be said at the end of the first century AD to the seven churches of Asia? What was the situation that required this message for believers to remain faithful to Jesus, a call to endurance?

Well, I have got to give you a little history. John, of course, is already in prison; he is already suffering as a political prisoner for the testimony of Jesus and the Word of God. So, he is already under pressure because he is a Christian, but there is something much more serious behind this book. It was written around AD 96. It was probably the last book, or one of the last books, of the

New Testament to be written, when John was a very old man.

Now, why? The answer can be found by looking back over the previous 100 years. Julius Caesar was the first emperor, a 100 years before this book was written. Julius Caesar claimed to be divine; he claimed to be a god. He was followed by a man called Augustus. Augustus not only claimed to be a god, like Julius Caesar, but he demanded that everywhere in the Roman Empire, temples should be erected to worship Augustus. Augustan temples were erected all over the Mediterranean world, where you could worship Caesar, Augustus Caesar.

Many of these were erected in western Turkey—what was called Asia. It was a centre of emperor worship. They were more enthusiastic about worshipping the emperor in Asia than in any other Roman province. All this is helping us to understand something. By the year 96, the Roman emperor, the Caesar, was called Domitian. He took emperor worship one stage further. He said, "Every year, every person in the Roman Empire must worship me by taking a pinch of incense in their fingers and throwing it on an altar fire, and as the incense burns, everybody must say three words: 'Caesar is Lord.'" He said, "If they don't do that, they will die."

Unsurprisingly, the Christians absolutely refused to say those three words. They said, "Jesus is Lord and we will never say 'Caesar is Lord.'" The emperor called the day of the year when this was done the "Lord's Day". That is the meaning of that phrase in Revelation 1:10. John says, "On the Lord's Day I was in the Spirit... —not *a* Lord's Day, *the* Lord's Day. In fact, in the Greek there the word "Lord" is not even a noun, it is an adjective. It says, "On the Lordy Day," or "the Lordly Day". That was the title that Domitian gave to the day on which everybody had to worship him.

Now, Sunday was never called the Lord's day in the New Testament. It was either called the first day of the week, or in some cases it was called the eighth day, but in the New Testament it is

Why Was it Written?

usually called the first day of the week. "The Lordly Day", that was something different. If it had simply been a Sunday, John would have said, "I was in the Spirit on a Lord's day," but he does not say that. He says, "On the Lordy Day I was in the Spirit."

That is very significant because it would be revealed to John; he would see that this was going to be the greatest test of the early Church that they had yet had. They would have to choose between denying Jesus, and as a result being allowed to live, and refusing to say "Caesar is Lord" and being killed. Emperor worship was more concentrated in Asia (Asia Minor) than anywhere else, and you can still see the ruins of Augustan temples all over western Turkey.

PHOTOGRAPH 2

Do you realise that those simple believers in the seven churches were about to face the greatest test of their faith? Would they endure? Would they remain faithful to Jesus? John himself was in prison for it, but he realised that from now on such faithfulness would result in death. That is why the book is full of the word "martyr". Now, you may not know that the Greek word *martur* means "witness". It does not mean to die at all, it simply means "to witness".

John realised that to be a faithful witness to Jesus would mean dying for him. That was when the word *martur* changed its meaning, and it became someone who is faithful unto death for Jesus. That does not mean faithful until death, but faithful unto death—that is the phrase. It is often used at the funeral services of someone who had been faithful until they died, but it really means faithful to death, as Jesus was obedient even to death—faithful to death.

The whole call is to Christians: "Are you willing to die for Jesus? Are you willing to be a martyr for Jesus?" I would give the book of Revelation a title. If I were asked to give it a title, I would call it "A Manual for Martyrdom"—it is a manual for martyrs. That is precisely why it was written—to help those simple Christians to stand firm for Jesus. That is the whole purpose of the book. It achieves that purpose in many different ways, as we will see, but it is encouraging the saints to stick it out and to see it through, and not just passively, but actively, to face it.

There is a passive word that is used all the way through: "endure". That means to suffer passively, not to fight back, to stick it out, to see it through. But there is a more positive word that is more frequently used, and it is the key word for the whole book. When you read a book or a chapter, look for the keyword. The keyword of Revelation is "overcome". If you underline your Bible, as I hope you do, you will find that this is a word that keeps coming up. "He who overcomes"; "he who overcomes"; "he who overcomes".

The whole book is written to persuade believers to be overcomers. That is not just to endure it—that is to be under something—but actually to triumph over it and come out on top of it. This word "overcome", of course, appears all the way through the New Testament. In John 16:33, Jesus says, "In this world you will have trouble. But take heart! I have overcome the world." The Bible promises trouble to Christians. We read in Acts 14:22 that Paul exhorts the disciples to "continue in the faith", saying, "We must go through many hardships to enter the kingdom of God."

I used to listen to some testimonies that depressed me enormously. People used to get up and say, "I came to Jesus and all my troubles were over." At first, I used to believe them; now I do not believe them. I do not believe it is true. My testimony is this: "I came to Jesus and my troubles began. Some years later, I got baptised in the Holy Spirit, and my troubles became much worse. I have been in more trouble in the last five years than in the previous forty—that is my testimony." It fits with Jesus' promise that I just quoted. But the call in Revelation is to be overcomers with Jesus and to be on top of the pressures, not under them.

I asked a friend of mine some time ago, "How are you?" He said, "I'm very well over the circumstances." I thought, "Only a Christian could say that." The world says, "I'm very well under the circumstances," but he said, "I'm very well 'over' the circumstances." That is a very Christian reply. The whole book of Revelation is designed to help believers be overcomers and to get on top of the pressures that they are going to be under. It is not just the message of Revelation, "Jesus wins." The message is, "He wants every believer to win." That is why it is written.

To achieve this, the book offers two kinds of incentives—a positive and a negative incentive to be an overcomer. The positive incentive is a reward. Many rewards are offered to overcomers in this book. Each of the seven letters to the seven churches of Asia finishes, "To him who overcomes I will give" this. Here are these seven promises given to the overcomers. To Ephesus: "I will give the right to eat from the tree of life, which is in the paradise of God." To Smyrna: "The one who is victorious will not be hurt at all by the second death." To Pergamum: " I will give some of the hidden manna. I will also give that person a white stone with a new name written on it, known only to the one who receives it." To Thyatira: "I will give authority over the nations— that one 'will rule them with an iron sceptre and will dash them to pieces like pottery'[1]—just as I have received authority from my Father, I will also give that one the morning star." To Sardis, "The one who is victorious will, like them, be dressed in white. I will never blot out the name of that person from the book of life, but will acknowledge that name before my Father and his angels." To Philadelphia: "I will make him a pillar in the temple of my God, and he shall go out no more. I will write on him the name of My God and the name of the city of my God, the New Jerusalem, which comes down out of heaven from my God. And I will write on him my new name." And to Laodicea: "I will give the right to sit with me on my throne, just as I was victorious and sat down with my Father on his throne."

All these are rewards that are held out to believers who are going to face the choice of being faithful to Jesus or denying him. The book says to look at the rewards that Jesus offers you for remaining faithful to him and for overcoming the difficulties. The negative incentive is one that again is not very popular to hear or to preach, but it is there. What about Christians who go under, who do not overcome, who do not endure, who deny Jesus, and disown him under pressure? Well, let me just give you two verses from the book of Revelation, which are very serious.

Number one: Jesus says to the church in Sardis, "The one who is victorious will, like them, be dressed in white. I will never blot out the name of that person from the book of life, but will acknowledge that name before my Father and his angels." Now, if you take that statement in its plainest, simplest sense. If language means anything, what does it mean for those who do not overcome? It means that their name can be blotted out from the Book of Life. It is there already if you believe in Jesus, but it can be blotted out, "rubbed out". Actually, the Greek phrase is "scraped off", because in those days, when they wrote on parchment, they had a penknife to scrape the ink off the parchment, they did not have rubbers. They scraped it off, and Jesus said, "He who overcomes shall be clothed in white garments, and I will not blot out his name from the Book of Life".

That is a serious warning; it means that it is possible to have your name removed from the Book of Life. Then, at the very end of the book, where the book describes the new heaven and the new earth and the New Jerusalem in the most beautiful terms, suddenly it says this: "He who overcomes will inherit all this, but the cowardly and the faithless, their place will be in the lake of fire." There it is again. So, there are both wonderful rewards offered and consequences of not overcoming. That is the thrust of the book, both negative and positive. We need to remember at this point that Revelation is addressed to saints, to believers, to Christians, to born-again people.

It is very interesting that the Gospel of Matthew is, of course, addressed throughout to disciples. It is not a book to put in unbelievers' hands. It is addressed to disciples all the way through. For example, in the beginning of the Sermon on the Mount, Jesus says, "Blessed are you when you are persecuted for my sake and the gospel's." That is not addressed to unbelievers; it is all addressed to believers.

I wrote a book entitled *The Road to Hell*, which was not my autobiography, despite it being advertised as such in a Christian magazine! That is not what it was, but it could be. Like Paul, I fear lest having preached to others I should be disqualified myself. But what I pointed out in that book is that most of our knowledge of hell comes from the lips of Jesus himself, and most of it comes from Matthew's Gospel.

Most of his warnings about hell were given not to sinners, but to born-again believers. This is totally consistent with the book of Revelation, which comes from Jesus as well. The strongest warnings of hell are given to Christians in the New Testament.

Very rarely did Jesus mention hell to sinners. He twice mentioned it to the Pharisees, but every other time it was to those who left all to follow him. Now that is serious.

The book of Revelation and the Gospel of Matthew together pretty well cover everything Jesus says about hell, but we need to ask, "To whom did he say it?" When he sent out his apostles two-by-two to heal the sick and cast out demons and to preach the kingdom, he said this to them in Matthew 10:28: "And do not fear those who kill the body but cannot kill the soul. Rather, be afraid of the One who can destroy both soul and body in hell." Who is he talking to? He is talking to Christian missionaries.

Now, all this is very important because Jesus himself said, "If you deny me before men, I will have to deny you before my Father and say, 'I don't know you.'" I think it must be the most terrible thing to be among those who are waiting for the Bridegroom and then hear him say, "I don't know you," and he said it so clearly. Paul sums it up, writing to Timothy. Paul says in a little poem, "If we endure, / We shall also reign with Him. / If we deny him, / He also will deny us." It could not be clearer.

So, this book is both an encouragement and a warning; it speaks to Christians who are going to be under pressure to deny Jesus, and it tells them not to deny him, not to throw away their future, and instead to remain faithful to Jesus. This is a call to endure and to keep faithful to Jesus. That is my summary of the whole book, in a sense. You see, the word "faith" and the word "faithfulness" are exactly the same word in both the Hebrew and the Greek language—there is no distinction.

Therefore, it is often a problem whether you translate the word into English with the word "faith" or the word "faithfulness", because to have faith in someone is to be faithful to them. It is the same thing. You cannot believe in Jesus one minute, then not believe in him the next, and say that you are a believer. A believer is someone who goes on believing. "The righteous person will live by his faithfulness," is the best translation of Habakkuk 2:4.

Why Was it Written?

Every time that verse is quoted in the New Testament, it is quoted in the terms of being faithful. "The just shall live by faithfulness."

For example, Paul, writing to the Romans in Romans 1:16–17, says, "For I am not ashamed of the gospel, because it is the power of God that brings salvation to everyone who believes: first to the Jew, then to the Gentile. For in the gospel the righteousness of God is revealed—a righteousness that is by faith from first to last, just as it is written: "The righteous will live by faith". Or take another example. In the New Testament, the word "believe" is usually in a special Greek tense called the present continuous tense. That means to go on doing something; not to do it once, but to do it regularly.

When Jesus said, "Ask and you will receive, seek and you will find, knock and it will be open to you," the literal translation is, "Go on asking and you will receive, go on seeking and you will find, go on knocking and the door will be opened to you." Now listen to John 3:16, the favourite Gospel verse of every evangelist, but listen to it in its true meaning: "For God so loved the world that he gave his one and only Son, that whoever go on believing in him shall not perish but have eternal life." Now, has that changed that verse a little for you? It should have done. But that is its true meaning, "Go on believing."

Faith is to be faithful—to go on believing in Jesus. This is why Jesus himself repeatedly emphasised, "He who endures to the end shall be saved." Now, this of course runs right across one of the most popular clichés on the lips of Christians that is not in the Bible, but is forever being quoted: "Once saved, always saved." Have you heard that? It is quoted as if it is in golden letters in Scripture. You cannot find that phrase in Scripture. What you do find is a constant encouragement and exhortation to go on believing, to overcome, to stay with Jesus, and not to disown or deny him under pressure.

Having given you that key to the book—and it really is the key to the whole book—you should be asking the following question as you read everything in it: "How will this help those Christians and us to remain faithful to Jesus?" That is the key, and you will always find a relevant answer to that in every part of the book. If you are just reading it to satisfy your curiosity about the end of the world, you will miss it.

You ask at every stage, "How will this particular revelation help Christians to be faithful?" because martyrdom now is a very common experience. When I last looked at the figures, I read that some quarter of a million people died in one year because they were Christian in their faith, and it is still happening. It is happening in parts of Africa; it is happening in many places. We need to wake up and realise that it is going to happen everywhere before the end of the world comes. Everywhere, Christians will have to choose between being faithful to Jesus and losing their job, or their home, or even their life. The book of Revelation is to help us to be ready for that.

Now, we are in a position to look at the book as a whole and begin to ask how it divides up. The first obvious division in the book is between chapters 1 to 3 and chapters 4 to 22. The difference between those two parts of the book is that the first three chapters clearly talk about the present and the situation that the churches in Asia were in already and the state they were in already, both inside the church and outside.

Jesus knew about what was happening in those churches, both inside them and around them. So, Jesus is telling those seven churches the things that must be put right now, because the churches are not ready for what is coming. I would say this is the most relevant part of the book for the churches in this country today. Persecution has just begun in England—there is much worse to come—but the sad fact is that the churches are just not ready for what is going to happen. Therefore, the first concern of Jesus is that the churches should be strong and pure and ready for pressure.

Therefore, to each of them, he has to point out things that they have got to put right now before the crisis hits them. You have got to get the anchor down before the storm begins if the ship is not to be driven onto the rocks. The first part of Revelation is very straightforward; it consists of seven letters to those seven churches telling each of them what is good about them and what is not so good about them, and what needs to be put right. In the next chapter, we will talk about those seven letters to the seven churches—things that must be put right now in the present.

Still to this day, 2,000 years later, I believe the first part of Revelation is one part of the Bible that we really need to be looking at, because in those seven churches, you can see a mirror of almost every kind of church today. Somehow, the mixture of things in those seven churches covers just about anything that can happen in a church. When we read those letters, we can ask, "Which of the churches of Asia is most like the church I am in?" If we do that, it will help us to know how to get it ready for the pressure that is going to come on us.

Then, in chapter 4:1, the change occurs and the angel says to John, "Come up here, and I will show you what must take place after this." So far in the book of Revelation, you are just looking at what is happening on earth in those seven churches, and anybody else could have seen it, but Jesus sees things more accurately.

Suddenly, the two dimensions of coming up to heaven and seeing what is happening up there and seeing what is happening in the future appear in chapter 4, and they stay in right to the end of the book, so that we are into different territory. There is much more symbolism now, more visions, more voices, so it is quite different. The next part of the book, from chapter 4 to chapter 22, is all future, so that is the first basic division in the book that we note.

Chapters 1 to 3 are about the present situation of the churches, whereas chapters 4 to 22 are about the future situation that they are going to be in. We can further subdivide the second part, which is the longer one, into two parts again, the first part of which is almost unrelieved bad news and the last part of which is all good news. So, you have a pretty bad patch all the way through the middle from chapter 4 to chapter 18, and then you have a wonderful patch from chapter 20 to chapter 22 when everything gets put right again.

Outline of Revelation

A. PRESENT (1-3)
THINGS THAT MUST BE PUT RIGHT NOW (2-3)

B. FUTURE (4-22)
IN HEAVEN
THINGS ARE ALRIGHT (4-5)
ON EARTH
THINGS WILL GET MUCH WORSE BEFORE THEY GET BETTER (6-18)
　　JESUS RETURNS (19)
THINGS WILL GET MUCH BETTER AFTER THEY GET WORSE (20-22)
NEW HEAVEN AND NEW EARTH

DIAGRAM 4

My title for these two sections of the second part of the book is chapters 4 to 18: "Things will be much worse before they get better." Then my title for chapters 20 to 22 is: "Things will get much better after they get worse." I cannot give you simpler titles than those. That is my simple outline, but I have missed something out. What changes the bad bit into the good bit? The answer is in chapter 19, we read of a Second Coming of Jesus Christ to planet Earth. That is when things completely turn around.

Why Was it Written?

It really is a simple book. If you keep this outline in mind as you read it, you will begin to understand much more. First of all, chapters 1 to 3 concern the present—things which must be put right now. Then chapters 4 to 22 concern the future, the first half of which is things will get much worse before they get better, and the second half of which is things will get much better after they get worse. In between, what changes the whole scene is that Jesus comes back to planet Earth, and he puts everything right again.

It sounds simple, almost naïve. Some people would dismiss it and say, "It's far too naïve a picture of the future." No, it is not; God is essentially simple in the way he does things; he is not too complicated. He has revealed that this is what he is going to do and this is how he is going to do it. It is all designed to get believers ready for the future. It is not designed to help people to profess faith, but to practise faithfulness—that is its real purpose. It asks us not, "Did you once have faith in Jesus," but rather, "Will you remain faithful to him when the pressure is on?"

When Jesus comes back, the one thing he wants to be able to say to us is, "Well done, good and faithful servant! You have been faithful with a few things; I will put you in charge of many things. Come and share your master's happiness!" (Matthew 25:23). He is not saying, "Oh, I'm so glad you believed in me 20 years ago." He wants to find people who are still faithful. One of my favourite verses in the New Testament is in Hebrews chapter 11. It talks about the faith of Noah, the faith of Abraham, the faith of Moses, and then it says this: "All these were still living by faith when they died." That is what it is all about. That is why it then goes on to exhort us to run the race and to keep running, keeping our eyes fixed on Jesus, the author and the finisher of our faith, the one who begins it and the one who rounds it off when faith turns to sight. So, the whole book is telling us to be faithful to Jesus.

Now, let us just take a quick overview of the book and see where people get into most difficulty. Very few people have difficulty with chapters 1 to 3. There are one or two questions that we shall certainly have to answer in the next chapter and look more closely at, but most people can cope with chapters 1 to 3, the letters to the seven churches. Most preachers can cope with those, too, and there are famous preachers—I could name a few—who have published books on the seven letters to the seven churches of Asia, who just have not preached the rest of it because they get out of their depth. In the first three chapters, you are paddling up to your knees in the water.

Chapters 4 and 5 are a little more difficult because now you are up in heaven and we have so little experience of heaven that it is all a bit strange to us to see this "sea of glass, like crystal", stretching as far as the eye can see, a throne of jasper, and this great rainbow—it is very colourful and dazzling almost. It is so bright. You see this great throne and all the creatures around the throne worshipping the Creator. There is a lot of singing and music there.

Many of our hymns come out of those two chapters, four and five. "' Worthy the Lamb that died,'" they cry, "' to be exalted thus'". Have you ever sung that? That is straight out of the book of Revelation. A lot of our hymns come out of the book of Revelation; it is a very musical book. Whenever you get up into heaven, you hear music; you hear the sound of many waters. I have a recording of some angels singing. It is the most wonderful music, heavenly music, quite different from earthly music.

But it is very musical. The sights and sounds are almost overwhelming when you get into chapters 4 and 5. I have so often heard them read in services of worship because it stimulates your worship to see God on his throne. Well, people do not have much difficulty with those two chapters. But as soon as they get beyond chapter 5 and into chapter six, and read about all the trumpets and the seals and the bowls of wrath, and all the weird animals running around and the beast doing things, that is when they suddenly feel, "I'm out of my depth."

Well, I am going to try to help you through that middle bit. It is pretty startling. Actually, when you look at it, it is not very complicated at all. But we have to ask what it all means, how it all fits together, and what time it refers to. One of the biggest questions is whether that middle bit, with all its horrors, is already past to us. Some Bible students say that it all happened in the Roman Empire, and it is a description of the fall of the Roman Empire. That is one answer. Or is it still happening in the present? Are we somewhere in these chapters? Those who take that view usually decide that we are living in the middle of about chapter 16. They try to correlate the events with our daily newspapers. Or is most of that middle section still future to us?

That is one of the questions we will ask in the next chapter, because there are different schools of interpretation. Some say it is all past, some say it is now, and some say no, it is yet to happen. Well, we have got to answer that. One scholar, when he got to the middle bit, said, "John was either suffering from indigestion at best or insanity at worst." I think he is in danger of committing the unforgivable sin there; I think he is blaspheming the Holy Spirit. But it does get you, and I want to try and help you understand simply what it is saying.

But then, when we get to chapters 21 and 22, it almost seems like we have come home again, and we feel comfortable again. "And God shall wipe away all tears from their eyes". What a beautiful verse that is. I have a picture of a parent with a little child saying, "Come here, let me wipe your eyes. It's all over; you don't need to cry any more. It's all over." That is a beautiful picture of God, isn't it? We love that last bit, and it seems to be read at every funeral I have been to.

Well, it is that middle bit that is the biggest problem, and I want to help you very much to get through that. I will have to tell you about the different schools of interpretation. I hope that will not complicate things too much or confuse you, but if you buy books on Revelation, you will find that they usually stick to one idea, one interpretation. I want to show you that I think that is a mistake. We need the right interpretation for each part of this book. Each part needs a different approach—that is the way I am going to approach it with you. But let us conclude this chapter by looking at the book as a whole.

First, let me repeat that the Bible is essentially a romantic book. It is a book of love. It is no accident that right in the middle of the Bible is a love song called the Song of Solomon. The whole Bible is a love story of a God who so loved the world and a God who wanted to find this Bride for his Son. That has to finish up in a happy ending—every romance should do, and this does. Paul says to some of his converts, "I promised you to one husband, to Christ, so that I might present you as a pure virgin to him" (2 Corinthians 11:2), but he does not say, I've married you to Christ. The marriage is yet to come.

I was talking to some children in a school, and a little boy asked me a question. He said, "Why wasn't Jesus married?" I said, "It's all right, he's going to be." Afterwards, the headmaster in the headmaster's study said, "What were you teaching my children?" He said, "I've never heard about Jesus getting married." "Then," I said, "you haven't read the whole Bible yet, because the Bible finishes up with a wedding, 'And the Bride has made herself ready,'" and then he understood.

The Bible is a romance, and it finishes up with a wedding, and they live happily ever after. Without the book of Revelation, the story would be unfinished. Can you imagine getting hold of an Agatha Christie detective novel out of your public library and finding somebody had cut out the last ten pages? Wouldn't it be frustrating to get that far and then find out you do not know how it is all going to end or who the villain was?

But from another point of view, the Bible is a book of history, but different from every other history book in that it starts earlier and it finishes later. It starts with the beginning of the world and it finishes with the end of the world. Once again, if we did not have the book of Revelation, we would never know how the world will end or that that end will just be the beginning of an even more wonderful world.

Do you realise that if the book of Revelation was not in your Bible, the last book in the Bible would be the letter of Jude? What a depressing ending that would be, because Jude is the picture of a church that is being corrupted in its creed, its conduct, its character, and its conversation—the four basic corruptions that can happen to any church. That sad picture would be the last word in the Bible if we did not have this book, but thank God it is not. We have got this book and it is a good ending.

There is one last thing to say about this outline of the second part about the future: things will get much worse before they get better; things will be much better after they get worse. I just want to say one more thing about those two periods of history. We can expect immediate history to get worse and worse, and ultimate history to be much better. The difference is in the time. The chapters given to these two sections are out of all proportion to the time covered. The worst period in history, when all the worst things happen, is found in this section in the middle. Do you know how long it covers? It only covers three and a half years. That is all.

The worst period of history is only three and a half years. That period of time is emphasised in so many ways. Sometimes it says three and a half years, sometimes it says forty-two months, sometimes it says 1,260 days, and once it just says, "a time and times and half a time", or three and a half times, and that is all it says. That is all that is. When you come to chapters 20 to 22, the first part of chapter 20 covers 1,000 years, and chapters 21 to 22 cover the whole of eternity.

Now, because so much of Revelation concentrates on those three and a half years, you could get things right out of proportion, couldn't you? What it is saying is this: For just three and a half years of trouble, don't throw away a thousand years of joy and the whole of eternity. There is just no comparison. In other words, this very brief time when things will be very tough and there will be thousands of martyrs for the faith—it is so quickly over. Do not go under and throw away that long, long time beyond. How foolish you would be to throw it away like that just for a bit of comfort for a few years—how silly.

So you see, when considering the message of Revelation, we should not just look at the proportion of pages that describe the bad bit; we should note carefully that although that tells us in detail just how bad it is going to be, it is such a brief period. Jesus himself had said in Matthew 24:22, "If those days had not been cut short, no one would survive, but for the sake of the elect those days will be shortened", so it is only for a short time. To quote Paul in Romans 8: "I consider that our present sufferings are not worth comparing with the glory that will be revealed in us". The suffering is not to be compared with the glory that shall be revealed, and that is the message of the book. Stay faithful to Jesus. It is going to be tough, but that tough time will be very brief, and then it will be over, and then there will be a good time coming for those who remain faithful to Jesus. He who overcomes will inherit all this.

That has given you an introduction to the book. In the next chapter, we are going to start looking at it part by part, but I wanted you to get this overall view. So often books on Revelation do not see the wood for the trees; they get so bogged down in discussing who the two witnesses are in Jerusalem in chapter 11 that they miss the whole picture. In this chapter, I have tried to give you the picture of the whole before we look at the parts. In the next chapter, we shall go on with that.

Chapter 3

THIS IS YOUR LIFE

Let me just begin this chapter by reminding you of the simple outline of the book of Revelation that I gave you. We need to approach every part of the book of Revelation with one thought in mind: why was it written? Why was the revelation given to us by Jesus Christ? The answer is it was given to believers, to Christians, and it was not written to anybody else. It was written to believers in seven churches in western Turkey who were about to face the biggest crisis of their lives and the biggest test of their faith and their faithfulness to Jesus.

I am giving the present the title, "Things which must be put right now." The letters to the seven churches are saying one thing: "You're not ready for the pressures that are going to come." This is one reason why I believe that this is such an important book to teach today. I believe we have only a short time in this country before persecution is on the Church—official persecution. It has already begun in a small way, but before long, I believe the Church in this country will be suffering the kind of persecution that many other countries are suffering. We need to be thinking even today of Christians in Africa and China, and a whole lot of other places, and it is going to come here. If the churches are not right before the storm hits us, it is like not having the anchor down before the storm begins.

So, the first three chapters, which we are going to study in the present chapter, are all about getting the churches ready to face the crisis, because the churches are a mixed bag, and they are not ready for the pressures that are coming. Those seven churches of Asia needed to be prepared, so things needed to be put right immediately in the churches before the crisis hit them. Of the chapters that address the future, 4 to 22 divide very neatly into two parts: chapters 4 to 18, and then chapters 20 to 22. Notice that I have missed out chapter 19 for a big reason.

Now I am going to take you through chapters 1 to 3, which are possibly the easiest part of the whole book and the most straightforward. Reading the book of Revelation is like going into the sea at the seaside. You are paddling up to your knees in the first three chapters, and everything is safe and straightforward. You begin to get into deeper water with chapters 4 and 5. By the time you get through to 12, you are up to your neck, even out of your depth, and we are going to have to go steadily through that middle section.

It is called a prophecy, "This prophecy", and yet it is also in the form of a letter. Every letter in the ancient world was on a rolled-up piece of scroll, and at the beginning of the letter, you had the sender and the address to which it was being sent. Now, I think that is sensible. People write me long letters thinking I have got nothing to do but read long letters about their questions, and they might send me 20 pages, but the name is always at the end. Isn't that a silly custom? You have to read right to the end of the letter to see who has sent it, or look at the end first.

In those days, they put the sender of the letter at the beginning: "This is from me to you at such and such an address." The whole book is in the form of a letter to the seven churches, and then within the one letter to them all, there is a specific letter to each of them, which is unusual. But the whole thing is addressed as a letter to all seven churches, and then within it there is a letter to each of the seven churches.

Let me just remind you where they are again so that you get it. John is in prison in Patmos, the Alcatraz, the Robben Island of those days. He is totally isolated from the churches that he used to travel around and preach to. They are all on a circular route, and the letters to the seven will be addressed in the right order:

Ephesus, Smyrna, Pergamum, Thyatira, Sardis, Philadelphia, and Laodicea. I can imagine him when he was free, walking along the road, preaching in each church; it was a kind of circuit of churches that he looked after.

So, we have one message for all the seven churches in chapter 1 and then in chapters 2 and 3, we have a letter for each of them. Yet each letter is read by the rest, which must have caused some embarrassment because each church must have been waiting and thinking, "I wonder what the letter to our church is going to say?" when they heard what the letters to the others were saying. But they were all read to all the churches, even though each letter was addressed to one.

Then, always after the sender and the address in every letter, there is a greeting. Greetings in the New Testament are usually a combination of a Jewish and a Greek greeting. The Jewish greeting was "peace", *shalom*, which sounds similar to *salaam*, as the Arabs say peace. The Greek greeting means more than peace; it was "cheer" or "grace", and *eirēnē* was the word, but it means cheer, grace. So invariably, New Testament letters put the Hebrew and the Greek together, grace and peace. That was their greeting.

Then comes the substance of the letter, the whole letter, which is: He is coming. That is the theme that runs right through the letter. The whole letter will tell us what will happen before he comes and what will happen after he has come, but it centres on the fact that he is coming, and every eye will see him. He is coming to the whole world. It says Jews in particular will weep, will mourn when they look on him whom they pierced. Why will they do that? Well, they will realise that for 2,000 years they missed it and suffered for all that time when they could have been right in the heart of the kingdom of heaven on earth, and they will mourn when they realise that the one who was crucified is in fact their king.

So, he is coming, and it is absolutely certain. Do you know

what the Jewish word for absolutely certain is? Amen. I wish people would not use that in so many different ways. I cannot stand preachers who use it with a question mark—Amen? Have you come across preachers who do that? Amen? They are using it as a question when the word means it is absolutely certain, and you should only ever use it when you are absolutely certain that what you have just heard is true. You should not say it at the end of a prayer unless you are absolutely certain that God has heard that prayer and is going to answer it. We should not use it as a sort of over and out to God. It means absolutely certain; he is coming, and every eye will see him. Amen! It is absolutely certain, so let it be, Lord.

It is a very important word, but it is as misused as the word, "Hallelujah", or even more misused than the word "Hosanna". Do you know what the word "Hosanna" means? The Hebrew word *Hoshana* means "Liberate us now!" It is not a heavenly hello; it is a cry for freedom. If it were translated into Hebrew, then the title of the Richard Attenborough film "Cry Freedom" would be *Hoshana, Hoshana*. We must use words properly. Jesus said, "Let your yes be yes, and your no be no."

Now we get a statement that behind that "amen" that Christ is coming, lies a God of history, a God who is and who was, and who is to come, which means that time is real to God. The Greeks used to say that God was timeless, that God was outside time. The Hebrew never said that. It is one of the most important things to grasp that time is real to God.

It is not so much that God is in time, but that time is in God, and history is his story. Let me prove it to you. To prove that God is not outside of time, that God is not timeless, ask yourself this question: Can God change the past? Think that one through. Can God change something once it has happened? He can certainly change the future, but can God change the past? The answer is no, he cannot. God is not outside of time. Time is real to God. He is the God who was and is and is to come.

He is, therefore, the God of history, and when God writes history, he writes far more than other historians can. Human history covers what has happened in the past, and it covers what happens on earth, but it is only part of history. All of history includes not only what happens here on earth, but also what happens up in heaven. All of history includes not only what has happened in the past up until now, but also what will happen in the future.

God knows the future as well as the past, and God knows what goes on in heaven as well as on earth. The book of Revelation covers that circle. That is why it is different from any other book in history. No other book in history mentions the future as well as the past, and no other history book tells me what is happening on earth and in heaven and how these interact *(see diagram 1 on page 18)*.

So, the first chapters, 1 to 3, are all concerned with the smaller circle. Then, in Revelation 4:1, the angel says to John, "Come up here, and I will show you what must take place after this."So that from God's angle, you can see up into heaven and the future, but from the human angle, you only have a limited view. That is another reason why chapters 1 to 3 are much easier for us to understand. It is because they read like a normal book written here concerning events on earth. They read like all the other epistles in the New Testament, like the letter to the Colossians or the Ephesians. So, 1 to 3 are down here, but the rest of the book is covering the whole wide circle.

In Revelation 1:8, the Lord tells us that he is "the Alpha and the Omega", and "who is, and who was, and who is to come, the Almighty". Before this book is finished, those same things will be said about Jesus, because at the end of the book, it is Jesus who is the first and the last, the beginning and the end. So, what you can say about God the Father, you can say about Jesus. That is an implied claim that Jesus is God.

The next thing that happens to John is that he sees something, and he hears something. That is how the revelation came to John. It is both visual and verbal; he hears things, and he sees things. Things come to his ear, and his eye, and it is very important to notice which things come to his eyes in vision, and which things come to his ears in voices. The first bit of the Revelation that comes to John in his prison cell is a voice. He hears this voice, and he turns to see who is speaking because the voice comes from behind him. How gently the Lord leads him into this astonishing vision. When he turns around, he then sees a Jesus whom he does not recognise.

Bear in mind that this John knew Jesus more intimately than anyone else. As mentioned, he had been closer to Jesus than anyone else. He always sat next to Jesus at the table, and literally leaned against Jesus, and whispered to him. He was nearer to Jesus than any other man. He was the disciple whom Jesus loved, but now he does not recognise the figure of Jesus because Jesus has changed so much. For one thing, as mentioned, his hair is now snow white, whereas when he had last seen him, his hair was dark, almost black. That is just one change. Now his eyes, which were so tender and loving, are blazing with anger, and they go on blazing with anger through the next few chapters, and John never saw Jesus' eyes like that. Then he goes down the body, and the whole body is different. He has a great golden sash around him; he is clothed in white, and out of his mouth there comes a tongue shaped like a sword.

Now, I do not know if you realise what that means. The Roman soldier had two kinds of swords. One sword was a long, thin sword, and another sword was a long, flat blade. An ordinary sword is a long, thin thing with a handle. That is all right for fighting one person, but the Roman soldier had another sword which was shaped like an old-fashioned hay knife, if ever you have seen one, with a heavy rib down the middle, and with a double handle. It was very heavy and terribly sharp.

You stood and held it, and you swung it from side to side, and one man could keep off 50 people with that sword. It was the broad two-edged sword, and if you went anywhere near it, it just sliced your leg or your arm off due to the weight and the sharpness. Can you imagine it? Now, it is exactly the shape of the tongue. That is why the Word of God is sharper than any two-edged sword; it really cuts down hundreds of people. You see, it is a very vivid picture, isn't it?

Here is this sword in his mouth, white hair, blazing eyes, golden sash, and feet shining like brass. Now, this is such a shock to John that he just falls in a dead faint. It is just too overwhelming. In spite of the fact, that the voice came first to let him down gently, the sight of Jesus like this is just too much, and he falls as though dead. Then the figure speaks and says, "I am the first and the last." Then he says this: "I was dead, and I am alive for ever and ever."

Let me read you a page from my little book, "The Resurrection": "Plato, Socrates, and Aristotle are dead. Julius Caesar, Napoleon Bonaparte, and Adolf Hitler are dead. Cleopatra, Boadicea, and Florence Nightingale are dead. Leonardo da Vinci, Isaac Newton, and Charles Darwin are dead. Confucius, Buddha, and Mohammed are dead. Karl Marx, Sigmund Freud, and Albert Einstein are dead. Abraham Lincoln, Winston Churchill, and John F Kennedy are dead. They were all alive and are now dead, but Jesus was dead and is alive forevermore."

That is the difference. Of every other person you say, "They were alive and they're now dead." Only Jesus can say, "I was dead and I am alive." That is a quotation from the book of Revelation. He is actually being seen now as a Judge. When he came the first time to earth, he had the appearance of a saviour, but when he comes back, he will have the appearance of a judge. People were not frightened by his appearance when he came the first time, except on a few occasions when he showed his anger against evil. When he comes a second time, it will be frightening. Here he is showing John a vision of what he will be like when he returns to earth.

From then on, we have the first of many sevens. We have seven stars, seven lampstands, and we know what they are. We are told, "These are the seven churches of Asia." As stated earlier, seven is the perfect number of God; it is the round number, it is the complete number, and we are going to find sevens all the way through. We are going to find seven seals, seven trumpets, seven bowls of wrath, and the final seven visions that introduce the new heavens and the new earth. It is all in sevens. These seven churches, in a sense, are a complete picture of the Church of Christ on earth. Somewhere in these seven churches, you can see your church, and just those seven have within them all that we need to know about the Church, even today.

We are familiar with letters from the rest of the New Testament. Paul wrote letters, James wrote letters, John did, Peter did, Jude did. I wonder if you have ever asked the question, "Why should God choose to reveal most of his New Testament in letters?" It is a very strange channel to use, isn't it? Letters are just from here to there, so why should God use letters? I think, first, because letters are very personal and, second, letters are very practical; they deal with real issues. Third, letters are very emotional; most letters have the heart in them, as well as the mind. But really, the basic reason is that letters are always geared to real life.

A person's letters reveal more of their life than anything else. Here we have John the letter writer, except that whereas Paul and Peter used to dictate their letters to a secretary, Jesus is dictating his letters to John. So, it is not John who is the author of this; he is simply the secretary who wrote it down.

It is much easier to study the seven letters to the seven churches side by side. Then, very quickly, you begin to notice things. As soon as you put them side-by-side you see how similar they are. Have you noticed that already? Certainly, they have the same outline, as we might say. They each have seven parts. Now I am going to give you my own labels for those seven parts. Each letter starts with the address, "To the angel of the church in

Ephesus"; "To the angel of the church in Sardis", or Pergamum, or whichever. So, each letter begins with the address.

> **1. ADDRESS**
>   "TO THE ANGEL IN...."
> **2. ATTRIBUTE**
>   "THESE ARE THE WORDS OF HIM WHO...."
> **3. APPROVAL**
>   "I KNOW YOUR DEEDS...."
> **4. ACCUSATION**
>   "YET I HOLD THIS AGAINST YOU...."
> **5. ADVICE**
>   "....OR I WILL COME"
> **6. APPEAL**
>   "HE WHO HAS AN EAR, LET HIM <u>HEAR</u> WHAT THE SPIRIT SAYS TO THE CHURCH<u>ES</u>"
> **7. ASSURANCE**
>   "TO HIM WHO <u>OVERCOMES</u>, I WILL...."
>
> *DIAGRAM 5*

The second part always gives you an attribute of Jesus, some aspect of Jesus' character that the church has forgotten and needs to be reminded of. We get some lovely descriptions of Jesus. "These are the words of him who", and then it tells you something about Jesus, and it is a different aspect of Jesus as he was seen in the vision by John. The vision includes things that the churches are forgetting about Jesus. I think today the churches are forgetting a whole lot of the Jesus of the book of Revelation, and we only see the Jesus of the Gospels. So that is number two.

The third part is this: Jesus then begins by conveying his approval of what is good in the church. So, thirdly, he gives his approval, and he begins with "I know". Jesus knows everything about every church in the world. He says, "I know". It is always, "I know your deeds", I know what you're doing. Before he ever criticises someone, Jesus always says something good about them. The interesting thing is that all the other letters of the New Testament do the same.

If Paul is going to correct the Corinthians, he says something good about them first. There is something we can learn from Jesus here. If you are going to criticise someone, say something good about them first, say something that you approve of. But after Jesus has said, "I know your deeds and they are good," he then comes to the important part of the letter and says, "But I have this against you", and he accuses the church of failing in a particular area and tells them what needs to be corrected now if they are going to be ready for the persecution that is coming. "Yet I hold this against you". Fifthly, he then gives his advice to them about how to put it right. He says that if they do not put it right, then he will come and put it right himself. But how will he put it right? If he has to come and do it, the answer is that he will close the church down. Did you know that Jesus was in the business of closing churches down? That is something that people forget. They think he is just building his church. He is, but that involves closing churches down from time to time. You know, the tragedy is that most of the seven churches of Asia are now closed down. He warned them that if they did not put things right themselves, then he would come and remove their lampstand. Now, that is a very serious thing for Jesus to say to any church of his. He is amazingly patient, but his patience can run out, and then he will come and close it down, because Jesus

This is Your Life

will not permanently allow churches to insult his name.

After that, you find a promise is given. I want you to notice that the promise is always addressed to the individual church member. It is not addressed to the whole church. "He who overcomes," which means quite simply that if you are going to be an overcomer, you will first of all have to overcome inside the Church. Before you can overcome the world, you must overcome the Church; you must overcome the trends in the Church which are not good. "He who overcomes"—"he", not all of you. He is assuming that some churches will not change, but he is saying that each member of that church can change and that you do not need to follow the trends in the church. Stay faithful to Jesus—not faithful to the church, but faithful to Jesus in the church.

You see, I find many people in England who say they cannot be faithful to Jesus because they must be faithful to their church. Have you heard that? Many vicars in the Church of England tell me that. I say, "You know what Jesus is telling you to do," and they say, "Well, I can't do it, I have to do what the church tells me." I say, "No, you don't. You have to do what the Head of the Church tells you, and you must learn to be an overcomer inside the church. If you can't overcome what's going wrong inside the church, you'll never overcome what's going wrong outside the church." That is why the book of Revelation begins with "To the one who is victorious and does my will to the end, I will give authority over the nations" (Revelation 2:26). That is a very important message.

So then comes the number six, but already you may have noticed that half way through number six and number seven change places. Do not ask me why, because I have no idea. But in the first three letters, it follows this order. Finally, every letter ends with an appeal. The appeal is, "He who has an ear, let him hear what the Spirit says to the churches."

What does that mean? Jesus was always saying that after he told a parable. Have you noticed that? When he told the parable of the sower, he said, "He who has an ear, let him hear". What does it mean? It is saying, "I want a reply," or "I want a response," because you could just hear this letter and forget it, but he wants people really to hear it to the point where they want to make a reply, a response to the letter.

I want you to notice that it is what the Spirit is saying to the churches and not to the Church. Jesus deals with every local church separately because the churches vary from place to place and from congregation to congregation. We need to hear from Jesus about our church, wherever that is, because what he wants to say to this church will be different from what he wants to say to that church. He does not address the whole Church; his Spirit speaks to the churches. That is a very important point because these churches were very close to each other.

They were just a few miles apart, so that you could almost see them all from one point, and yet Jesus still addresses himself to each local church. The Head of the Church is directly interested in every local church. The only variation in that order is that after the first three, six and seven change places. But that is the only variation, and the beginning and the end are identical *(see diagram 2 on page 21)*.

Now, when we study them side-by-side, we find that each place is quite clear. In the above map of the region that I mentioned, it is a circle of churches beginning with Ephesus and going right around to Laodicea, but why is it addressed to the angel of each church? The word literally is "messenger", but that is usually used of angels, although not exclusively. Some people say, "Well, it means the minister, the preacher in each church, the messenger in each church," but I would say I am convinced that it means the angel.

The book of Revelation is full of angels, and it does look as if every local church has an angel assigned to it, who is a kind of messenger between that church and Jesus. I have a tape recording of angels singing, which, if you heard it, would make you realise how real they are. It would take your breath away.

But whenever we meet for worship, the angels watch us, and if just one sinner repents, they have a party up there, and we need to be aware of this. When Paul talks about our hairstyle in church in 1 Corinthians 11, he says, "That's because of the angels." We need to remember that angels are bound up with the life of each local church.

But there is another reason why I believe it is addressed to the angels, and that is the fact that John had no way of communicating these letters to the churches if angels did not take them. Now, angels are very practical beings—they can open locked doors. It was an angel who let Peter out of prison. They are very good cooks, did you know that? Don't you remember that Elijah had a hot meal cooked for him by an angel? You see, we read these things, but they do not always register. Well, they are very practical, and these angels were needed to be the postmen to take these letters around the churches.

So, I have no difficulty or problem with angels. If you go to a Church of England church, every time you have Holy Communion, you say the words, "Therefore with angels and archangels and with all the company of heaven we laud and magnify your holy name." I look around sometimes and think, "I wonder how many of you are thinking about angels?" It can just be just words, if you are not careful. People can be like the London secretary who said, "I've got a new pair of earrings," and one of the earrings had "In" written on it, and the other had "Out"! I am afraid that words can go in and out very easily without us registering them.

Then comes the sender, Jesus—I am going through the points again—and Jesus does not use his human name once. He does not say, "This is Jesus." He gives himself all sorts of titles. In Revelation 1:17–18, he says, "I am the First and the Last. I am the Living One; I was dead, and now look, I am alive for ever and ever!". In Revelation 1:14 we are told that his eyes were "like a flame of fire", and in the next verse, his "feet were like fine brass, as if refined in a furnace". Revelation 3:7 says that Jesus is "he who is holy and true, who hold the key of David. What he opens no one can shut, and what he shuts no one can open." All these lovely titles of Jesus really are saying to the church, "You've forgotten something about me which you need to remember." He tells each church something about himself that they have forgotten.

Do you remember from chapter 1 of the present book how many names and titles Jesus has? The answer is 250 in the whole of the Bible, and a lot of them are in the book of Revelation. A lot of those titles he gave himself, which I do not think anyone else in history has dared to do to that extent. Nobody in history has ever had so many names and titles. But it is important to notice which name or title he gives to each church, because that is the one they have forgotten, and that is the one they need to think about.

When we get to his commendation, this is very personal. He always says, "I", and "I know". You see, the most important opinion about the church that you go to is Jesus' opinion about it, not the members' opinion or the minister's opinion or the outsiders' opinion, but what Jesus thinks about the church you go to. Have you ever asked him? Have you ever tried to find out? Ask him sometime and see what he says to you. He says, "I know your works, your deeds, your actions," and this is very important. A Christian is justified by faith but a Christian is judged by works.

That is a very important truth that many Christians overlook. We may be justified by faith at the beginning of the Christian life, but we are judged by works at the end of the Christian life. We are justified by faith, but Jesus judges us by the actions that that faith leads to. In every mention of the Day of Judgment, we are judged for what we have done—not for what we believed or did not believe, but for what we have done. So, Jesus justifies by faith, but he judges by deeds. So, he says, "I know your deeds."

Now, as soon as you look at this, you notice that he has nothing good to say about two of the churches. Have you noticed that? He says good things about five of them, but about two of them, he has nothing good to say. Yet they are the most successful churches in men's eyes. Isn't that striking? They are the churches that are full and have big congregations and big collections and people say, "They're rich, they're successful," and Jesus has nothing good to say about Sardis or Laodicea. But he does have good things to say about the other five.

To Ephesus, he says, "I know your deeds, your hard work and your perseverance. I know that you cannot tolerate wicked people, that you have tested those who claim to be apostles but are not, and have found them false. You have persevered and have endured hardships for my name, and have not grown weary." (Revelation 2:2–3). Crucially, then, they tested and rejected false apostles and did not accept every travelling ministry that came around.

If only churches would check on travelling ministers. The number of churches I know that have got into trouble because they have been impressed by a visiting preacher and got involved with him without checking him out—it is so important. We really need to test and reject false apostles.

If you walk down the main street in Ephesus with modern tourists wandering down it, you are walking where Paul walked *(see photograph 3 on page 76)*. You can see the pagan temples at the far end. Paul was taken into the theatre at Ephesus when there was a riot. We know more about the church in Ephesus than anywhere else. To this day, you can find the tomb of John the Apostle and the tomb of Mary, the mother of Jesus, whom he took there to look after. You can find those still today in those ruins.

Here is what Jesus says about Smyrna in Revelation 2:9: "I know your afflictions and your poverty—yet you are rich! I know about the slander of those who say they are Jews and are not, but are a synagogue of Satan."— people claiming to be Jews who are not. Then, in the next verse, Jesus says to them that " the devil will put some of you in prison to test you, and you will suffer persecution for ten days." Jesus knows.

PHOTOGRAPH 3

When we come to Pergamum, Jesus says, "I know where you are, you are where Satan's throne is." I wonder if you know what Satan's throne means? Towering above Pergamum on the hillside was this pagan temple. It is in the shape of a letter "U" so it looks

This is Your Life

PHOTOGRAPH 4

like a gigantic armchair. They called it "Satan's seat".

Do you know where that is today? It is in Berlin, and there are Christians who are praying that it may be sent back to Turkey. It was brought stone by stone from Pergamum in modern-day Turkey to Berlin where it was re-erected in a gigantic museum. So, Satan's seat is in Berlin now. It was brought there just before Hitler came to power. Many Christians have prayed there that it might be removed. Can you imagine the little city of Pergamum and above it this gigantic armchair building, Satan's "seat"?

Jesus said, "I know where you are, but you didn't deny your faith under pressure."

This church, Pergamum, had the honour of having the first martyr for Jesus. They had a church member who had died rather than deny Jesus. We are told in the letter that his name is Antipas, which means "against everybody". Antipas: "against all". What an interesting name, and that man stood firm against everybody and was the first martyr in western Turkey, or Asia, as it was called then.

To Thyatira, Jesus says, "I know your deeds, your love and faith, your service and perseverance".Philadelphia was another place that did not deny Jesus. They had already had some pressure because again, there was Satan's synagogue. It is amazing how many Christians in England say this to me after I have asked them, "How are things with you?" They say, "Oh well, it's very hard here, there's a lot of Satan worship in the area." Have you heard that kind of thing?

I say, "Great, that's one of the best places to be a Christian," isn't it? But they are kind of excusing the poor church life because, "Oh, satanic worship." Since when was Satan stronger than Jesus? You see, it is crazy to blame Satan worship on the poor state of the Church there. They are making an excuse. It is the very place to be faithful to Jesus and show that greater is he that is in us than he that is in the world. So, you notice that Satan is quite prominent in these letters, and there is a foreboding; there is looming trouble in the letters. To the church at Philadelphia, Jesus says, "Since you have kept my command to endure patiently, I will also keep you from the hour of trial that is going to come on the whole world to test the inhabitants of the earth." (Revelation 3:10)

When we turn to the criticism of the letters, the negative things that Jesus says, again we notice that he does not have anything bad to say about two of them. Did you notice that? He does not have anything good to say about Sardis and Laodicea, but he does not have anything bad to say about Smyrna or Philadelphia. But he does have bad things to say about the other five. About Ephesus, he says, "You have forsaken the love you had at first." Bible scholars argue about whether that is their love for God, or their love for each other, or their love for the lost. Which do you think it is?

You cannot separate those three things. If you do not love your brother, you cannot be loving the Lord. It is all three, and they have lost their first love. That includes their love for the Lord, their love for each other, and their love for the lost. So, we do not need to argue about it because it is all that same agape love. You cannot lose one of those loves without losing the others. It is altogether, absolutely right. "Ephesus, you have forsaken the love you had at first."

Regarding the church at Pergamum, Jesus identifies syncretism and promiscuity. I just want to say that I meet church after church after church in England where those two things are there. Syncretism is mixing Christianity with other religions. I remember watching Nelson Mandela's televised inauguration as president of South Africa. I saw a Muslim reading the Quran, a Jew reading the Old Testament, and there were about six different religions reading one after the other; then Desmond Tutu led in a prayer, a Christian prayer. I just thought here we go again. This is what we call syncretism; you put all the religions together as if they are all different ways to God. That is syncretism, and it is rife in the church in England.

The other thing is promiscuity—the spirit of Jezebel had gotten into the church in Pergamum. Do you know, I hardly go into a church today without finding Christians living in adultery? Jesus said, "To divorce and remarry is living in adultery," and that is in almost every church I go to. The church in Pergamum is very familiar, and Jesus said that they have got to clean that church up before the pressure comes, or they will not be ready to stand for him and be faithful.

There was a lot wrong with Thyatira: "You tolerate that woman Jezebel, who calls herself a prophet. By her teaching she misleads my servants into sexual immorality and the eating of food sacrificed to idols".

Sardis, I find it interesting. He had nothing good to say about Sardis, and what he did have to say was negative. He said, "You have a reputation for being a live church," and yet he said, "I've got nothing good to say about you." Isn't that striking? Then he said about Sardis, "Nothing you start is ever finished." There is something, isn't it? Sardis was good at starting things, but it never got them finished. I know Christians who are wonderful at starting things, but they do not get them finished. Jesus is not impressed with starters, but with finishers.

Next is Laodicea, and I want to say quite a bit about it. On the next page is a picture of Laodicea. This might surprise you. It shows a white mountain because there are hot springs that gush out of the mountainside, and they have covered the mountain with salt and left little pools of salt. It is a wonderful place to go and sunbathe because the sun reflects off the white mountain, and you can bathe in the hot springs of water that it has left. It is supposed to be good for your health. It is a health resort; it is a kind of Bath or Harrogate of western Turkey. Actually, I saw a picture in a modern tourist brochure advertising holidays at Laodicea, encouraging people to go and sunbathe and dip in the hot springs.

Now, when this water full of salts reaches the town of Laodicea, a mile and a half from the mountain, the water is lukewarm. It comes out hot; these are steaming springs, but it is lukewarm. If you drink it when it is lukewarm, you will be sick. It acts like an emetic; it just makes you throw up. Then, by the time it reaches the Aegean Sea at Ephesus, it is cold. You can drink it when it is hot, you can drink it when it is cold, but if you drink it when it is lukewarm, you spew it up. Jesus says to the church at Laodicea, "Lukewarm churches make me sick."

Isn't that interesting? He knew all about this and he says, "You're neither hot nor cold." He says that he can cope with a hot church and he can cope with a cold church, but what he cannot cope with is a lukewarm church. Yet how often do we use the word "warm" of our churches? "We give you a warm welcome." We pride ourselves on being a warm fellowship. We should say, "We give you a hot welcome. We preach the hot gospel here," you see? Jesus would rather we were cold than be lukewarm.

This is Your Life

PHOTOGRAPH 5

This was a very rich church because the tourist industry came here even in Jesus' day. They were very wealthy, and they got big collections. They were a holiday resort church, and often they are quite wealthy. Jesus said, "You are poor, you are blind, you can't even see that I don't attend your church meetings." He said, "I'm outside your church." Then comes a verse which is probably the most misused and misinterpreted verse in the whole book of Revelation: "Here I am! I stand at the door and knock. If anyone hears my voice and opens the door, I will come in and eat with that person, and they with me."

That has nothing whatever to do with conversion or with evangelism. It should never be used in counselling an unbeliever because it gives a totally false picture of what the real situation is. The real situation is that a sinner is the one on the outside who has to knock on the door to enter the kingdom. It is not Jesus who is on the outside knocking to get into your heart, and I am afraid that using that verse has done untold damage. It has "brought people to Christ" without any mention of water baptism, without any mention of receiving the Spirit, and without any mention of repentance.

That is serious, and it makes Jesus so little. It makes him a little Jesus knocking on my heart, wanting to get in. That is not what this verse is about. It is a word to the church, and the door on which he is knocking is the church door. What he is saying is, "I can get back into a church that has lost me if just one church member gets up and lets me in." Now, I think that is a wonderful promise. It means that even for the deadest church, there is hope if just one member will invite Jesus to come in. But this rich, successful church was carrying on without Jesus.

I have another picture—a reproduction of a famous painting of the inside of a cathedral. This picture speaks to me very much. In the picture, the altar is all lit up with the priest, and there is a poor woman kneeling down and weeping, and there is Jesus, and he is not up there with all the priests; he is at the back with this one woman crying out to him.

I wish you could see the original painting because it is a beautiful painting. It is a picture of Jesus coming. He is not coming to all the paraphernalia at the front and all the ritual and the liturgy, though; he is coming to that one woman who needs him. That just speaks to me. That is the church of Laodicea.

Now comes this very strong appeal: "To him who overcomes". In particular, he is appealing to the men of the church, because so often the strength and the weakness of a church is in its men. Are there men in the church who will overcome what is happening in the church? It is an appeal to the individual member. He does not say, "Leave your church" or "Go to another church." He says to overcome what is happening in it.

As we saw in chapter 2 of this book, to those who overcome Jesus makes so many rich promises, from the promise to "give to eat from the tree of life, which is in the paradise of God", to the promise that "I will grant to sit with me on my throne, as I also overcame and sat down with my Father on his throne". What a list of promises to each church member who overcomes the compromises that are taking place in the church in which they worship. All the rewards are for all the overcomers, and it is most striking that all these awards pop up again in the last three chapters of the book of Revelation. They are all promises about the future and about life in the new heaven and the new earth.

Then, finally, comes the call: "He who has an ear, let him hear what the Spirit says to the churches." Jesus was always saying that, and he is really saying, "Have you really heard?" There is an old English word, "harken". Have you heard that word? It means to "pay attention". Jesus is really saying, "You've heard this letter, but have you really harkened to it?" I wish that word were more frequently used, and we could use it.

Have you ever heard an angry parent saying to a little child, "Did you hear what I said?" Have you heard a parent saying that? Well, that is what Jesus is saying: "Did you hear what I said?" It is like a parent saying to a child, "Now go to bed," or, "Put that down," and then the child does not go to bed or does not put it down, and the parent says, "Did you hear what I said?" Well, "He who has an ear, let him hear."

I want to reply to this, and so as we read these seven letters to the seven churches, we are asking the question, "What is Jesus saying to me in my church through these letters?" Somewhere you will hear the voice of the Lord. If you are really hearing this, you are not just studying it to get a diploma or certificate from a Bible college. We are to listen to Jesus, and he is asking whether you are overcoming what is happening in your church or whether you are going along with it because everybody else is.

The churches in England are in a state of crisis, and there are very few people who have the courage to stand up and say, "I'm not going along with that." But the Church is getting conformed to the world in so many ways. I need not outline them as I am sure you are aware of them. Jesus is looking for individual members who will overcome that and say, "I'm not going to go that way. The whole church may go that way, but if it's against the teaching of Jesus, then I'm not going to take part in that." And we need to remember Jesus' promise: "He who overcomes will sit with me on my throne." Well, we have explored the first three chapters. I have not covered everything in them, but I have given you enough to help you to read them in the right way.

Chapter 4

HOW HAS THE BOOK BEEN INTERPRETED?

In this book, I am taking you through the next section of the book of Revelation, and in the following chapter, I am going much deeper and looking at some of the controversial issues, because if you read different books on the book of Revelation, you can finish up in confusion. There are so many schools of interpretation. So, in this, and also in alternate chapters, I want to take an aspect of controversy where Christians disagree with one another and look at it carefully. Now, in chapter 4:1, as we have seen, there is a change of perspective from the present to the future.

Chapters 1 to 3 are only concerned with the state of the contemporary churches in Asia on earth, but we suddenly have the change from earth to heaven, "Come up here," and from the present to the future, "and I will show you what must take place after this". Now, the book of Revelation is full of predictions. Altogether, there are 56 separate predictions about the future. Out of 404 verses, 256 (or 63 per cent) contain a prediction. In other words, two-thirds of the book of Revelation is about the future and predicting future events. But the question is, how far into the future? When will these predictions be fulfilled? Have they happened already? Are they happening right now, or have they not happened yet?

Certainly, the predictions are future to the time of the first readers of this book. Clearly, the book was written around AD96, so those churches at the end of the first century were being told about the future. But our question is: are these predictions future to us as well, or have they already happened, or are they even now happening before our very eyes? That is where there are different schools of interpretation of the rest of Revelation from chapter 4 onwards. There are four different ways of interpreting the book. You can go to any Christian bookstore and pick up commentaries or books about the book of Revelation, and they will drop into one of these four categories of interpretation.

You cannot interpret it all these ways, so we have got to ask which category of interpretation is right. You may or may not have heard of these four labels, but I shall run through them and explain them. The four schools of interpreting this book are called the *preterist* school, the *historicist* school, the *futurist* school, and the *idealist* school. They each give you a different answer to the question: when are the predictions of Revelation taking place? When will they be fulfilled? The preterists say that all the predictions in the book of Revelation were fulfilled at the end of the first century AD or during the first few centuries AD and that the predictions were all fulfilled during the Roman Empire and the fall of the Roman Empire.

Therefore, they take Babylon, the city that falls in the book of Revelation, to be the city of Rome, and certainly Rome was called Babylon by some Christians. The first letter of Peter finishes, "Those who are in Babylon salute you", and yet it was quite clearly written in Rome. Furthermore, it says, "Babylon is a city sitting on seven hills," and it is obvious that Rome sits on seven hills. So, this school says that Babylon is Rome, and in fact, all these predictions were fulfilled immediately following the first-century AD, and therefore, the things predicted are nearly all past to us.

Babylon did fall. The Roman Empire fell. The predictions in the middle chapters of Revelation are concerned with the decline and fall of the Roman Empire. Therefore, as far as we are concerned, we are reading history in this book. The historicist takes the line that between chapter 4 and chapter 18, we have, in fact, the whole history of the last 2,000 years, meaning that Revelation unfolds for us the entire Church age between the first and the Second Coming of Christ.

According to the historicist, you can trace the past 2,000 years of history in these chapters and find out where you are today and find out exactly where we are. In other words, this is the belief that the whole book of Revelation covers the whole of history between the first and the Second Coming of Christ, and each chapter takes us through the next few centuries right up to the Second Coming. I have a little book by E J Watson entitled "Studies in the Revelation: The Historicist Viewpoint Concerning the Seals, Trumpets, and Vials". Just opening it at random, I read what it has to say about the seven seals. For example, Watson says that seal number one covers the period from AD 96 to AD 180, seal number two 183 to 212, seal three 212 to 235, and so on. That comes a bit nearer up to date where we get to the seven bowls. Let us see where he thinks we are.

The first bowl of wrath covers 1792 to 1794; namely the French Revolution. Then the second bowl is 1796 to 1801; the third bowl is 1796 to 1801 as well; the fourth bowl is 1805 to 1807; the fifth bowl is 1808 to 1815; the sixth bowl is 1820 to 1917 — nearly where we are. We are in the middle of the sixth bowl of wrath. That is what is called the historicist point of view. I will be looking at each of these in a moment, but it says that Revelation was not fulfilled in the first century AD, but through all the centuries AD. Now, having said that, there are two versions of it, and this gets a little complicated. The linear version of the historicist position says that the whole thing covers in one line the period from AD 100 to the Second Coming.

But the cyclic version of it says that it keeps going back to the beginning and starting again, and that each series of seven covers the whole period, so that in fact the book keeps going around in a cycle and starting again and covering the same period, so that there are in fact a number of series of visions covering the whole period. So, the linear says there is just one account of the whole of the Church age. But the cyclic says there are a number and it keeps going back to the beginning, and coming back to the present, and going back to the beginning, then coming back to the present.

I do not know if you have read the book by William Hendricksen called "More Than Conquerors". That is one of the most popular books on the book of Revelation. He takes the cyclic or historicist position so that, in fact, he says, the book keeps recapitulating, keeps going back to the beginning and starting again. So, you have a number of reviews of Church history from different angles. The linear says there is only one review of church history. I will just add now that I find the historicist view to be totally unconvincing, but you will come across books that say this.

The futurist takes the line that the middle chapters of Revelation are still future to us and have not happened yet. That is what the word "futurist" means, that in fact those middle chapters describe the end of the age, the final few years of big trouble when history is at its worst—what is known as the Great Tribulation. That, in fact, all the predictions are squeezed into comparatively few years right at the end of Church history and just before Jesus returns. That is the futurist interpretation.

The idealist says that these predictions do not relate to time at all. They are simply an allegorical, mythological presentation of the struggle between good and evil that goes on all the time. They are simply stories or pictures to help us to interpret any time at all; they show that the struggle between the devil and God, between good and evil, goes on in every age, in every century, every year, and these visions help us to interpret and understand what is happening at any time. You must not expect a particular fulfilment at one time, but this is a kind of picture of what is going on all the time.

That is very much Greek thinking. The word "idealist" is a Greek word. It comes from Plato. The word "ideal" comes from that, and really, it is just the same form of interpretation as that used by people who say there were never such people as Adam and Eve, that that was a story to give us a picture to understand our present situation. In other words, it is saying it is a myth. But it is a myth with the truth in it. It is like Aesop's Fables; it is stories.

In other words, it treats the whole thing as a parable, as a fictional story, but one that gives you truths by which you can understand what is going on. Now, those are the four, or if you count these as two, the five positions. You will probably find that every single book on Revelation that you pick up will fit into one or the other of these views. Of course, it makes a great deal of difference in how we handle the book. Are these predictions in the book past to us, or are they present to us? And if the latter, are we in the middle of them, or are they yet to come? Or are they not going to happen specifically at all, but are just there to help us to understand the struggle between good and evil that we all find ourselves in?

I am going to go on to ask what are the grounds for each view and how do we cope with them, because I am afraid it depends very much on what church you go to or what your minister believes or what the preacher you have heard believes, as to how you approach the book of Revelation.

I just want you to understand clearly the different approaches so that you can recognise them. Then, if you borrow a book on Revelation and you read it, you will recognise straight away where the author is coming from. These authors are well-known Christian preachers who would be widely respected, but they take different views. Let us look in more detail at these and evaluate them. I will try to say what is good about each view and what is not so good about each view. That is following the pattern of our Lord in his words to the seven churches in Asia, so I will say what is good about each view and what is wrong about each view.

Let us take the preterist. What is good about that view is that it recognises that this book was written for the first century AD and therefore it must have been meaningful to the people then;

it was written to help them then, so all of it must be shown to be relevant to the first century AD. Our first interpretation of the book must be, "What did the original readers understand by it?" After all, it was for them before it was for us. Now, that is what is good about the preterist. What is not so good is that if all of Revelation is past to us, then it is not of much value to us except by way of historical example. It would simply be looking back and learning from the past, as you look back and learn from the past in the book of Kings, for example.

In other words, it would not help us to face the future, but it would be of historical interest and therefore an example to us of how they faced it. But the biggest thing that is wrong with this is that most of the predictions were not fulfilled in the fall of Rome. The things that Revelation says will happen did not, in fact, happen to Rome, and in fact, have not clearly happened yet. So, to say that it was all fulfilled in the decline and fall of the Roman Empire is simply not true, and it does not fit. Above all, if it is purely preterist and was all fulfilled so long ago, why should it be included in the New Testament? Why should it round off our New Testament as it does?

That is the preterist, now the historicist. What is good about that is that it does claim to have a message for every different age of church history. It does at least say there is something in this book that is relevant to you, which is a good point. The bad point is that no two people can agree on the dates of each bit, and it is almost impossible to line up Church history with the predictions of the book of Revelation. As I quoted above, the fifth bowl has been matched to 1820 to 1917, but when you look at the details, it is a very forced correlation. I find it totally unconvincing.

Every different historicist comes up with a different pattern, lining up this with that. There is no discernible consistency in this approach. This kind of book leaves you very unconvinced and very unsatisfied. You say, "Come off it; you are really forcing it to fit into church history." What is good about the futurist is that the predictions do seem to lead directly to the Second Coming and the end of the age. All the predictions do seem to relate to the Second Coming rather than the first coming of Jesus, and to lead directly up to it. Since he has not come back yet, it makes sense that these predictions have not come true yet. The other thing that is good about the futurist is that most predictions have not been fulfilled yet, so that to take the line they are still yet to happen in the future makes a lot of sense.

Against the futurist view is the criticism that it means that most of the book of Revelation was not relevant to the Church for the last 2,000 years and that it was talking about things that were of no direct interest to the Church all through the last 2,000 years. Would God have given us a book that would only be of any interest or relevance right at the end of history? It seems unlikely, doesn't it? The other thing is that the futurist interpretation invariably leads to an excessive interest in speculation, in calculation, in working out charts, schedules, and maps. Have you seen all these, working out exactly the order of events at the end of history? Well, this approach leads to a curiosity about the future rather than an application to Christian living.

I am afraid that many Christians who get fanatical about Revelation get into this kind of clairvoyant approach, a kind of horoscope reading of the book of Revelation that is purely satisfying intellectual curiosity. The good thing about the idealist interpretation is that it does have a message that is relevant to all Christians in all places at all times. It provides a key to interpreting the struggle between good and evil. But what is bad about this idealist approach is that if you turn it all into myth, into non-historical stories, then we lose any understanding of how the world will end. It simply becomes a fable or a picture of what is going on all the time ad infinitum; we lose any understanding of the last days. It becomes an interpretation of all days instead of an account of the last days.

Above all, it is essentially the Greek thinking that God is

outside time and that time does not matter to God, and that therefore history is not heading towards a goal or a conclusion; it is just going to go on and on as the struggle between good and evil. Basically, the idealist view kills the Second Coming as a historical event. It tends to say, "Jesus is always coming to us in the struggle."

Can you tell which I am yet? I have given you good points and bad points for each of these approaches. Well, I shall keep you guessing a bit longer. I want you to go on thinking hard, because if you are going to study Revelation you have got to tackle this kind of question.

I want to say four things and then I am going to tell you, but let me make four observations. What do we conclude from this evaluation of the four schools of interpretation? Number one: it is obvious that no one key unlocks it all. If you force the book of Revelation into one of these interpretations, you will damage it at some point. So, no one of these unlocks the whole book.

The second thing is I believe that each school has some value and some truth but not all of it. There is no harm in using more than one. Texts can have different meanings and applications, but the important thing is to ask which approach in a particular passage opens up the meaning that was intended by the divine Author and the human writer that they wanted to be understood by the human reader. In other words, we need to be flexible in our interpretation.

Thirdly, the emphasis may change in different parts of the book. We may use one of these keys for one part of the book and another for another. The main questions, of course, are about the middle part of the book; that is where there is most disagreement.

Fourthly, parts of each school of interpretation may be helpful, but as a whole, none of them is because there are some elements in these four schools that are frankly incompatible with each other. All of those four statements mean that we have got to be flexible with each section of the book.

Now I will tell you what I am. I am different things in different parts of the book. There are three main sections in the book, as I have told you, and I use different interpretations for sections depending on which is (or which are) appropriate for that section. Let me show you what I mean.

Do chapters 1 to 3, which we looked at in the previous chapter, apply to the first century AD? The answer is yes.

So, the preterist is at least one correct interpretation of those chapters. Now, the historicist would say that those seven churches represent seven phases in church history, that Ephesus represents the first few centuries and that Sardis represents the next few centuries. You see, they split them up over the Church age and usually come to the conclusion that we are living in the Laodicean age and that the whole church today is like Laodicea. Does that convince you? That is the historicist interpretation of the first few chapters. I am not convinced because I do not think the whole church is Laodicea today. I think maybe a lot in Europe are, but the ones I know in Africa and Asia are not.

So, I cannot see that you split church history up, and each of these churches represents part of the history of the whole Church. That is the historicist approach. So, I question that.

The futurist approach to the seven churches of Asia is that before Jesus comes at the end of history, there will be a church in Ephesus and a church in Sardis and a church in Pergamum again and a church in Laodicea again, that these are seven churches that will reappear at the end of 2,000 years, and that when Jesus comes back each of those towns will have a church again. That is the futurist. Are you persuaded by that? I am not persuaded at all; I just do not believe it.

But the idealist says that these churches between them give you a picture of the Church in any age in any place. Now, are you beginning to understand the flexibility that we need? Most commentaries you see take one of these interpretations and fit everything into it. That to me is a mistake. When we come to the middle section that is the bad bit where things get much worse. Which of the interpretations is appropriate? I do not think the preterist is because in fact those things did not happen when the Roman Empire fell.

So, I rule that one out. I do not look for a fulfilment in the past because the events just did not happen. The historicist view, which I read to you, treating those middle chapters as a complete picture unfolding through the whole of Church history, does not convince me, and I just cannot see it. It is so forced, and no two scholars can agree on what represents what. It just seems to me that it is trying to make it say something that it does not say.

But the futurist, I really can see. In other words, I do believe that most of the predictions in that middle part will happen at the end of history before the Second Coming in the time of great tribulation. Basically, I treat that middle section as futurist.

But I also use the idealist view for this reason. We know that the final Antichrist will come, but John says in his letter (2 John 7–8) that there are already many antichrists in the world. We know that the False Prophet will come, but there are already false prophets. We know that big trouble will come worldwide, but there are already big troubles in China and local areas in Sudan and Angola. In other words, the Great Tribulation is foreshadowed all the way through Church history on a local scale. Therefore, although these troubles will only actually happen at the end of history, already their shadows are cast before them, and we can already see things like them happening.

In other words, I did not believe that Saddam Hussein was the Antichrist, but I did believe he was an antichrist. I did not believe that Hitler was the Antichrist, but he was an antichrist. In other words, we can see events like the end happening already. Therefore, I can apply these middle predictions to any time in Church history. I am not saying that the prediction is related directly to what is happening now; I am saying that what is happening now is a little foreshadowing of that, and it is going to be like that, only worse. Do you follow me?

I believe Antichrist will be worse than any of the people I have mentioned already, but I see him in them. I see the man of lawlessness in the lawlessness of our age. Therefore, I can use this middle section to interpret what is happening now. It is the beginning of that. For example, since 1971, there has been a major shift in the world's weather.

My brother was on the TV for weather forecasts, and he has shown me that from 1971 onwards, the weather worldwide has been far less predictable than it was before, far more extreme. There are greater floods and greater droughts now than there were 30 years ago. There are more earthquakes now. The earthquakes are doubling every ten years and happening in places that never had them before. I see all that as a foreshadowing of what the book of Revelation talks about gigantic hailstones.

The book of Revelation talks about hailstones a hundred weight each. It talks about the whole ocean and all the rivers being so polluted that people cannot drink from them. But I see the beginnings of that. I see so many things around me that remind me of the book of Revelation, only it is far worse there.

So, when I interpret the middle chapters, I do not bother with the preterist; the historicist does not convince me, although some people are convinced, but I certainly use the futurist and I use the idealist. I see these are future events, but I can see them beginning to happen already. So, those are the two that I use for the middle part. Those are the two that I use for the first part.

When I get to the last bit, I have really only got one interpretation. I cannot believe that the new heaven and the new earth and the New Jerusalem came in the first century AD. I cannot believe we are in it now. I just cannot, except in spirit, where citizenship is in the heavenly Zion, but I cannot see the New Jerusalem on earth yet. I certainly believe it is coming. I am not sure that I can see foretastes of it because it is going to be a brand-new earth and a completely new city built out in space and coming down out of heaven. So, it seems to me that the futurist is the only interpretation that you can apply to that last section.

So, when we go through the sections of Revelation, I find I have to shift from one key to another to unlock it. That seems to me the approach that we should take. It is when you pick up a book that says, "It's all this," and it presents one part and has nothing about another part, that I feel the author has got into an artificial situation where they have forced their interpretations to fit a system. Almost every book on Revelation that I have studied does just that; it is forcing the book into a particular line of interpretation, and it just does not work. I am always very wary of people forcing the Bible to say what they want it to say.

I want to remind you, finally, that the overall purpose of the book is practical. If you are not careful with these different schools of interpretation, you get away from the practical and into what I call the speculative. Some people are just curious to know what is going to happen and when it is going to happen, whereas really the book is written not to tell you what is going to happen or when, but to get you ready for what is going to happen so that the crisis will not cut you out and you will not be surprised by it.

That is a very important point because when we get into those middle section chapters (4 onwards), one of the things that hits you straight away is that it is terribly difficult to put the predictions in order because sometimes the revelation jumps backwards and there is a kind of flashback, a recapitulation, and sometimes it jumps right forward to the end. Although there are some sequences like the seals and the trumpets and the bowls, there are bits in between that make you wonder where they fit in. In other words, if Jesus was giving us a timetable, a schedule, an order of events so that we would know exactly where we were when they happened, then frankly, he has not done a very good job.

It is messed up because he should have given it to us in the exact order, because it is written for simple people like us. When you try to fit all the events into an order, into a timetable and write them out so that this will be first, that will be second, and that will be third, you find it almost impossible to do. So why has Jesus made it so difficult for us to fit these things together? Well, the answer is that he does not want you to know the order. He wants you to know what is going to happen rather than when it is going to happen. Because his interest is not in satisfying your curiosity so that you can say, "Ah, we're living in the middle of chapter 16." That is not his interest. His interest is to help us to be so prepared for the worst that when it happens, we will remain faithful to Jesus.

For example, I keep getting asked questions about the identity of the two witnesses in chapter 11. Who are the two witnesses that get killed in Jerusalem? I do not know who they are. I have no idea. When it happens, I will know and I will tell you. The point is, it is to help me to be ready so that when it does happen, I will say, "Oh, well he told us this would happen, and it's going to be all right."

This means that when the worst happens, we can lift up our heads and say, "Hey, it's getting near." It is all happening according to Jesus' plan. That is the beauty of it, which means that nothing is going to happen that he is not ready for, and nothing needs to happen that we are not ready for. Now that is the purpose of the book. As mentioned, you make a big mistake if you think of it as a kind of Old Moore's Almanack, so that you can predict the future, so that you can be in the secret knowledge of the future. It is nice being in the know, isn't it? And saying, "I know what's going to happen and you don't." It is not for that at all. It is so that we can be ready for it when it does happen, and not be predicting or forecasting when it will happen, but saying what will happen.

I just love preaching the book of Revelation, but I do not try and do it in such a way that it just satisfies people's curiosity about the future, but in such a way that they know what is coming—not *when,* but *what* is coming. The important thing is that they know *who* is coming. Now, let us begin on the next section, chapters 4 to 19, to which I give the title "Things will get much worse before they get better." Yet the first part of this section is a surprise. Instead of getting straight into telling us what is going to happen, the Revelation shows us God on his throne in heaven. As you read chapter 4, an incredible sense of peace comes to you.

If you have read it already, you will know what I mean. You see the most beautiful, peaceful picture, and you see God sitting down on a throne without moving, just sitting there. You see in front of him a glassy sea, the calmest sea, just like a mirror that stretches from horizon to horizon. Above the throne, you see this beautiful rainbow, and the colours of it are breathtaking. You just see God sitting on his throne in this complete peace, and before you are told about all the troubles down on earth, you are told that God is on the throne. That is so that you will not be so disturbed by what comes later.

You get this tremendous sense that God is not worried about the future. God is not disturbed. God is not struggling with Satan—we are, but he is not. It is terribly important to know that Satan cannot do a thing without getting God's permission first. Do you realise that? He cannot touch you unless God says he can do so. You read the first chapter of Job. Now, that gives a wonderful sense of this. Nothing has got out of God's control. God has not lost control of history. We may think he has because all we see is what is happening on earth, and we think, "God's lost control of the situation." He has not at all. He is sitting calmly on his throne because it is all working out his way, and history is in his hands.

Do you remember the little girl I mentioned running home from Sunday school singing, "God is still on the phone. God is still on the phone." She got it a little wrong; the chorus is, "God is still on the throne." You see, the picture we are given in chapter 4 is before you see all the disturbing events, all the crises, the tragedies, the disasters that are going to come before the end of history. God is just sitting on his throne, as if to say, It's all right.

Everything's under control. It's going my way. I know how I'm going to finish it. You get this tremendous sense of worship.

The book of Revelation is full of worship. It is full of music. It is full of the most wonderful sights for your eyes and sounds for your ears. Many hymns are based on the book of Revelation, and of course, lots of Handel's *Messiah* comes out of the book of Revelation, including the Hallelujah Chorus. It is full of praise to God, the God who made it all, who is running it all; that God is still in total control of everything. That is why he has made a promise to every Christian—you will never be tempted more than you can bear. There is no situation in which a Christian has to give in. God has promised never to allow you to be tempted more than you can say no to.

I meet many Christians who ask me to deliver them, requesting the ministry of deliverance from something they cannot say no to. But God has promised that they will never be in that situation. God is in total control of Satan, and he will not let Satan tempt you too much. It does not say he will not let you be tempted; otherwise, you would never grow up if God made it easy for you. You will be tempted, but he will never let you be tempted too much. He has a piece of rope around Satan, and he only lets him go so far. That is a lovely promise.

We are shown this picture of God surrounded by the creatures he has made, surrounded by the angels; they are all singing away. They are singing hallelujah; they are singing glory to God before ever the book of Revelation tells you about any of the troubles coming on earth. It says you must get your eyes fixed on God and realise that he is at peace. He is the God of peace. He is not disturbed. He is not worried, and he is not surprised by anything that is going to happen. He knows it all.

You see, that is our security, isn't it? To know that God is not worried is a big help to me, because when you are in a situation where you are afraid, isn't it great to be with someone who is not afraid? When you are disturbed and upset, isn't it great to have someone alongside you who is not disturbed and upset? Somehow, they communicate their peace to you. That is how it is.

Chapter 4 is fundamental to the book. Isn't it kind of Jesus to let us see that before he shows us what is going to happen? Then, in chapter 5, John realises that God has written down the end of history on a scroll, and that he has written down everything that will happen before the end of the world and then rolled it up and sealed it with seven seals, and that he cannot bring history to a conclusion until he finds someone worthy to break the seals. God the Father has decided that he himself will not bring history to an end. He wants a Man to do that. He wants history to be in a Man's hands. He wants a Man to end history, a Man to break the seals, or as we would put it, a Man to press the button for the countdown of history.

I meet many people who are afraid that a man will press the wrong button. North Korea has the atom bomb now. Who is going to press the button and cause the Holocaust that brings the world to an end? I am not worried about that because no man can get his finger on that button. John begins to weep because God cannot find a man good enough to press the button to bring history to an end. He wonders whether that means that evil is going to go on forever. Does it mean that this world with all its suffering, with all its sin, and with all its vice and crime, cannot be brought to an end? He weeps over that. Frankly, if you knew that this world was going to go on forever in the state that it is in now, wouldn't you weep? No, it has got to come to an end; someday evil must be dealt with.

Someday it has got to be wound up, and only the good things will survive. It has got to happen. But John wept because nobody was found worthy. Then suddenly he sees somebody standing by the throne who is like two animals. Now, here I want to correct a wrong impression. He sees somebody who is like a lion. That is a good impression, the king of the jungle, a lion of the tribe of Judah. But it also says that he looks like a lamb. As explained in chapter 1, I think that is the word that really misleads us. The word should be "ram", not "lamb". Unfortunately, when people read the phrase, "Lamb of God", they think of a little cuddly white thing a few weeks old that cannot hurt a fly, which you see in stained glass windows in churches, in children's Bibles, and in picture books.

Again, it is important to emphasise that the lamb always had to be one year old. By that time a sheep is fully grown, and a male lamb of one year has horns, and you would not like to be shut up in a room with a one year old ram. Recently, I was reading in Exodus, and it said, "The Passover lamb could be either a sheep or a goat." Did you know that? They could have used a male goat for the Passover. Would you like to be locked in a room with a male goat that is one year old? Would you feel you wanted to go and cuddle it, or would you stay at the far end of the room? Here we are told that this lamb has seven horns. Now, Jacob's sheep have six. Have you seen sheep with six horns, with three on each side? But this has one in the middle as well.

If you saw a one-year-old ram with seven horns, I do not think you would want to go and play with it. It is a very strong picture, and so whenever I get to the word "lamb" in my Bible, I cross it out and put "ram", because it is wrong to picture the Jesus of Revelation as a little cuddly woollen thing. It is a totally wrong picture. He is a full-grown ram. When you put together a ram with seven horns and a lion, you have got a pretty strong animal.

Yet John sees this animal, and he sees that it has been slain. It still bears the marks of someone who has been killed. Then comes the voice, "He is worthy to break the seals," on the programme of the final age of history. That is when the action begins to happen, with the breaking of those first seals.

But, you see, before the action of the end of history happens, you have got this very static picture of God unmoving on the throne around a glassy sea. You have got this picture of stability. You have got this picture of unchangingness, and it is from that throne that there comes the scroll of the fearsome events which wind up history and bring evil to an end. The picture of Jesus breaking the scroll, the seals, and releasing the disasters would be quite wrong if it immediately followed the letters to the seven churches. You see, this is against the background of a God who is totally at peace, in total control, is not going to be caught by surprise at anything, and now says, "Now you can start it". This is the end of history. I will just mention the first four seals, and then we must finish this chapter.

The first four seals are four horses, and straight away, we are into symbolism. The key to those four horses is their colour. The colour of the first horse is white, the colour of the second horse is red, the colour of the third horse is black, and the colour of the fourth horse is pale green. These four horses ride out into the world, and they are often referred to as "the four horsemen of the apocalypse" — have you heard that phrase? Well, in every series of seven, we find that the first four of the seven go together — that is just a clue to help you with the later series of sevens. The first four seals belong together; they are the four horses with different colours. What do they mean?

From the rest of the Bible, we know exactly what they mean and, indeed, they are explained here. The white horse is always the horse used by a military aggressor. It is the horse of a conqueror. Jesus himself comes on a white horse at the end of the book. But here it is a symbol of military aggression, of imperialism, of somebody wanting to expand his empire or territory, riding out to conquer others. Inevitably, anyone who does that brings about the appearance of the red horse, which is bloodshed. When people are trying to take territory from others, they invariably cause bloodshed.

The black horse is the colour of famine. Human flesh goes black when there is famine. It talks about the shortage of food, and a huge amount of money is needed to buy a little bit of food if you read on. It is the horse of famine. When there is a shortage of food, invariably the fourth horse follows. Pale green is the colour of disease, of plague, of sickness. Those four horses are very clear, aren't they?

Military aggression leads to bloodshed, which leads to shortage of food, which leads to disease, pestilence. I can see the four horses in Europe today. I can see them in Africa. But those four horsemen will one day ride through the whole earth. They have been riding so many times already. I can see the foreshadowing, but here they ride out into the whole world, and you see shortly afterwards that something like a quarter of the world's population has perished.

Well, that has never happened yet, has it? It has just not happened on that scale, but in certain countries, it is happening on that scale. So, we can see it coming. That is the beginning of the disasters that are unfolded in the middle of the book of Revelation. But they make so much sense to me. Yes, I know it is in symbolism, I know it is in a picture, but they stand for those simple four things: aggression, bloodshed, famine, disease. It is an inevitable progress, and it is happening now locally, but will one day happen on a world scale. Yes, it is frightening, but do not forget that God is still on the throne and God is still reigning over the whole scene. He is allowing it to happen, yes, because these things must happen, and Jesus said, "I've told you beforehand so that your heart will not be troubled." I just thank Jesus that he has been so honest with us. He said, "If it were not so, I would tell you." He has told us the worst so that we may be ready for it.

Well, we have got into the beginning of chapter six, and in the first half of the next chapter of this book, we will look at chapter 6 through to about chapter 16 and really get to grips with that. That is when you get out of your depth, usually, but we will get to grips with it and we will study it carefully.

Then in the next chapter, I want to look at one very important question, and it is this. There is a teaching that is very widespread in the Church today. It began in about 1830 and it is now almost universal, and that is that the Church will be taken out of the world before all these bad troubles come. I am sure you must have heard of this. It is sometimes known as "the secret Rapture of the Church", and I want to look very carefully at that because it is the most important question when we read that middle bit of Revelation: when the trouble is at its worst, are we going to be in it or not? That is a very important question, and it is one on which Christians differ, but one on which we need to be sure of what we believe. I will tell you what my position is then.

Chapter 5

BIG TROUBLE

We are now in the very heart of the book of Revelation, the most difficult part, the most difficult to understand, and the most difficult to apply to our daily living. So let me just recap a little to pick up the threads. We are in the second of three major sections of the book of Revelation. You will remember that we divided the book of Revelation into the present and the future. Chapters 1 to 3 talk about the present, and I will give that section the title "Things which must be put right now". It deals with the condition of the seven churches of Asia, which represent all churches.

But in chapters 4 to 22, we are into the future. John is invited to come up into heaven and look ahead, so from now on, he sees not just things on earth but things in heaven, and he sees not only things in the present but things in the future. Now, I have divided the second half of the book into two parts. The first part is chapters 4 to 18, to which I will give the title "Things will get much worse before they get better". Then, in chapters 20 to 22, "Things will get much better after they get worse". Now, I have missed out chapter 19 because in chapter 19, we have the Second Coming of Jesus, and it is that which makes all the difference in terms of moving from things getting much worse to things getting much better.

So, we are right in that middle section when things will get much worse before they get better. Let me just remind you of chapters 4 to 5. Before we look at the dreadful things that are going to happen at the end of our world, we get this tremendous picture of the Creator and his creatures in heaven—a most colourful, beautiful, peaceful, powerful scene with God on his throne, quite undisturbed by what is happening down here on earth. There are a lot of threes in that chapter. God himself is called holy, holy, holy. He is also described as the God who was, and is, and is to come. And, as you know, God is a Trinity.

Then there are 24 elders with crowns and thrones around God, and many people ask why 24. The only answer I can give is that there were 12 tribes of Israel and 12 apostles. Right at the end of this book, in the new city called the New Jerusalem, you find 24 names inscribed on the city—12 tribes, 12 apostles. It is saying that the old and new covenant peoples of God belong together; Israel and the Church are together God's people, or will be at the end. So that is why there are 24 elders. Then there are four creatures.

Now, these are rather weird creatures, and again, I do not have the complete answer to what they are, but if you go to Coventry Cathedral, you will find above the high altar a weird, if not grotesque, tapestry. It is an incredible piece of work. There are literally millions of stitches in that huge tapestry. In the original architect's plans for Coventry Cathedral there was to be a beautiful rose window there done by the same artist who did the baptistery window, which is sheer poetry in glass.

I think it is a great tragedy that they cancelled the rose window and decided on this huge tapestry. It really is quite weird, but it is a tapestry of Christ in the book of Revelation, of Christ in glory, and around him are those four living creatures. They are quite grotesque. They certainly are not only living creatures.

Basically, one is a lion, one is an ox, one is an eagle, and one is a man. I think between them they represent all God's creatures from the four corners of the earth, although some people say they represent the four Gospels, which I think is a bit far-fetched. But there are the four creatures on that tapestry around Christ, representing every other creature in the four corners of the earth.

Then in chapter 5, we have the picture of the lion and the lamb, or rather, as I said in the last chapter, the ram. It is a much stronger

Big Trouble

picture than a little lamb. Here we have at last a human being who is worthy to "press the button" and start the countdown to the end of world history. God the Father was looking for a man to do this. But a man must be worthy of that, and Jesus proved himself worthy to end history by dying for everybody within history and coming first to save everybody from a dreadful end. That makes Jesus worthy to end history itself. So, we get the picture of Jesus actually ending history. It is this that makes us really quite fearful of Jesus unless we are in a good relationship with him. You see, after he opens the scroll and the countdown of world history begins, we have the expression, "The wrath of the Lamb".

This is the day of the Lord's anger. Again, here is a picture of Jesus that you do not get very often in the Gospels; only about half a dozen times in the Gospels is Jesus so angry with people that they run away from him. It was his anger that cleansed the temple once, and he actually whipped people. That is not gentle Jesus meek and mild. That is a Jesus who, from time to time, showed his anger when he was on earth. He was very angry when they would not let him bless the little children. He was very angry when they did not want him to heal a man with a withered hand on the Sabbath. But, he was most angry when he found that the temple was a place of commerce and fraud. He just said, "How dare you turn my Father's house into a den of thieves?"

However, those little glimpses of Jesus in anger on his first visit are really nothing compared with the view of Jesus that we have in the book of Revelation. Listen to these verses at the end of chapter 6: "Then the kings of the earth, the princes, the generals, the rich, and the mighty, and both slave and free, hid in caves and among the rocks of the mountains. They called to the mountains and the rocks, 'Fall on us and hide us from the face of him who sits on the throne and from the wrath of the Lamb! For the great day of their wrath has come, and who can withstand it?"

Now, that is going to be a very different Jesus from the one that many people think they will meet one day. It is the time when the Lord will boil over in anger at what people have done to this beautiful world. That is really what we are talking about. That anger results in a whole lot of disasters, which we are going to look at now. They come one after the other and are released when Jesus breaks the seals on the scroll. We are now into a period of very great trouble. It is called here "The Big Trouble" or "The Great Tribulation"—that is the phrase. I call it the Big Trouble, a time of distress worse than anything the world has yet seen.

Many of these troubles are not difficult to understand. Let us look at them. There are three series of seven troubles called seals, trumpets, and bowls. When you look at the meaning of all these 21 things, it is not hard to understand them. In fact, they have become entirely credible in our day, and it is very easy to understand these things happening. But when you add them together, it is a lot of trouble. It is one trouble after another. Well, we are in the middle section of Revelation, which is bad news. Things will get much worse before they get better. So, we have wars and famines and earthquakes and hailstorms and polluted rivers and oceans and diseases killing a third of mankind. Do you find all that difficult to believe? I do not. It is entirely credible now.

Now, the problem is to discover the order of these events, but let us go through the events themselves before we go any further. In the last chapter, I introduced you to the first four seals, which come to us in the form of four horses of different colours: a white horse, a red horse, a black horse, and a green horse. Those colours have always been symbols of military aggression; conquerors usually ride on white horses, and Napoleon did for one. A red horse symbolises bloodshed. A black horse symbolises famine because that is the colour that human flesh turns to under malnutrition. The green horse symbolises disease, which usually follows famine when the physical resistance is low.

That is a series of four things, which you can see in local situations in many parts of the world—aggression, then bloodshed, then famine, then disease. We can see them in parts of Africa; we can see them in many parts of the world. But here we are not only seeing them in local countries, but on a worldwide scale, a greater scale than before.

Numbers five and six are quite different from the first four. Number five begins to talk about the troubles that God's people will have, in addition to the general troubles there will be for everybody. In other words, God's people will suffer more than others because they will suffer the general natural disasters as well as being a kind of scapegoat for those disasters. People have to find someone to blame.

God's people are going to be hit worse than others, but then that has always been the case. God's people suffer more than other people. We suffer from the normal things that go wrong in the world. We also suffer because we do not belong to this world. So, God's people have a double portion of suffering. It is normal for God's people to suffer, but it will be worse at the end. So here we have seal number five, persecution of Christians and, in Revelation 6:10, the believer's prayer to God, "How long, Sovereign Lord, holy and true, until you judge the inhabitants of the earth and avenge our blood?"

Then, in number six, we go back to the world of unbelievers, and we have huge earthquakes and terror from those earthquakes. I have never been in an earthquake. I was once at the top of a skyscraper in Seattle, in America, when there was a tremor and I thought at first it was me beginning to faint. But then I realised the whole building was swaying, but it was not too bad. But people who have been in a bad earthquake have told me that the most terrifying part of it is that there is nothing to hold on to because there is nothing that is stable. The whole world is shaking.

That is seal number six, and then number seven is quite a surprising one—silence in heaven for half an hour. What is so surprising is that it tells you that heaven is quite a noisy place. Well, we know it is a very musical place. There is a lot of singing there, but all seven seals are greeted with total silence in heaven for half an hour. That is probably unheard of in heaven.

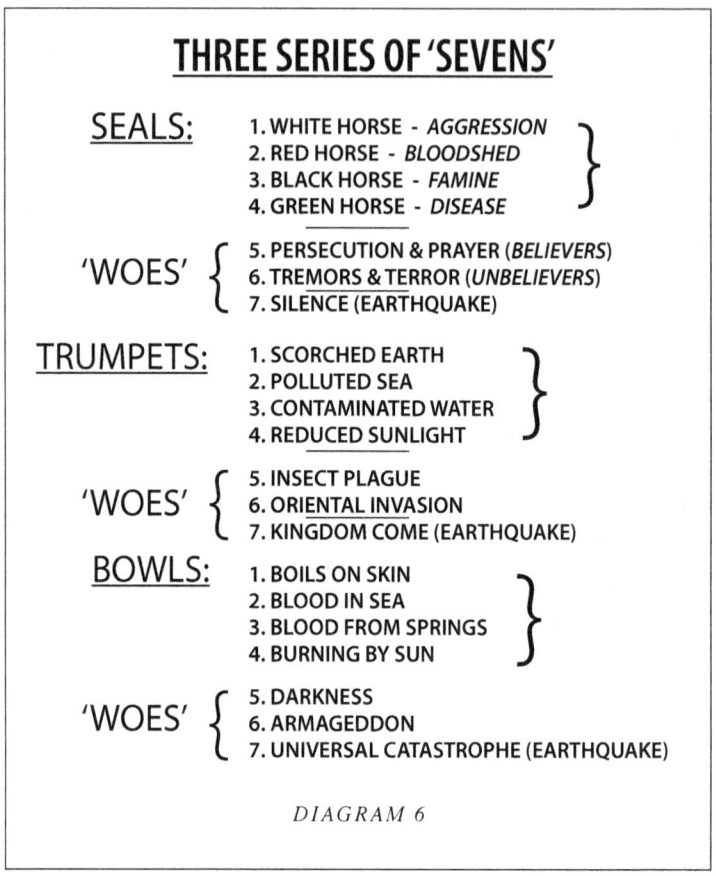

DIAGRAM 6

So those are the seven seals, and I want you to notice something about this. The first four belong together, but the next two, five and six, are different from the first four. The seventh is totally different from the other six. In other words, there is a series of four, two, and one. We will find that this is a common pattern all the way through to the end of the book of Revelation; a series of seven is always composed of four, and two, and one. So, the first four belong together in a pattern, then the next two go together, and the final one stands on its own. We notice that the seals five, six, and seven are described as woes.

Now, that word "woe" is a curse. It is a word we should never use. I tremble when I hear a parent say to a little child, "Woe betide you if you do that again." We should be very careful in our use of words. Woe is the opposite of blessed, and Jesus uttered as many woes as he uttered the word "blessed". Did you notice that? For example, in Luke's version of the Sermon on the Mount Jesus says, "Blessed are you poor", then "But woe to you who are rich". He says, "Blessed are you who weep now", but "Woe to you who laugh now". Blessed, woe, blessed, woe. Jesus once said this to five large cities. For example, in Matthew 11:21, he said, "Woe to you Chorazin! Woe to you Bethsaida!" Then, in Matthew 11:23: "And you, Capernaum, will you be lifted to the heavens? No, you will go down to Hades"; and if you go to Galilee today where all those cities were, you will find that they have all gone and there is not a trace of them left, just a few ruins.

However, there was one city on the shore of Galilee that Jesus did not say 'woe to':the city of Tiberias. That is where you will stay if you go to Galilee, because it is the only city still standing. There were 250,000 people living in Galilee in Jesus' day, and modern tourists get there and say, "Oh, isn't it beautiful and peaceful?" I'm not surprised Jesus loved this. But there were a quarter of a million people living there in five cities, and Jesus said, "Woe to you because you didn't believe the miracles I did in your streets." When Jesus says, "Woe", that is a curse. So, every city that Jesus said "Woe" to has disappeared. The only city that he did not say "Woe" to is still there. That is why you must notice this word "woe" when it occurs. It is a very serious word.

The last three seals are called woes. We are going to see that the last three trumpets are called woes, and the last three bowls are called woes, meaning that the last three in each series are much worse than the first four. There is the element of cursing coming into the climax of each of the seven series.

Let us, therefore, look at the seven trumpets. One, two, three, and four again go together. They are all concerned with the environment, with what we call ecology now. The first is a scorched earth, a dust-bowl earth that cannot grow food; a polluted sea is the second; contaminated fresh water is the third, and reduced sunlight is the fourth. Of course, sunlight is the source of our life and energy, the source of our food. It is the source of so much.

So, these first four trumpets are natural disasters. The first four seals were caused by human beings, but these four are now the environment going wrong—seriously wrong—and therefore unable to support the population. Again, five and six are rather different to the first four. Five is an insect plague. Locusts are mentioned. I have only once been in a locust plague in Kano, northern Nigeria. I had never seen anything like it. At eleven o'clock in the morning, the sky went dark. I thought it must be an eclipse, but it was not. It was a locust swarm. I measured them; they were flying at 12 miles an hour, and it took three-quarters of an hour for the swarm to pass.

I was just watching a whole tree, and after they had passed, there was not even bark on the tree. It was just like a white skeleton. The poor Africans were trying to save their little cabbages, but they could not. You could hear them all chomping. Have you ever seen a locust swarm? There are millions upon millions of these little things, and they just eat everything in their path. Well, that is number five.

Number six is a human invasion by a vast army from the direction of China, coming from the Oriental world. I do not know if it will be Chinese or who it will be, but there is a monumental invasion by a vast army from the East somewhere. But, in number seven, once again, we have a complete change and now an announcement (in Revelation 11:15) that "The kingdom of the world has become the kingdom of our Lord and of his Messiah, and he will reign for ever and ever."

So, once again, we have a series of seven with the first four going together, the next two taking a different turn, and the last, the seventh, taking a completely different turn. Notice the pattern here. There is a clear pattern emerging. When we come to the bowls, we have some serious things happening, which will have an immediate effect on worldwide health.

The first bowl leads to an outbreak of terrible boils on the skin, terrible ulcers and sores on the skin. The second is blood in the sea. That happened in the western Pacific some years ago. You may remember when the whole western Pacific off the shores of South America went blood red. It has happened locally before. It is a weird sight to see an ocean of blood, but here the whole sea, all of it, and similarly the same thing happening from the springs of water. Finally, there is intense burning by the sun—presumably a reduced ozone layer, which would lead to an increase of cases of skin cancer. Well, these four things clearly and directly attack human life and make it extremely vulnerable; they can be painful and even fatal.

Then we have five and six taking a different turn. Five is total darkness over the face of the earth—terrible darkness. Other parts of the Bible also talk about the sun, moon, and stars losing their light. Then number six announces for the first time the last great battle of this age, Armageddon. It just mentions it and then leaves it. We are going to see it in much fuller detail when we get to chapter 19. Finally, seven, bowl number seven, a universal catastrophe which will shake the whole earth. Once again, five, six, and seven are called woes.

Let us summarise these three series. First of all, each series splits into three parts: four, two, and one. That is very important to understand. The last three, that is the two and the one, numbers five, six, and seven. In other words, the last three in each case are called woes, which are curses, and therefore, they are somehow worse than the other four.

The second thing that I want you to notice is that each series of seven is worse than the previous series in terms of its effect on human life; for example, in one of the seals, a quarter of the world's population dies, but in one of the trumpets, a third of the world's population dies. Now, it is a third of what is left, but a third is a larger proportion, so there is an intensification here of things getting worse and worse. They are not the same. The trumpets are worse than the seals, and the bowls are worse than the trumpets. Next, we notice there is an acceleration, as well as an intensification. The things get shorter as they get worse. Things move more quickly as they get worse, so there is a speeding up, as well as an intensification of the tragedies.

Now, what does all this that we have gone through remind you of? Does it remind you of anything elsewhere in the Bible? Rivers turning to blood, locusts, the plagues in Egypt—it is astonishingly like what happened to Pharaoh, only much worse. But it looks as if the plagues in Egypt, of which there were ten, were a kind of foretaste. What God did to Pharaoh, He will finally do to Antichrist. Do you see the parallel? It is remarkably similar.

Next, I want you to notice that the seals have human causes: aggression, bloodshed, resulting in famine and disease. That is all caused by man. The trumpets have natural causes. They come from the environment. But the bowls have supernatural causes. They are poured out by angels. There is no mention of angels doing this until the bowls.

So, once again, there is a clear progression of human disasters, natural disasters, and supernatural disasters caused by angels. So, I hope you have got this picture of what we call an exponential curve, a kind of climax building up. Then comes another big question: How do these all relate to each other, the three trumpets, the three seals, and the three bowls? Let us look at the ways in which people have tried to relate them to each other. There are three ways in which people have related them.

CHAPTER 6 -16
A. SUCCESSIVE
SEALS	TRUMPETS	BOWLS
1234567	1234567	1234567

B. SIMULTANEOUS
SEALS	1234567
TRUMPETS	1234567
BOWLS	1234567

C. SUCCESSIVE, SPEEDED, SIMULTANEOUS
SEALS	1234-56		7
TRUMPETS		1234-56	7
BOWLS			1234-567

DIAGRAM 7

First, there is what we call the "Successive Way", which means simply that the seals are followed by the trumpets, followed by the bowls. Many commentators have simply said, "That's how they relate," that you have one, two, three, four, five, six, seven seals; one, two, three, four, five, six, seven trumpets; and then one, two, three, four, five, six, seven bowls. Well, I am going to say that I do not think that is the answer for the simple reason that number seven in each case seems to be the same one, and while they are different from one to six, seven is always the same, and it is a worldwide earthquake. So, it is not quite as simple as just having seven seals followed by seven trumpets followed by seven bowls.

So, some other people have come up with an alternative, which is called the "Simultaneous Way" of relating them to each other.

The simultaneous way of relating them is to say they are parallel, that each goes back to the beginning again. This acknowledges that number seven is the same in each case, so therefore people say, "Well, it must come at the same period." You are just looking at it from different angles, so that the seals look at the same period of trouble from the human angle, the trumpets look at the same period from the natural angle, and the bowls look at the same period from the supernatural angle. That view is to be found in William Hendricksen's "More Than Conquerors". We tend to call it the recapitulation theory for obvious reasons, because people are just going back and back. Well, that does not seem to fit either.

It seems to me that both the successive and simultaneous have some truth in them, but we actually need both to understand how they fit. So, there is a synthesised approach that says that one to six seals are followed by one to six trumpets, which are followed by one to six bowls, but the seventh always looks forward to the same event, the very end. So, we have the seals one, two, three, four, five, six, but the seventh moves right along ahead to the end. Then following the sixth seal, we have the six trumpets, one, two, three, four, five, six, and then number seven looks along to the very end.

The sixth trumpet is followed by the six bowls, one, two, three, four, five, six, and then the seventh looks at the very end. So that the seventh is the same event, but all the others are different. I have tried to explain it as clearly as I can. That, I think, is how those three series relate.

But then we have some more complications on top of that, believe it or not. The complications are that we have some chapters inserted in all that, which are clearly interludes. Between the sixth and the seventh seal, chapter 7 is inserted, which is not part of the series. Between the sixth and seventh trumpet, chapters 10 to 11 are inserted; they are not part of the series.

Since the bowls are all so close together right at the end, there is no way to put an interlude in there, so that, in fact, it is put in before the seven bowls. But chapters 12 to 14 belong to the seven bowls, so that there are six seals and then right at the end, number seven. Then in the gap we have chapter 7, then on the next line after the sixth seal we have six trumpets, and then an interlude, chapters 10 to 11, and then the seventh.

Then we have an interlude before the bowls that fits into the last series, which is so close together that they cannot fit it in. We then have one, two, three, four, five, six bowls and then the seventh. Now then, why is it all so confused? Jesus was an excellent teacher, so why could he not give it to us in a more straightforward manner? Well, I have done this to show you that, in fact, Jesus was not intending us to work out a timetable. He was telling us everything that would happen, telling us the worst that could happen, but he did not want us to concentrate on the order of events because that is not the most important thing in this middle section. That is my reading of it. If Jesus were simply giving us a timetable of the events of the countdown of history, then he could have given it to us very much more clearly than that. But he has not done so.

Therefore, I believe that by concentrating on the order of events, we are actually concentrating on the wrong aspect of all this. Right in the middle of chapter 13, there is a call to the saints to endure and to be faithful and obedient to Jesus throughout the Big Trouble. That is the real point of all this. Not so that you can sit down and work out a nice order, but so that you can be ready for everything. That is the major thrust of it, not to get it all nicely tabulated, but so that you can be ready. But I have given you virtually what is the outline of this middle section.

There are six seals, then chapter 7, then the seventh seal, six trumpets, then chapters 10 to 11, then the seventh trumpet. Chapters 12 to 14, then all seven bowls. That is the order, and I think if you have got that pattern in your mind, then we can tackle the bits of it. But you see, the order is really too complicated for the ordinary reader, and therefore I am quite sure that Jesus did not want us to concentrate on the order of events.

Let us look now at those interludes. I have looked at the seals and the trumpets and the bowls. Wouldn't it be much simpler if that were the extent of the content in the middle section? But it is not. There are interludes, and there are two other factors, which make the order even more complicated. Factor number one: there are constant recapitulations; there is constant going back to something earlier. In addition to that, there are anticipations of things that have not even been mentioned yet, like Armageddon. We do not know what that is about yet.

We do not know what things like the fall of Babylon are about yet, so that is all jumbled up. You have got the basic seals, trumpets, and bowls, but in between you have got things that look back to the beginning, things that look on to the end, and you have got all these interludes. In other words, the whole thing is jumbled up, and I think that is to prevent you from trying to get it all neatly worked out in your head.

But, it is important that you read this not to work out the order but to realise what is coming, so that you will be ready for it. That is why we read. The interludes expand on a number of other things that we need to know about concerning this period of Big Trouble at the end of history. When we look at the three interludes, they all tell us about two of something. For example, chapter 7 has two groups of people in it. Chapters 10 to 11 concentrate on two witnesses, and chapters 12 to 14 mention two beasts.

So, let us look at each of these interludes, as it were, that come in between the series of seven seals, trumpets, and bowls. The first interlude is chapter 7. Now, these interludes are far more concerned with what will happen to God's people, whereas the seals, trumpets, and bowls tend to be concerned with what is going to happen to the world. These three interludes tell us about what will happen to God's people in all this. In chapter 7, there are two groups of God's people mentioned. The first group is Jewish, and the second group consists of Christians. The first part of chapter

7 tells you what will happen to the Jewish part of God's people during this time, and the second part tells you what will happen to Christians during this time.

So, the first group is a group of a limited number, a group that you can count and the number given is 144,000, which is 12 by 12 by 1,000. It is a round number. It specifically says that there will be in this number people from every tribe of Israel. By the way, that means that none of the 12 tribes is lost. People talk about the ten lost tribes. I do not know that they are lost. They are lost to me, but they are not lost to God because God knows where all of them still are. He intends all those 12 tribes to be represented in the New Jerusalem, so he is keeping tabs on them all.

It says here that during the Big Trouble, God will protect a limited number of them, that he will ensure that there is a number protected by him through all this trouble from each of the world's trials. I find that fits in beautifully with Romans 11, where Paul teaches clearly, "God has not finished with the Jews." They may have rejected him, and they still do, but he has not rejected them. He intends to save them at the end.

So here we have a picture of a limited number of Jewish people protected by God throughout this period. When we turn to the Christians, we find that they are a number that cannot be numbered, a multitude too big to count. Furthermore, whereas the Jewish people are largely protected on earth, we have here a picture of Christians being comforted in heaven. We are told that this great multitude is coming out of the Great Tribulation. The verb there means "are continuously coming out", not in one big group, but one after another, they are coming out of the Big Trouble. We know exactly how they are coming out. They are coming out through martyrdom.

The Christians are not like the Jews, protected from death. The Christians are comforted after dying for Jesus. You find the book of Revelation is packed with martyrs from beginning to end. At one stage (Revelation 6:10) the souls of the martyrs lying under the altar cry out to God, "How long, Sovereign Lord, holy and true, until you judge the inhabitants of the earth and avenge our blood?" The answer God gives in verse 11 is that they are to "wait a little longer" until the full number of martyrs is complete. In other words, during this time of big trouble, there will be a huge number of Christian martyrs. Indeed, the book of Revelation, as I have described it, is a manual for martyrdom; it is to help people to be willing to die.

I was reading some Church history, and reading one case after another of people who, through the ages, paid for their faith with their lives. It really humbled me to read all this and to consider the fact that it is already millions. It is astonishing how many have died for Jesus through the ages. But there will be a climax to that at the end. We read in Revelation 7:14, "These are they who have come out of the great tribulation; they have washed their robes and made them white in the blood of the Lamb." They are coming out of it, they are escaping from death.

As soon as they have got out of the Big Trouble, it says, "'Never again will they hunger; never again will they thirst. The sun will not beat down on them, nor any scorching heat. For the Lamb at the centre of the throne will be their shepherd; he will lead them to springs of living water. And God will wipe away every tear from their eyes" (Revelation 7:16–17). God is saying that it is all over, it is all right. You are out of it now. Dry your tears. It is a wonderful picture of God. Have you ever seen a parent pull a handkerchief out and say, "Don't cry, it's all right. It's over. Stop crying."? That is what God will do to this multitude coming out of the Big Trouble by martyrdom.

That is chapter 7. Let us look at chapters 10 to 11, which is the interlude between the sixth and the seventh trumpet. Between the sixth and the seventh trumpet, we have these two chapters, both of which concentrate on prophesying. There will be a lot of true prophecy at the last, as well as false prophecy at the last. Chapter 10 is a serious interlude, and it says to John, "The last and the worst part of the revelation is now to be given."

John is given a little scroll on which much more detailed descriptions of the future are contained. John is told to eat it. He eats this scroll and describes it as "sweet" to taste, but it turns his stomach "sour". Sweet and sour, where did you hear that? Do you like Chinese food? Well, actually, the front of the tongue tastes sweet things, and the back of the tongue tastes sour things. So, all the time you are eating, you are tasting sweet and sour—sweet on the front of your tongue, sour on the back. John says that when he read this scroll, his first reaction was that it was nice. It was sweet. But then as he went further in it turned sour.

Do you know, I find the whole book of Revelation sweet and sour, don't you? It is exciting to read, and then when you stop and think about what you are reading, it turns sour. I hope you are really feeling that you are getting to know this book and that you will understand it more when you read it. It is exciting stuff. It really is. Yet when you just stop and think about what is going to happen, it goes sour in your mouth. You wish you had not eaten it. That is exactly how John the Apostle felt when he was given this little scroll. For you see, the whole of Revelation is a prophecy. It is described as a prophecy, and John is being given this prophecy about the future.

That is chapter 10, but in chapter 11, our attention is focused on Jerusalem, the city where Jesus was crucified. It says that before the end, it will be under the feet of Gentiles. So, Jerusalem will yet see itself under Gentile trampling again. It says that when that happens, there will be two prophetic witnesses who will walk through the streets proclaiming the truth about God. Now, I am always being asked, "Who are the two witnesses?" The answer is very simple: I do not know. Until it happens, no one knows. People say, "Is it Elijah and Moses?" or Who is it? Look, we do not know because this has not happened yet.

But God will make sure that there will be two witnesses because out of the mouths of two witnesses, truth can be established. At the very last, there will be these two prophetic witnesses in the city where Jesus was crucified, telling the truth. Now, here we have for the first time two things mentioned. Number one, the length of the Great Tribulation or the Big Trouble, the period of it. For the first time, a figure is given. It is going to be repeated many times in different forms, but, as we have noted, the figure is forty-two months. It is also given as 1,260 days, which is the same period. It is also given as three and a half years. It is given in verse 14 of chapter 12 as a time, times, and half a time, which adds up to three and a half.

So, here we have expressed in many different ways the first mention of the period covered by the biggest trouble. It is only three and a half years. It is only forty-two months. It is only 1,260 days. Well, I think that it is a tremendous comfort to Christians that when things get really bad, we can say to each other, "Hang on, it's just forty-two months. Tick them off, just 1,260 days. We can count them. It's only three and a half years, that's all." I find that a tremendous comfort. Jesus himself talking about the Big Trouble, said, "Unless those days were kept short, even the elect might be lost." But they will be kept short.

So, while it takes a long time to describe all these troubles in the book of Revelation, it is really describing a very short period. What a concentrated trouble that period will be. But if we know it is only three and a half years, we can surely hang on. This is a call to the saints to endure. It is such a short time. Hang in there. The other thing that is mentioned in chapter 11 for the first time, which we will not find again until chapter 13, is the beast. At this point, we do not know what that is. It just says, "a beast". So, you can see the revelation is constantly looking forward, looking back, then looking around. It is all jumbled up because the important thing is not for you to work out the timetable but for you to be ready for everything.

Now let us go back to these two prophetic witnesses in Jerusalem. An extraordinary thing happens to them. They are put to death, and their two bodies are left lying in the street. After three and a half days, they stand up again and come back to life and go up to heaven, and people see them. It says that in the very city where Jesus was crucified and three days later came back, and from which he ascended into heaven, the exact cycle will happen again to these two witnesses at the very end. Now, it has not happened yet, and I do not know who they are, but one day this extraordinary demonstration will take place in the city of Jerusalem. What happened to Jesus himself, God will do with those two last prophetic voices in the heart of the Middle East. Amazing, isn't it? I mean, who would have thought this up if we had not got the book? It has to be divine inspiration; human imagination could not have worked all this out.

Now, let us look at chapters 12 to 14. This is the interlude in the bowls, but because the bowls are so tightly packed together, the interlude cannot come between six and seven; instead, it comes at the beginning. But it is an interlude that belongs to the third series. I am trying to help you; therefore, to read it with intelligence and be able to see something of the pattern.

The six seals are over, but not the seventh. The six trumpets are over, but not the seventh. Now, the last and worst series of disasters is about to happen. It will be the worst for the world, but primarily it will be the toughest of all for the Church. That is why chapters 12 to 14 give us the worst news for the Church. Let us look, then, at chapter 12, then 13, then 14. We will give chapter 12 the title "War in heaven". We have an extraordinary picture given to us of a pregnant woman, only clothed with the sun, and about to be attacked by a dragon. Actually, there is some kind of representation of the picture that was done by an artist in the East End of London when he was reading this book *(see overleaf)*.

Now, this is probably the most difficult chapter of Revelation to interpret. Who is this pregnant woman, and who does she represent? Now, let us try and feel our way into this, because it is a very difficult piece of symbolism, and you will find that when you

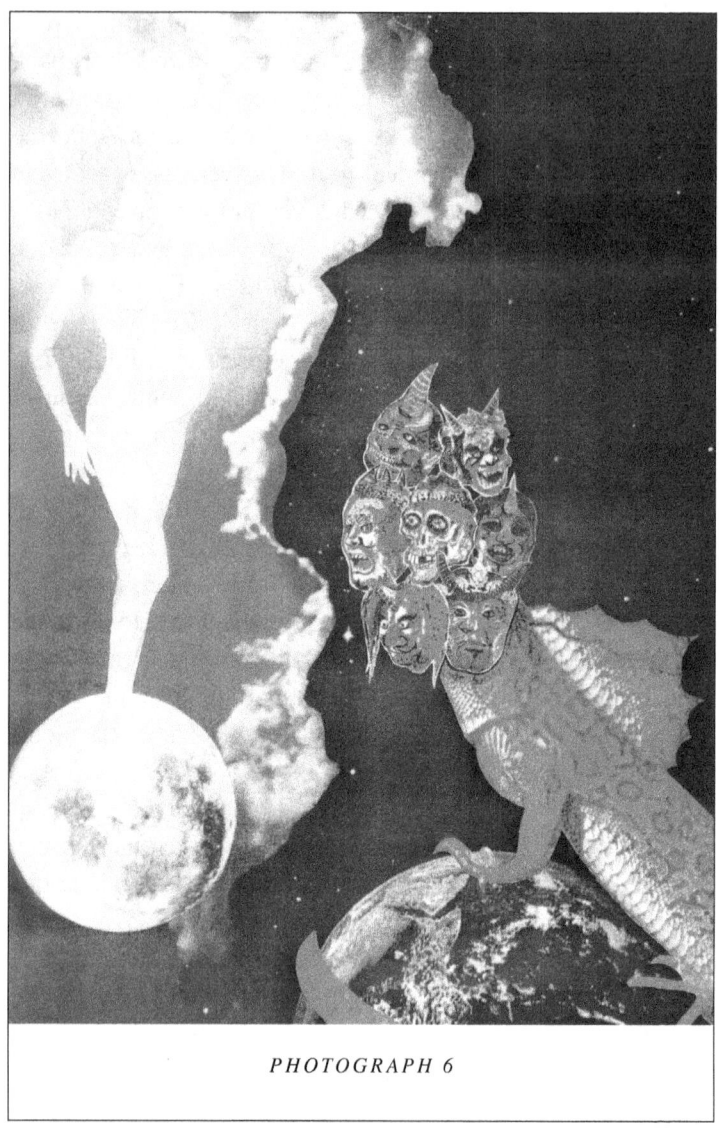

PHOTOGRAPH 6

read books by Bible scholars, it really is the most controversial little bit of the whole of the book as to what it means. Now, the dragon is no problem. Who is the dragon? Well, it tells us. It says the dragon is "that old serpent, called the devil". So, we know who the dragon is. By the way, it says that the dragon drags down with him a third of the stars of heaven. That is an amazing piece of information.

It tells you that altogether one out of every three angels has gone with the devil. The devil is an angel, and he has persuaded one-third of the heavenly host of angels to become demons with him. A demon is nothing else than an angel following Satan, and Satan himself is an angel. In other words, there are good angels and bad angels, and the good ones outnumber the bad ones two to one. Here we have this dragon, this devil at the head of an army of a third of the angels, now called demons. He is going for this pregnant woman dressed in the sun. He is waiting for her to deliver her child so that he can kill the boy child.

Now, of course, as soon as you read that, who do you think of? Mary. I am afraid that is the first person many people think of, and it is the official Roman Catholic interpretation of this chapter. You can understand that because of their veneration of the Virgin Mary, they see Mary in many places. But there are three possibilities. The first possibility is that it is Mary and the boy child is Jesus, and the devil is seeking to destroy the boy child as he did through Herod at Jesus' birth. But what is all that doing in the book of Revelation and in the middle of a description of the Big Trouble? It really does not fit at all.

The second possibility, as just mentioned, is that the mother is Israel, the Jews. But who is the male child then? Again, those who take that line say the male child is Jesus. I want to put a third possibility to you, which puts it back into its setting. What is it doing here in the book of Revelation towards the end of the Big Trouble? Well, bear in mind first that all women in the book of Revelation are not individuals; every woman in the book of Revelation represents a large number of people. We shall see the scarlet woman representing Babylon. We shall see the Bride, the New Jerusalem, representing God's people. This woman is a representative woman, what we call a corporate symbol.

It says that though her man-child is killed, the rest of her children flee to the wilderness and are saved. So, is the male child an individual or is it a group of people? Is it a picture of the martyrs? We notice that in the book of Revelation, it says that Christ will rule the world with a rod of iron, and it also says that Christians will do the same. In other words, we are seeing in these chapters that what happened to Christ will happen to Christians at the end of history. Then comes the real clue, because in connection with this woman, it says that she flees to the wilderness for 1,260 days. That is the period of the Big Trouble. So, we are not talking about Jesus' birth at all.

We are talking about the Big Trouble, and I therefore understand the woman to represent the Church, and the male child, whom Satan is wanting to kill, as the martyrs, and the rest of her offspring as those who have managed to survive the Big Trouble by fleeing to the wilderness. Now, that I believe is the picture here, and that picture fits perfectly with where it comes in the book of Revelation. Those are the three major interpretations. There are others, but I leave you to take your pick.

First, that the woman is an individual and it is Mary, and the devil is seeking to kill her male child Jesus, but all that is back in the Gospels. Second, that it is the nation of Israel. But who is the male child? Jesus, but what is the point of bringing in at this point the devil trying to kill Jesus at birth? It just does not make sense. But if this woman represents the Church of Christ and her offspring are going to be treated as Mary's offspring (Jesus) was, then there will be those who seek to kill her offspring. However, some of her offspring will escape by getting out into the country areas for 1,260 days and hang in there and somehow survive. You see, there will be some people still alive on earth when Jesus gets back. Not all Christians will be martyred. I leave you with that thought.

What it does say is that there is war in heaven. Let us go back to Coventry Cathedral. Outside Coventry Cathedral, against the baptistery window, there is a remarkable sculpture on the wall of the cathedral. Have you seen it? It is a picture of the Archangel Michael defeating the devil. It is there in Coventry Cathedral. It is taken straight out of chapter 12. What it says is this: Satan right now is in the heavenly places. He is not in hell. Nobody is in hell yet; hell is being prepared for people, but not even the devil is in hell.

Demons are in heavenly places, which is why we do not wrestle with flesh and blood, but with principalities and powers in the heavenly places. You see, the devil is an angel, and the demons are in heavenly places. But there will come a day when an archangel kicks the devil out of heaven, and he will be unable to return. If you read Job chapter 1, you will find the devil attending the council of heaven and arguing with God. But there will come a day, says chapter 12, at the very end of history when the devil will be thrown out of heaven and a third of the stars with him, all his demons, they will be right out of heaven. But it says they will be so angry that their anger will be directed against earth.

That is why things get so terribly bad right at the end, because the devil is finished; he is out of heaven. He has one last opportunity to mess up the earth. It is that frustration that leads directly to what he will do on earth when he is finally kicked out of heaven for good. Chapter 13 tells us what he will do. The answer is he will raise up two beasts.

In chapter 13:1–10 talk about the first beast and verses 11 to 18, the second beast. Both are human beings, and together they will form the last totalitarian regime that the earth will see. The first beast is political, the second is religious. They are elsewhere known as the Antichrist and the False Prophet. Together with the devil, they form an unholy trinity; instead of Father, Son, and Holy Spirit, we have the devil, Antichrist, and False Prophet. It is a hellish substitute for the holy Trinity. Together, these two puppets of Satan will control the earth for a very brief period.

Let us look at the two beasts of chapter 13. The first one is political, a world dictator who is given authority over every tribe, people, language, and nation. He is also allowed to fight and conquer the saints. He is also called "the lawless one" in 2 Thessalonians chapter 2. Now, to clear up one thing, "anti" does not mean against. It means "instead of". Antichrist means instead of Christ. It is interesting that the devil once offered Jesus the post of Antichrist. Did you ever realise that? The devil said to Jesus, "I'll give you all the kingdoms of the world if you'll bow down and worship me."

Had Jesus been tempted and accepted the devil's offer, we would now be talking about Jesus Antichrist, but we talk about Jesus Christ because he refused that job. One day, a man will accept this position. He will demand that people worship him, which is the ultimate blasphemy, and he will do this for three and a half years. Now, at this point, there are some details about his kingdom that we will not understand until it appears, but he talks about ten horns and seven heads, one of which is fatally wounded but miraculously healed.

Clearly, there is a coalition of nations here. People ask me whether I think the European Union will be it. I do not know. I will wait and see. It has now got far more than ten heads in it, so that puts some people off who, when the European Community had ten in it, asked, "Is this the Antichrist's community?" We do not know. It now has many more than ten member states. We will wait and see, but the reference to ten heads clearly means a coalition of ten nations with seven rulers. Again, I do not know for certain, but it seems as if some of those rulers will have more than one nation under them. But of those seven rulers, one will be fatally wounded but miraculously restored, which will impress a lot of people.

But out of all that will come *the* beast, out of all that will emerge this powerful ruler. He has not emerged yet. Some people thought it was Gaddafi. Others thought it was Saddam Hussein. They once thought it was Napoleon. There have been many antichrists who have gone into the world, but *the* one has not come yet. I will tell you his name when he comes, if we are still around.

The second beast in verses 11 to 18 is the False Prophet, who can back up his words with signs and wonders. The devil will give him power, and he will be the religious leader underneath the political leader to bring people into a one-world religion and under one-world government. I have mixed feelings about all the desires that I come across that we should all be in one nation under one government.

I believe we will be under Christ, but I do not want to be under Antichrist. So, I have mixed feelings about all the talk about world government because it is all heading up to this. But the practical side of all this is very important. In the middle of chapter 14, it says, "This calls for patient endurance on the part of the people of God who keep his commands and remain faithful to Jesus." In chapter 13, it says that when the first beast controls the world, you will not be able to buy food [at the supermarket] unless you have his number tattooed on you [to pass over the checkout]. We will have to find our food somewhere else. But it becomes entirely credible all this. It is just around the corner—a lasered number on your body to use instead of money. Plastic money is here, and the next step is a tattooed or lasered number on your hand or forehead so that you can swipe it at the checkout, and that will be it. This is just around the corner, and it is already being talked about along with how the Antichrist will control that number.

Now, it is at this point where the number 666 comes. What does it mean? As mentioned in chapter 1 of this book, I do not know for sure. I think we have got to be honest and say about these things in the future that we will not know until they have happened. There has been much speculation. I do not know if you know that 666 is now banned from personal licence plate numbers for your car. They will not do it now. It became a very popular number with different letters, and you could buy a personalised number plate with 666. Well, not now.

The authorities in Swansea said no longer because they had a stream of complaints that the number is jinxed and makes the car take on an evil mind of its own. You see, there is going to be an awful lot of superstition surrounding all this. Believe me, when I hear someone following a superstition, I always correct them. I was talking to one of my neighbours and I said, "How are you?" I said, "Has the trouble you had with your heart gone away now?" because he had suffered a heart attack. He said, "No, touch wood." I said, "You're not superstitious, are you?" "Well," he said. I replied, "Do you know what that began with? That began with people touching the crucifix, touching the cross." I said, "Did you want to touch the cross?" We had quite a chat, but it is amazing how superstitious people are.

Thirteen—we are in a row of houses and it goes 7, 9, 11, 11a, 15, 17. Do you know why they will not have 13? It is because 13 sat down at a table one night, and 24 hours later, two were dead, Judas and Jesus. That is where it goes back to. There is going to be an awful lot of superstition around towards the end. This will be capitalised on. The second beast will capitalise on and exploit superstition to bring people under the power of the Antichrist.

Chapter 14 simply describes three angels. This vision in chapter 14 somehow compensates for the horrors we have been reading about. It is a little chapter of good news with a little foretaste of the future in it. The three angels each bring a comforting message. The first message is a call to fear and worship God, and it is a warning that judgment is coming, but that the gospel is still available for anyone who will believe it, and there is still a chance to be saved.

That is the message of the first angel. An angel flying through the air with the everlasting gospel to preach to all the inhabitants on earth. Right there in the middle of the book of Revelation, it tells us that the gospel is still available at this point. Right in the middle of all this trouble people can still get saved. That is good news. The second angel says, "Babylon will fall." Do you know what that means? I will not discuss it in detail until the next chapter. But that is a little look forward again and it is good news that Babylon will fall. That will be spelled out fully in chapters 17 to 19. But the book of Revelation keeps looking back and it keeps looking forward; it keeps jumping around all over the place.

The third angel has a warning for believers, for the saints, that they could finish up in hell unless they are faithful and obedient. The third angel warns believers that this may mean martyrdom for you, but you haven't got to live. I remember a man telling me once that he had to compromise in his daily work because he said, "I've got to live." I said to him, "No, you haven't got to live. Jesus didn't have to live." Apparently, that word just set him free.

He went to his boss. He was working for ITV and he was writing a sitcom, a situation comedy for them, and they had told him he must put a gay person into the sitcom. He told me he had to. He was a freelancer and dependent on this money. I said, "No, you don't have to live. Jesus didn't." That set him free. He went to the ITV authorities and told them he would not put a gay person into the sitcom, and they accepted the sitcom, and he continued working for them. But it was just saying to him, "You haven't got to live." Do you see? "We've got to live,"—No, we have not, we can die for Jesus.

Now comes this beautiful thing in Revelation 14:13. The angel says to John: "Write this: Blessed are the dead who die in the Lord from now on."Unfortunately, I have heard that read at so many funerals. It is for Christian martyrs, and it is especially for the martyrs at the end. From now on, says the angel, "Blessed are the dead who die in the Lord". "Yes," says the Spirit, "that they may rest from their labours, and their deeds will follow them." That is a word of comfort to believers there. Hang in there, be faithful, endure.

If you die for the Lord, you are blessed. You are really blessed, and what you have done for the Lord will follow you, go with you. It is a tremendous promise. Now two more angels appear, followed by seven more with the bowls of the last plagues. We are into the worst of all.

Earlier, we discussed how to interpret the book of Revelation. I looked at the different ways that people interpret it. There are those who put it all into the first few centuries (the preterist approach). There are those who spread it over the whole of Church history (the historicist approach). There are those who see it primarily as the last part of history (the futurist), and there are those who see it as applying to any period of time as a kind of mythological picture of the struggle between good and evil (the idealist approach).

I think you will realise from what we have been saying that I regard these central chapters of Revelation as primarily futurist—not as having happened yet. Having said that, there are things like them happening in different parts of the world even now. They cast their shadow before them, and I can see many antichrists in the world, but not *the* Antichrist. I can see many false prophets, but not *the* False Prophet. I can see countries where Christians are experiencing all this already, but only in certain countries. What we are looking at in Revelation is these things happening on a worldwide scale over a brief period.

But let me finish this chapter by saying this: always remember why Revelation was written. It was written to help us overcome when the pressure comes. You are only told all this not so that you can be in on the secret, not so that you can work out a beautiful timetable on a strip of paper on your wall and be able to say to people exactly where we are, but so that you can be ready for the worst that can happen.

It is a call for patience, for endurance, for obedience, for allegiance, and for perseverance. Those are the five things that Revelation seeks to communicate to you. All those add up to overcomer. That is what it is all about, and there is both encouragement and warning all the way through—the blessing for those who overcome and the torment awaiting those who do not. Regarding the latter, in chapter 14:11, it says this: "And the smoke of their torment ascends forever and ever; and they have no rest day or night for those who worship the beast and his image, **or** for anyone who receives the mark of its name."

So, we are given the promise of blessing if we overcome and the warning of eternal torment if we give in to these pressures. Finally, let me mention one verse, Revelation 16:15. I am looking ahead. Jesus says, "Look, I come like a thief! Blessed is the one who stays awake and remains clothed, so as not to go naked and be shamefully exposed." Do you know that in Matthew 22: 1–14, we have the same picture of being clothed for when Jesus comes? There we have a parable of a wedding feast, and a man turns up for the wedding without having changed his clothes, and he is thrown out of the wedding.

We find this in Luke's Gospel as well. Jesus says in Luke's Gospel, "When I come, will you be wearing the right clothes?" It is quite a picture. The clothes are righteousness, perseverance, patience, and endurance. That is how he wants us to be when he comes.

I have taken you all the way up to the end of the bowls of wrath. In the next chapter, we will look at chapters 17 to 19.

Chapter 6

WILL CHRISTIANS ESCAPE BY SECRET RAPTURE?

In this book, I am looking at some of the big questions about which Christians differ very deeply. In the previous chapter, I made one huge assumption, and that was that there would be at least some Christians all the way through the Big Trouble and that the only escape from it would be through martyrdom. You may have heard a different view from this. We are discussing what is called the Rapture. Have you heard that word, the "Rapture"? Actually, that comes from a Latin word *rapto*, which means "to be snatched up", and is in fact in the Latin Vulgate translation of the Bible in 1 Thessalonians chapter 4, where it says, "We shall all be snatched up to meet the Lord in the air." We will all be "raptoed" and from that it has come into English as raptured.

The word "Rapture" is, of course, ambiguous. Originally, it meant to be snatched up physically, but nowadays, to be raptured means to be snatched up emotionally, or to be terribly excited or fall in love or something: "I'm in raptures over it." Well, forgetting the word "the Rapture", I believe in the Rapture in that we shall be caught up to meet the Lord in the air. The question is not whether you believe in the Rapture, but when you believe it and when that is going to happen in the series of events Revelation gives us.

Now, many Christians would disagree with me here that we will only escape the Big Trouble by martyrdom. There is a widespread teaching that at the beginning of the Big Trouble, all the Christians will vanish and be snatched up secretly. It is called the Secret Rapture before the Big Trouble starts. Of course, that has profound implications, the biggest of which is that we will not know when the Big Trouble has started because we will have gone. This means that the next event that we could discern would be this secret Rapture, or it means, in simple terms, the "any moment" theory of our Lord's return—that he could come tonight.

If what I have been saying to you is the right approach to Revelation, then Jesus cannot possibly come tonight, or even this week, or even in the next few years. It would be at least three and a half years because the Big Trouble does not seem to have started yet. So that is really what hangs on this—when you expect Jesus to return. If he is coming for us before the Big Trouble, then he could come at any moment, but if he is not coming until after the Big Trouble, then it cannot be at any moment, although it could be within our lifetime. Every Christian hopes it will be in his or her lifetime, because I do not want an undertaker measuring me for a box. I hope he will come before I die, but I do not expect him tonight. That is the big difference.

Now, this teaching of a Secret Rapture of the Church before the Big Trouble is comparatively new. It has only been known for the last 160 years; before that, there is no trace of it whatsoever. It is part of a system of interpreting the whole Bible in quite a different way, which began in about 1830, and we call this system "dispensationalism". It is a horrid, long word, but it is a totally different and complete way of interpreting the Bible, which has been made very popular, more in America than in this country, but I am quite sure you have heard of it. In particular, it uses a text from 2 Timothy 2:15, "rightly dividing the word of truth". The word "dividing" is in fact "ploughing". "Rightly ploughing the truth", but the emphasis of the dispensationalists, as we call them, is on rightly dividing the truth, as if we have got to divide the Bible up.

Let me show you roughly some of the things that this system called dispensationalism does with the Bible, bearing in mind that it makes a great deal of this word "dividing"—"rightly dividing the word of truth". The New International Version translates it much better as "correctly handles". The word is actually not "dividing", but unfortunately, that word is seized on by the dispensational system of interpretation. It makes three very important divisions in the Bible which affect your whole understanding of the whole Bible.

The first huge division it makes is that it divides history into what it calls "dispensations", periods of time in which God deals quite differently with people. That is the heart of dispensationalism. So, it divides the Old Testament into five periods, or dispensations; it divides the New Testament into two dispensations or periods. So, it divides the whole Bible into seven separate periods. If you were brought up among the Brethren, you will be familiar with this dispensational approach because that is where it originated.

So, the periods, or dispensations, in each of which God relates to man on a quite different basis to the others are as follows. The first dispensation is called the Dispensation of Innocence, and that is limited to the one generation of Adam, and even then, only to that part of Adam's life before he sinned—the Dispensation of Innocence. Secondly, the Dispensation of Self Determination from Cain to Enoch, after which the Flood altered things enormously and started a new dispensation. So, the sin of Adam moved from the first dispensation to the second, and the Flood moved the world from the second to the third.

After the Flood, there were three dispensations in the Old Testament. The third was the Dispensation of Human Government from Noah to Abraham. The fourth was the patriarchs from Abraham to Joseph—four generations. Then the Dispensation of Law from Moses on to Christ. In other words, the rest of the Old Testament is the Dispensation of Law.

Then, the first coming of Jesus started a totally new dispensation called the Dispensation of Grace. So, the law came through Moses, but grace came through Jesus. The Second Coming will mark the end of this dispensation and the beginning of the seventh and final dispensation, the Millennium. We have not reached that yet in the book of Revelation. In the next chapter, we will, and I will give you the different Christian views on that.

Now, that is essentially the division of the Bible into seven dispensations. At the opposite end of the spectrum are those who treat the whole Bible as one covenant of grace. Calvinists do that, and Reformed Theologians talk about one covenant of grace covering the whole Bible. So, at one end, you have seven dispensations; at the other end, you have one covenant. I find the Bible fits into a division of two: the Old and the New Covenant. So, I am right in between these two extremes. I do not divide the Bible into seven; I divide it into two, and my Bible happens to be in two halves, the Old and the New. I believe we only need to work with the Old and the New to understand the whole Bible.

Having said that, I do find there is grace in the Old Testament. God is revealed as a God of grace all the way through. It was his grace that brought the Hebrews out of Egypt, so I cannot limit grace to the New Testament as dispensationalists do. I cannot go into all this in greater detail, but I believe they have over-divided the Word of God up into seven. I believe that at the other end, there are people who under-divide it and make no distinction between the Law of Moses and the covenant of Christ, and therefore regard Christians as still under all the law. But I find the simple division into two of what belongs to the old covenant, which is now obsolete, and what belongs to the new covenant for the rest of eternity, is the simpler way of looking at the Bible.

The second division which dispensationalists make is to divide the destiny of the Jews from the Christians forever. They see the future destiny of the Jews on earth, the new earth and the future destiny of Christians in heaven. Now, once again, I believe this is a false division because it keeps Jews and Christians apart forever. So, God, they say, has two divine and distinct peoples; the earthly people are the Jews and the heavenly people are the Christians.

That is why they go on to make the most serious division: they divide the Second Coming into two comings, the first of which is secret, a coming for the saints, the second of which is public, coming back to earth with the saints. So, the saints go up before the Big Trouble and come back down with him a few years later, publicly. Again, I find all these divisions are too divisive, but it does mean that if he is coming first secretly for the saints then he could come at any moment. But if he is coming after the Great Tribulation only, then, of course, he could not come tonight but he could come within our lifetime.

We are going to concentrate on this last part of dispensational teaching, but I want you to realise that it is part of a whole system of interpreting the Bible. Let me therefore concentrate on this third part. Most books that emphasise the Second Coming that are available today are written from a dispensational view. Hal Lindsay has written what is probably one of the most popular books with "The Late Great Planet Earth". I am sure you have heard of Hal Lindsay. But most books are written from this point of view, and therefore most preaching on the Second Coming has been done from this point of view and not from any other. That is a pity because that has caused many Christians to stop talking about the Second Coming and to stop thinking about the future, because this is the only interpretation they have heard, and to me, that is tragic.

So, we have two comings, a private Rapture for the saints or *of* the saints and a public advent with the saints, with a gap in between during which the Big Trouble takes place. The implications are two-fold. First, Christians escape the Big Trouble. Therefore, chapters 6 to 19 of Revelation are of no concern to Christians; they are purely for curiosity; they have no practical message to Christians; they are of interest only to those who will be on earth at the time—the Jews. Therefore, the whole middle section of Revelation ceases to have any practical significance for Christians.

Quite frankly, that makes me wonder why on earth Jesus should tell us about it. What good could it possibly do to tell Christians what others are going to go through? Do you follow me? The only answer I can get from dispensationalists is that these middle chapters are to frighten unbelievers into conversion. I honestly cannot see that a book that is deliberately addressed to the seven churches should suddenly become an evangelistic tract, but there we are.

The second implication is that the Rapture is the second prophetic event on God's calendar and that there are no prophecies to be fulfilled before we are to be caught up to meet the Lord in the air. Now, those are two huge implications, so we are dealing with very big issues. Now, let me say straight away that this position has tremendous appeal. You have probably heard the word "eschatology". Well, this view turns eschatology into "escapology", doesn't it? Studying the book of Revelation becomes a study in "escapology"—how to get out, how to escape.

Frankly, it is very comforting to think that none of these troubles will come to touch Christians. That, of course, is why this view has tremendous appeal. Not only does it produce comfort, but it is also used to challenge unbelievers. Again, I have met so many people brought up among Brethren, for example, who were frightened into conversions as little children by the thought that they may find mummy and daddy gone, and that has been used in preaching too.

I believe that is wicked. I cannot find that kind of preaching in the New Testament even to adults, never mind children. But the thought of little children being so scared stiff that they might run into mummy's bedroom in the morning and find that she has been raptured, I find that very, very hard to take. But many have made decisions for Christ on the thought that Christ could come back tonight, and it has been widely used in preaching. So, it is a very strong appeal, a comfort to the believer and a challenge to the unbeliever. But the question is, is it right, is it true?

Now, let me give you the history of this position. It began

around 1830. There is not a trace of this approach to the Word of God before 1830. There are three strands that came together. It was an Englishman, an Irishman, and a Scotsman. Do not read anything into that, but it just happened to be! The Irishman was a Church of Ireland curate called John Nelson Darby—J N Darby, the founder of the Brethren movement. The Englishman was Dr Henry Drummond, who lived just outside Guildford in Surrey, and the Scot was a Church of Scotland minister called Edward Irving, and there was a lady prophetess called Margaret MacDonald, who lived in Port Glasgow.

It all began when Margaret MacDonald gave a prophecy to the effect that Christians would not have to go through the Big Trouble. That was accepted by the minister Edward Irving. It was discussed at a conference in Dr Henry Drummond's house in Guildford to which came John Nelson Darby. Somehow that idea found its way into Darby's thinking and became a fundamental part of Brethren teaching, although I hasten to add that many of the Brethren did not go along with it in the early days. Some of the finest Brethren never accepted it.

I suppose the finest brother who did not accept it was a man called George Müller of Bristol. I am sure you have heard of Müller's Orphanage. George Müller was a lovely, lovely brother, but he said to Darby, "You're wrong on this, I can't accept this." But, I am afraid Darby was the stronger personality in the Brethren movement. There were others like Benjamin Newton and a man called Tregelles, who opposed Darby and said he was wrong, but in the end, Darby won, and most Brethren today would be dispensational.

Now, Darby went across to America and persuaded a lawyer called Dr C I Scofield to adopt this position and Scofield decided to produce a Bible with notes in it, interpreting the Bible in this way, called the Scofield Bible. Have you heard of that? Well, that is what did the damage. Never buy a Bible with human notes in it, because when you are reading the Bible and you see a human interpretation on the same page, if you are not careful, you will think you are reading the Word of God when you are just reading one man's views.

The Scofield Bible was the best selling Bible in the States; it sold by the million, and people read Scofield's interpretation like this. They assumed that the Bible says that history is divided into seven periods, the Jews' future is divided from the Christian future, and there are two Second Comings. Now, you can find all that in the Scofield Bible, but I cannot find any of that in my Bible because my Bible has no human notes in it.

Again, I urge you to never buy a Bible with human notes in it. Buy notes, by all means, buy them as commentaries, but never get a Bible with one man's views in it. It is the most dangerous thing you can do because you read the Word of God, then you go on reading down below, and your mind must stop and say, "That is not the infallible Word of God, it's just one man's view." But you cannot mentally do that on every page you read and you tend to read the whole lot.

So, many people thought they found all this in the Bible, but they found it in the Scofield Bible. This led to whole Bible colleges which only taught this view of the Bible, of which the most famous is Dallas Theological Seminary. You cannot be a student there if you do not accept all this. It was from Dallas that came a student called Hal Lindsay. Well, that is the history of it. An Englishman, a Scotsman, and an Irishman, crossing the Atlantic, giving it to Scofield, who puts it into the Bible, and Dallas produces Hal Lindsay, and that is how we have it.

The majority of evangelicals in America hold this view of the Bible. This is not the case with the majority over here, but it is still very influential because we get books from over there, and the Scofield Bible is sold here. I was speaking at Filey Holiday Crusade—that was before the Spring Harvest days—and somebody found a dustbin full of Scofield Bibles and the rumour went round that I had told people to throw their Scofield

Bibles away.

Well, I do not like it for the reason I just gave, but I did not tell them to throw them away. What had happened was that it had rained unexpectedly on the open-air bookstore and all these Bibles were ruined in the downpour and that is why they had been thrown away. But for years after that I was the preacher who tells people to throw their Bibles in the dustbin! You see, that is how rumours start in the Christian bush telegraph!

What is the basis for this view of the Second Coming that it could be any moment and will be secret? It is a view that is now in films. Have you seen a film called "Thief in the Night"? That film is pure dispensational teaching, and you have got to be very careful lest you are swept into it and lose your critical faculties.

Well, there are seven reasons that are given for this view that there will be a secret Rapture of all the Christians before the Big Trouble. There is no clear statement in the New Testament to this effect. You can only infer it from data in the New Testament. I just wish there was one verse in the New Testament that simply said, "Don't worry, you will be raptured before the Big Trouble." There is not a single clear statement. But the arguments for it are all arguments from inference. That is to say that it looks as if, or here is a hint, or this might indicate. That is what we mean by inference, and there are seven inferences which are claimed to be the biblical basis for this secret Rapture.

Do you know the word "exegesis"? Exegesis means getting something out of the Bible. There is another word, "eisegesis", which means reading something into the Bible. What we are asking is whether people are getting it out of the Bible or are they reading it into the Bible? When you get into the realm of inference, that is when you start reading things into the Bible that are not clearly stated there.

Here they are. The first is that there are many statements about the speed of the Second Coming: "I am coming soon"; "I am coming quickly"; "I stand at the door". So, that is the first.

So, regarding the statements about speed, "I'm coming soon", "I'm coming quickly", they said, "That implies any moment. We can infer that he could come at any moment from these statements." But actually, we have got to qualify "soon" and "quickly". It has been at least 2,000 years. It is "soon" and "quickly" from God's point of view because to him a thousand years is as a day.

Secondly, there are the statements about surprise, such as those in chapter 3:3: "Therefore, if you do not wake up, I will come like a thief, and you will not know at what time I will come to you." All those statements about being surprised infer that he could come at any moment.

Thirdly, there are differences in language; there are different words used about the Second Coming. Words like *parousia*. Words like *apokalupsis*. There are different words even in English: "the Day of the Lord" and "the Day of Christ", his "arrival" and his "appearing", he is "coming for" saints and he is "coming with" saints. Now, using this language, these words have been divided up by the dispensationalists to infer that they do not all refer to the same event, that his arrival and his appearing are two different things, and that is why two different words are used.

Fourthly, the early disciples expected him at any moment, according to dispensationalists. That is the belief that in the New Testament they expected him within their lifetime, based on Jesus' words, "Truly I tell you, this generation will certainly not pass away until all these things have happened." (Matthew 24:34), and just before that in verse 33: "when you see all these things, you know that it is near, right at the door." There is this constant emphasis on being ready in the New Testament, which has led to this belief that the early Church expected him at any moment.

Fifthly, there is the absence of the word "Church" in Revelation chapter 6, right through to the Second Coming in chapter 19.

The word "church" does not occur in that whole middle section describing the Big Trouble; therefore, the Church cannot be there.

That is another inference. Now, of course, the word "elect" and the word "saints" are used in those chapters, but that is said by the dispensationalists only to refer to the Jews still on earth, but not to Christians. The word "church" is not there.

Next, there is the emphasis on comfort and encouragement in passages about the Second Coming, 1 Thessalonians 4:18 says, "Therefore encourage one another with these words". In other words, what comfort is it to tell people they are going through the Big Trouble? Surely comfort means telling them they will not go through it. Finally, again, there is an inference: if the Big Trouble is the pouring out of God's wrath on the world, then surely believers are not under God's wrath. We have been delivered from God's wrath; we are not under it, and therefore we cannot experience it when his wrath is poured out in the Big Trouble. 1 Thessalonians 5:9 is often quoted: "For God did not appoint us to suffer wrath," and therefore, since the Big Trouble is the outpouring of his wrath, we are not going to suffer it.

I am going to go through these seven points and examine them more carefully. I think you have realised where I stand on this, but I want you to make up your own mind. We turn to the statements about speed: "soon", "quickly". I believe these must be seen from God's time and not ours. Time is different for God. Now, 2 Peter 3 discusses the delay of Christ's coming quite clearly. Even in the New Testament Church, people were asking, "Where is the promise of his coming? Everything's going on as it always has done; there's no sign of it, what's happening?" Peter answers that by saying that a thousand years is like a day to God. God is on "flexi time".

Einstein was once asked to explain simply his theory of the relativity of time, and he said, "Well, quite simply, one minute sitting on a hot stove seems much longer than one hour talking to a pretty girl." That is the relativity of time simply explained. Well, I like that, but to God, time is flexible. A day can seem like a thousand years to God. I can think of one day that did, can you?

But a thousand years to God can seem like a day.

Therefore, it has only been a couple of days that Jesus has been away, from God's point of view. In other words, the Bible thinks of time from God's angle and not ours. But Peter goes on to say, "But thank God he is delaying his return, because it means more people can repent and get saved, and it's because he loves us that he's delaying it."

James says in his letter, "Learn patience from the farmer." He is talking about the Second Coming. He says, "The farmer waits for the harvest; you must learn to wait for the second coming, slow but sure. But the great Saint Bernard of Clairvaux said, "Dost thou call that a little while in which I will not see thee? Oh, this is a long little while." I like that. That is a real saint crying out for the Lord's return: it is "a long little while". But what I am saying is I do not think we can infer from the words "soon" and "quickly" that it is going to be at any moment.

Secondly, there are the statements about surprise. Yes, Jesus did say, "I will come like a thief, and you will not know at what time I will come to you.", and people will be totally caught out, but he prefaces that with the words "if you do not wake up". Also, in 1 Thessalonians 5, it says believers will not be caught out. The surprise element is only for the world. The believers will be alert, awake, and watching because they are children of the day and not of the night, and they will see the signs of his coming. Now, that is a very important point.

The New Testament teaching on surprise in relation to the Second Coming is always directed at two groups of people: the unbelievers and the sleepy believers who are not watching and praying. They will be caught out. But to the believer who is alert and watching, he will not come like a thief in the night, because a thief comes to take things away from you; he comes to rob you, but Jesus is not coming to rob alert believers.

So, what does the word "watch" mean when Jesus says, "Watch for my coming"? Does that mean I should walk down the street looking at the clouds? If he is coming any moment that is what it should mean. It is pretty dangerous to live like that! I met a young girl who spent all her spare time in a cemetery because she wanted to be with the saints when they rose. That girl was becoming neurotic. What are we to watch for, then, when we watch for his coming? Are we to do this? No, we are to watch for the signs.

Jesus told a parable of a man who heard a rumour that a burglar was coming, and he did not go to bed, but he stayed awake, and he watched, and he saw the signs of the man coming and was ready for him. In other words, Jesus is saying that he will not come like a thief in the night to you because you will stay awake and watch, and you will see the first signs of his approach. So that argument does not hold.

Regarding differences of language, the three Greek words used are *parousia, epiphaneia, apokalupsis*. *Parousia* means to arrive. D-Day was a *parousia*. That is a perfect use of the word—an army arriving to liberate or a king arriving.

An *epiphaneia* means to appear as you are. So, when the Queen appeared on TV recently, she wore a pink hat and a raincoat so she did not appear as the Queen. They knew she was the Queen because they recognised her and the band played when she arrived, but looking at her dress, you would not have recognised her. If you had just seen her from the back in the raincoat and hat, you would not have said, "That's the Queen." An *epiphaneia* is when she appears with her crown on and her robe, when she appears in glory. An *apokalupsis* is an unveiling, and it means to be seen, and the things that you have hidden are now visible. The things in your character, the things in your ambition, are now unveiled, and people see right through you.

Now, all those three words are applied to Jesus' coming, as well as many other words. The word "gathered" is used: "He will send his angels, and gather his elect" (Mark 13:27). But when you look at these words in the New Testament, they are used interchangeably; they are used synonymously; they are all used of the same event. You cannot say this is the *parousia* and this is the *epiphaneia* because both words are used interchangeably. Then how do we reconcile the two phrases, "Coming for his saints", and "Coming with his saints"? It is very simple. I will explain what the word *parousia* means when it is used of a royal visit.

Supposing the Queen is coming to visit a city in England, say Birmingham, and she is flying in. So, her helicopter, or one of the Queen's flight aircraft, lands at Birmingham Airport, and there is going to be a big parade in Birmingham; she is going to be driven around the streets. Do you suppose that everybody in Birmingham waits in Birmingham and that nobody meets her when she arrives at the airport? No. What happens? All the dignitaries go out to the airport and come back with her in cars following her, don't they?

That is what the word *parousia* means. It means to go out and greet the visitor and accompany him back into town. Have you got the picture? That is exactly what the word *parousia* means. We are going to meet the Lord up in the air before he touches earth. So, he is coming for his saints, and we will meet him outside the earth, as it were, and come back with him, accompany him on the final part of his journey. That is what *parousia* means. So, he is coming *for* and *with* at the same time, and that is clearly the picture that the language gives us.

Now, what about the early Church? Did the early Church expect Jesus to come back any moment? Because really this is the heart of this view, that Jesus could come back at any moment, and the claim is that in the New Testament, the early Church believed that Jesus would come any minute. Well, let us look at the New Testament. Jesus told the apostles that they would be his witnesses "to the end of the earth". Do you think those who were told to take the gospel to the ends of the earth believed that he would come back at any moment? When would they do it all? It is obvious that they needed time to do that before he got back.

Next, in John 21:18, Jesus predicted Peter's crucifixion when he was an old man. So how could Peter expect him at any moment? Clearly, he was telling Peter that he would die in old age before he came back, which is why Peter then asked Jesus, "But Lord, what about this man?" Jesus replied, "If I will that he remain till I come, what is that to you? You follow me." John, putting that at the end of his Gospel, points out that Jesus said "*if*" because a rumour went around the early Church that John would live until the Second Coming. But John says, "Yet Jesus did not say to him that he would not die, but rather 'If I will that he remain till I come, what *is that* to you?'" So how could Peter expect Jesus any minute when Jesus had told him he would die of old age?

There are numerous parables about the Second Coming, all of them indicating a long wait. Take the parable of the bridesmaids, the ten virgins. I must tell you something funny here. In the old City temple, a preacher once said, "You young men in the gallery there, where would you rather be: in the light with the wise virgins or in the dark with the foolish ones?" From the gallery, he got a unanimous answer from the young men. It was not the answer he wanted, I am afraid. Preachers, beware of asking a congregation questions! But note that it says, "The bridegroom was a long time in coming".

That is followed by the parable of the talents: "After a long time the master of those servants returned." Here is an extraordinary verse from Luke's Gospel immediately before the parable of the talents: "He [Jesus] spoke another parable, because he was near Jerusalem and because they thought the kingdom of God would appear immediately." (Luke 19:11) Then he told them a parable about a long time.

The real test of whether you are ready for the Second Coming is not how you behave if you think he is coming tomorrow, but how you behave if he does not come for another thousand years, because the real thing is not what Jesus finds you doing at the moment of his return but what you have been doing while he has been away. Having the panic motive of "He may come tonight" means, frankly, and to put it crudely, that I would not make love to my wife tonight in case Jesus found me at it. How foolish to think that way.

Do you see what I mean? It is not, "Oh, he might come tonight and find me doing this." That is a panic motivation. It is when he comes that he will say, "David, what have you been doing while I've been away?" You see, it is not those who think he is coming tonight who will live right, but those who realise that whenever he comes, he will ask you what you have been doing while he has been away.

Paul corrected the Thessalonian Christians who thought the Day of the Lord had arrived because they had a forged letter in Paul's name. Paul wrote his second letter to correct that, and he told them that Jesus could not possibly have come back yet because the man of lawlessness must appear first. He is telling believers, "You will see the Antichrist before you see the Christ," and the Antichrist is only seen in the Big Trouble. Now, what is true is that the early Christians did hope that it would be in their lifetime. Paul hoped that, and so do I, but there is no trace in the New Testament of "any moment".

Next, there is the absence of the word "church" from Revelation 6 to 19, and also from Matthew 24, which covers the same period. Why isn't the word "church" there? Well, let me point out that Matthew 24 and Revelation 6 to 19 are both addressed to disciples; they are not addressed to sinners. Revelation—the whole of it—is addressed to the seven churches in Asia, to the believers. As I said before, why give all this information to people for whom it is of no practical use? I just cannot get around that one.

Is it so we can say to the world, "Blow you, Jack, I'm all right." I cannot conceive that Jesus wants us to think like that. "Oh, you poor lot, you're going to go through all these troubles. But I'll be out of it, I'm okay." Is that why he told us? I cannot believe it.

It does not sound like Jesus at all. What he did say (in Matthew 24:23–25) is this: "Then if anyone says to you, 'Look, here is the Christ!' or 'There!' do not believe it. For false christs and false prophets will rise and show great signs and wonders to deceive, if possible, even the elect. See, I have told you beforehand." It is so like Jesus to warn us of what is coming and tell us ahead of time so we should not be thrown by it.

Next, the words "elect" and "saints" are in these chapters and are normal New Testament words for Christians and the Church. Again and again in the New Testament, born-again believers are called the elect of God and the saints of God. Every epistle is addressed to the saints in a particular place, such as the saints in Rome or the saints in Ephesus. If the absence of the word "church" means that a Scripture is not for the Church, then there are at least six epistles which do not have the word "church" in them.

So, does that mean that they are not for Christians? Rubbish. They are, in fact, 2 Timothy, Titus, 1 Peter, 2 Peter, 2 John—the word is not there. And the Epistle of Jude, which does not use the word "Church", does use the word "saints". However, could there be a reason why the word "Church" is avoided in Revelation? Well, the word "chosen" and the word "elect" are used 55 times in the New Testament, of which five are for Jews and 50 are for Christians. The term "holy ones" is also used of Jews as well as Christians; that is the same as the word "saints".

I believe that the reason the word "church" is not here is because the words "elect" and "saints" are to keep together God's concern for Jews and Christians, primarily for Christians, but also for his Jewish people. Do you remember Revelation seven, the two groups, and God protecting Jews and God comforting Christians? It goes right through this double concern until finally, in the New Jerusalem, both Jews and Christians are living together in Christ. Jesus said, "I have other sheep which do not belong to this fold, but there must be one flock and one shepherd."

I believe the destiny of Jews and Christians is one, not two, and that Jesus will bring us together at the last. Therefore, the reason that Revelation does not use the word "church" regarding the Big Trouble is not because the Church is not there, but that the term "elect" is used, which covers both Christians and Jews, because God has a concern for both. Incidentally, the word "Church" is not in any of the passages which describe the Rapture.

That is interesting, isn't it? 1 Thessalonians 4, which dispensationalists love to quote, does not have the word "Church" in it, so I could equally say, "Well, the Rapture doesn't include the Church because the word "Church" isn't there." It is so crazy to make that argument just because the word "Church" is not used.

Next, we turn to the emphasis on comfort and encouragement. The encouragement is that the Lord will see us through the Big Trouble, not that he will take us out of it. The New Testament promises trouble to believers. Jesus said, "In the world you will have trouble". He promised us this. But he added, "But take heart! I have overcome the world". I have overcome, so you can. You can be overcomers because you have got the Overcomer with you. I am the overcomer, so cheer up. I asked a friend of mine recently, "How are you?" He said, "I'm very well over the circumstances." Now, that is overcoming. In Acts 14:22, Paul says to his converts, "We must go through many hardships to enter the kingdom of God." Jesus spoke of the shallow rooted, who when trouble or persecution comes, they quickly fall away.

The last argument: Christians are not under wrath, for God did not appoint us to suffer wrath. Of course, in the Great Tribulation, saints will suffer worse treatment than others and will be persecuted and martyred in huge numbers, a multitude that no man can count. Now, let us realise that even today, saints suffer because the wrath of God is on our society. Romans 1:10 tells us that violence, dishonesty, lawlessness, and homosexuality are all symptoms of God's wrath on our community, and Christians suffer because of this general wrath upon society. There is no guarantee that a Christian will not be mugged or raped.

I remember having tea with Helen Roseveare when she was just back from Congo. She told us how the Congo rebels came and took her away and locked her up with a Roman Catholic nun, and then they came back and raped both of them repeatedly. I remember Helen saying to me, "You don't discuss denominational differences when you're both being raped on the same bed, you cry to the same Jesus." There is nothing in my Bible that says Christians will not suffer in a sinful world and that we are going to escape all the signs of God's wrath upon our world. We are not; we live in it. But when the wrath of God is poured out on the world, there are seven things I can say about it.

First, we will know that it is not personally directed against us. That is the first thing. God is pouring his wrath out generally on the world, not on us. We are caught up in it, but it is not personally directed at us.

Secondly, it will not lead us to the lake of fire. For others, there is something worse than the Big Trouble, and that is hell.

Thirdly, we know it will be short.

Fourthly, we will know that Jesus' coming is very near.

Fifthly, some of us will escape the worst by fleeing to the wilderness, by getting away from the urban centres.

Sixthly, the worst that can happen to us, martyrdom, only rushes us to heaven early. So, is that so terrible?

Seventhly, it will be no worse for us at a personal level than it has been for the Christians through the ages, because these things have already happened locally, and Christians have already been through them in their local situation. For the individual, it will be no worse.

Eighthly, we know it is not the final expression of God's wrath. The final expression of his wrath is hell, the lake of fire, and that we shall never see.

Having said that, I believe that God will give some of his people special protection in that time. I was reading again about the plagues of Egypt, and again and again God said to the Jewish people, "I will make a distinction between you and the Egyptians," and none of those plagues actually touched his people. In Revelation 3:10 there is this promise to one of the good churches in Asia, the church in Philadelphia: "Since you have kept my command to endure patiently, I will also keep you from the hour of trial that is going to come on the whole world to test the inhabitants of the earth." So, there are special promises to the overcomer. There is not the promise to escape martyrdom, but rather the promise to be protected from the worst of the Big Trouble. It is those who live who will suffer more than those who die.

Finally, I think I ought to mention that there are four different views about the Big Trouble, the Great Tribulation. The view that I have been giving to you, which I have been convinced by through my Bible study, and the only one I can find in my Bible, is called the post-tribulation view that Christ will come after the Big Trouble. But there are three others.

The pre-tribulation is the dispensational view that all Christians will be taken out of the world before the Great Tribulation. That is the dispensational view that I have been dealing with in this chapter. There is a second view, which is becoming more popular. It still says that the Church will be taken out of the trouble, but in the middle of it. It just postpones the Rapture a little bit, a secret Rapture of all Christians after the seals and trumpets, which are warnings, but before the bowls of wrath. That is a view that is gaining a little ground.

So, there is the pre-tribulation Secret Rapture of all Christians before the Big Trouble, and the mid-tribulation Secret Rapture of all Christians after the seals and the trumpets but before the bowls of wrath are poured out. That is how Christians escape wrath. The third view is the partial Rapture, and that is still a Secret Rapture of overcoming Christians before the Big Trouble, as if Jesus is saying, If you overcome the pressures, I'll secret rapture you; if you don't overcome, you've got to see it through.

So that means that not all Christians get the Secret Rapture, but some do who deserve it. But frankly, that makes no sense to me, because how can you prove yourself an overcomer in the Big Trouble before it has happened? But, the secret Rapture, the partial Rapture, is the third view.

I am driven by all my study of the New Testament to the post-tribulation view, which is by far the major tradition of the Church through the centuries. All the other three are very recent. I mean by that, in the last 200 years. Before that period, the Church from the earliest days had been post-tribulation, believing in one coming of Christ at the end of the Big Trouble, and the only escape from the Big Trouble being martyrdom.

Now, have I explained those four views clearly? But the fourth view, I am afraid, is by no means the most common view today. The other three together are far more common and have gained tremendously in popularity. But I sense quite a strong swing back to this fourth view. But having said all of that, I would say two things to close. First, we should not divide from Christians with different views on this.

Some churches, some missionary societies, insist on only one view if you are going to be a member. Since it has not happened yet, it seems so wrong to be so dogmatic about the future that you will not have fellowship with Christians who take another view. That is the first thing. So, whether you are a post-, pre-, mid-, partial, or whatever, I want to have fellowship with you. I do not believe this is a ground for division. That is the first thing.

The second thing I want to say is this: I would rather be wrong my way than wrong with any of the other three. I would rather tell other people to get ready for trouble and then have the delightful surprise that they do not have to face it than tell them they do not have to face it and then they find themselves in it. So, I would rather be wrong my way than with any of the other three.

I will tell you who persuaded me of this—a dear, dear saintly lady called Corrie Ten Boom. Now, Corrie Ten Boom, for the last few years of her life, was completely paralysed. She had a very bad stroke. The only two things that she showed any response to were, firstly, music, so they used to play her tapes of music constantly, and secondly—and I only found this out later—somebody gave her my tapes, and she would listen to my tapes of Bible teaching.

But before she was paralysed, Corrie made a visit to China, and this is what she wrote when she came back, and I want to finish with this: "I have been where the saints are already suffering terrible persecution. In China, the Christians were told, 'Don't worry, before the tribulation comes, you will be raptured.' Then came a terrible persecution. Millions of Christians were tortured to death. Later, I heard a bishop from China say sadly, 'We have failed. We should have made the people strong for persecution rather than telling them Jesus would come for them first.' Turning to me, Corrie said, 'Tell the people how to be strong in times of persecution, how to stand when the tribulation comes, to stand and not faint.'"

So, Corrie went on: "I feel I have a divine mandate to go and tell the people of this world that it is possible to be strong in the Lord Jesus. We are in training for the tribulation. Since I have already gone through prison for Jesus' sake and since I met that bishop from China, now every time I read a good Bible text I think, 'Hey, I can use that in the time of tribulation.' So, I write it down and learn it by heart."

Now, I think that is a wonderful statement. You see, when she was paralysed and unable to do anything, that was her tribulation, but she had prepared for it and stored up the Word of God in her spirit for it. I would rather be wrong my way than the other way. Jesus said, "See, I have told you beforehand," and I think he did it because forewarned is forearmed. Let us get ready for trouble, realising that when it comes, it is only for a short while and then he is coming back. Amen.

Chapter 7

HALLELUJAH CHORUS

We have now reached chapters 17 to 20. We are still in the Big Trouble, but at the very end of it. Events now hasten to their denouement, the climax of world history. The totalitarian regime that we looked at in the last chapter of this book is mercifully very short in duration. We finally looked at the unholy trinity of the devil, the Antichrist, and the False Prophet—a kind of hellish inversion of the Father, Son, and Holy Spirit.

I am afraid that at the end of chapter 16, there are some very sad words. In spite of all the disasters and all the troubles and all the warnings that God has given, people refuse to repent. They are so stubborn, so obstinate that even in all those disasters, they will not turn to God. Indeed, they do worse than that; they curse God for the disasters instead of repenting. Jesus was once asked about a natural disaster, a tower that fell, and he said that "the people killed in that disaster were no worse than anybody else", but he said, "Unless you repent, you will likewise perish."

Every disaster is a reminder to us that we need to be right with God... They are messengers of mercy—they are calling us to repent. Yet at the end of chapter 16, people refuse to repent and instead curse God.

As you may know, in every air crash, they try to find the little black box, as they call it; it is actually orange, but they try to find it in the wreckage because it has recorded the conversation right up to the moment of the crash. They always, or nearly always, edit the tape before it is played publicly. The reason is that almost invariably, the last words of the pilot are curses against God, and they always cut that out before it is made public. That is what someone involved in investigating air crashes told me.

Now, you realise that of the unholy trinity—the devil, Antichrist, and False Prophet—two of these are human and all of them are male. The rest of the book is dominated by two female figures, and from a very male sort of situation, suddenly we are looking at two women. One is a very bad one and one is a very good one; one is a filthy prostitute and the other is a pure bride, and these two women take us right to the end of the book of Revelation.

Neither of them is human; indeed, neither is a person. Both are what we call personifications; they both represent cities, and therefore, they represent a good city and a bad city. Each of them is a symbol of a city, and we could describe the rest of the book of Revelation as a tale of two cities. The two cities are Babylon, which stands for everything evil, and the New Jerusalem, which stands for everything good.

In chapters 17 to 20, we are wholly concerned with the bad one, with the scarlet woman, the whore; she is described in various ways representing Babylon. But what does Babylon represent? Babylon has been mentioned twice before, but purely in passing. In chapter 14, there is just a mention of Babylon without saying where it is, what it is, but that it is going to fall, that it is going to come to an end. Those are little glimpses, a kind of looking forward, but now we get the full details in these chapters.

In the Bible, cities in general are bad places. The very first mention of cities is in the line of Lamech, and he was a bad man, notably associated with weapons of mass destruction and the manufacture of armaments way back there in Genesis. Now, cities are usually regarded as bad places because they concentrate people, and therefore, they concentrate sinners, and therefore, they concentrate sin.

Sin seems to become more blatant and more concentrated in cities. There is less community in a big city and more anonymity, and therefore, there is greater freedom to do wrong without people knowing. In particular, there are certain sins which concentrate very much in cities. The sin of anger tends to concentrate in cities. It is in cities that you get riots, and violence rarely happens in the countryside, but somehow a mob of concentrated people is capable of violence that, individually, or even in small groups, they would not be. Lust concentrates in cities. Over half of the homosexual people, gays and lesbians, in England are in London.

Cities concentrate sins, but the two sins that are concentrated more than any other in the city in the Bible are greed and pride. Greed and pride somehow come together. Within the City of London, you have the concentrated finance of our nation. You have got people living for money and trading money without any exchange of goods or services of value. An awful lot of gambling is going on, which is gaining money at the expense of other people, to their loss. It is concentrated in this part of London, which is called the City.

So, there is greed, trade, and money-making; money concentrates in cities, and therefore, greedy people are drawn to the city to make money. Then there is pride, ambition, and aggression. All forms of human pride (thinking how great we are) concentrate in cities. I was studying the grandeur of the buildings as I walked there. You do not find buildings like that in Little-Puddlecum-in-the-Marsh! There is a concentration of "We are the biggest and best; we have the tallest tower." Canary Wharf is a symbol of human pride.

Now, all that is what the Bible says about the city—it is where mammon is worshipped and its architecture is a series of monuments to man's achievement and man's pride. I was looking at Saint Paul's Cathedral and trying to think of the day when all around Saint Paul's were only two- or three-storey houses, and it must have towered above them. Now it is dwarfed by the NatWest bank and by the Post Office tower. Churches are now hidden by the achievements of man—they are monuments to man's greatness.

It is in cities that hostility to God's people is most concentrated, and that is why in Revelation 12, for example, the woman, who I believe represents the Church, flees to the wilderness. She gets out of the city. She gets into the countryside where it is possible to survive. The Jews have always been in ghettos in cities. Somehow, the city concentrates anti-God feeling.

Now, the first city really to do this was Babylon. It begins with the Tower of Babel. From that, we get our word "babbling", because it was there that languages were first confused by God. It was by the great Euphrates River. That was on the main trade route between Europe, Africa, and Asia. The main trade route ran down the Euphrates River valley, and the Tower of Babel was at the centre of world trade in its day, a strategic position.

It was founded by Nimrod, a mighty hunter of animals who then became a mighty hunter of men and a mighty fighter, a mighty warrior. It was founded on aggression and war. It was founded on the belief that might is right and the belief in the survival of the fittest. Typically, it built mighty edifices; we are told they were built of brick stuck together with bitumen. It is a little touch of the Bible that proves its accuracy, because there is no rock or stone or mountain there, just a flat, clay plain. All they can build with is brick.

Let me describe for you the Tower of Babel as it was and as it is today, just so that you get some idea of what it was like. It was a mighty Ziggurat, as we call them, built up in stages, a tremendous tower for the priest to go up to the top and for the people to stand at the top. I am afraid that if you went there today, there would not be much that you could see, but millions of bricks were needed to build it.

There is natural bitumen around; you can actually see the brick courses there. But that is all that is left for you to see of the Tower of Babel today, if you went there. God judged that tower, and he came down and confused their languages. It was the first time that God gave the gift of tongues, and he gave it for the first time to separate people. Centuries later, he gave that gift again, and people came together and united. The first gift of tongues was at Babel. I sometimes read books which say there is no mention of the gift of tongues in the Old Testament. I wonder if people have read it. It is right there in Genesis 11.

Now, at the heart of Babel was humanism, which is the deification of man. The reason they built the tower was that they wanted to build a name for themselves. It was purely for their own reputation and pride. By way of contrast, let me jump ahead to something else which I took from *Time Magazine*. Some time ago, *Time Magazine* talked about the race that is on now to build the highest tower reaching to heaven. Isn't that interesting? It had pictures and descriptions of some of the giants in the old days, including the Empire State Building. That was the highest in the old days.

When that was built, that was the proudest monument to man's building achievement. That is nothing compared with what is going on now, with fancy buildings of astonishing heights. Talk about Babel, this is the race that is now on. It is notable that most of the biggest buildings are around the Pacific Rim, which is where the money is now. Japan, China, Taiwan, that is where it is all heading, that is where man is building his Tower of Babel again.

By complete contrast, Jerusalem is not on a trade route, it is not on a road, it is not on a river. It has no reason to be there. It is up in the hills, completely surrounded by hills; it is relatively inaccessible. Nobody goes to Jerusalem to make money. The only reason it is there is that it is God's city. It is where he put his name. In all these other places, man wants to make a name for himself, but Jerusalem makes a name for God. It is a complete contrast.

Actually, the city of Jerusalem is not on the top of the hills; it is in a hollow completely surrounded by hills that are higher than itself. Somebody has said it is like a night light in a bowl. That is a good description because even when you are in the temple, you still see the earth as well as the heavens, whereas the pagan high places did not want to see the earth. They built them on top of the mountain instead.

But you worship the Maker of heaven and earth in Jerusalem, so you see both, and you are below the horizon. It is in a little hollow in the hills, but it is not a trade centre at all. All the business is in Tel Aviv; you do not go to Jerusalem for trade. To this day, Jerusalem has no strategic significance whatever. It only has spiritual significance for Jews, Christians, and Muslims. They will go on fighting about it, I am afraid, because they all claim it to be their holy city.

These two cities became related in the Old Testament: Babylon and Jerusalem. The King of Babylon, when it was only a little city, had a little king. He heard that King Hezekiah of Israel was ill, so he sent him a get-well card. He sent it by the hands of two or three Babylonian citizens: "Dear King Hezekiah, hope you'll get better soon. Love, King of Babylon." *Ezekias*, or Hezekiah, as we call him in English, was so chuffed, we would say, by this, so pleased to be noticed by the king of faraway Babylon that he said to the visitors, "Would you like to see around my palace?" They said, "Oh yes," and then he said, "But I can show you something even more wonderful. I will show you the treasures of the temple."

He took these Babylonian visitors, who had brought a get-well card, around the temple in Jerusalem. At that point, after they had departed, Isaiah the prophet came into the palace and said, "Who were those visitors, O king?" "Oh, a couple of men from Babylon. They brought a get-well card. Rather nice of them." Isaiah said, "What did you show them?" "Oh," he said, "I showed them the palace. I showed them the temple and all the treasures." Isaiah said, "The king of Babylon will take from you everything you showed them."

It is a remarkable prophecy, isn't it? You will find it in chapters 36 to 39 in the book of the prophet Isaiah. Sure enough, King Nebuchadnezzar, when he extended Babylon from a city to be a whole country and then to be an empire, set his face against

Jerusalem. It was ultimately Nebuchadnezzar who came and took away all the treasures from the temple, burnt the temple and the King of Israel's palace to the ground, and ransacked Jerusalem.

Now, Nebuchadnezzar was ruthless. He not only destroyed buildings, but when he conquered a country, he cut down every tree, and he killed every sheep, cow, and horse. He left a country completely devastated. You will read about this in Habakkuk chapter 3, because God told Habakkuk that the Babylonians would come and just obliterate the whole country. That is why Habakkuk came to sing a little song: "Though the fig tree will not blossom and the vine will not bear her fruit, though there are no cattle or sheep in the stall, yet will I rejoice in God."

Habakkuk is an amazing little prophecy; it is all about the Babylonians coming. Not only destroying the city and taking the people away into exile, but destroying every tree, every animal, everything living. That happened, and they were taken away into exile in Babylon. They settled by the canals of Babylon, by the waters of Babylon.

Babylon, then, embodied everything that was anti-God. If you read Jeremiah or Ezekiel or Daniel or even Isaiah, before the exile, you will read about the doom of Babylon. Sure enough, it fell. Babylon is a place where the people of God do not belong. They belonged in Jerusalem. When they got to Babylon, they say in Psalm 137 that they could not even sing the Israel songs there: "We hung our harps upon the willows". The Psalmist cried a curse on himself: "May my tongue stick to the roof of my mouth and my hands forget their cunning if I sing the songs of Jerusalem before we get back home." It is an amazing curse on themselves.

Babylon became a name of all that was anti-God, where the people of God did not belong and needed to get out of there and come back home, and after 70 years, they did because Babylon fell. It became a total ruin. The biggest city in the then-known world is now a heap of rubble. It is dust; only wild animals can be found in its ruins. Can you imagine a preacher in the London City temple saying, "London will be left desolate with nobody living in it?" Nobody would believe him, and nobody believed Isaiah. But it happened. When God says Babylon will be destroyed, it is.

Now, there have been many Babylons in history, just as there have been many antichrists, so where is Babylon today? There is still an ancient Babylon. The famous Hanging Gardens were one of the Seven Wonders of the World, and one of the biggest tourist attractions.

I have seen the Ishtar Gate, a gigantic gate through which the triumphant armies with the king's chariot returned from battle. I saw that archway in that same Berlin museum where the altar of Pergamon has been rebuilt. It is blue glazed brick; it is beautiful actually, but there are the weirdest animal symbols all over the royal blue coloured glazed brick tiles. It is from those symbols that Daniel undoubtedly began to see the pictures of the weird creatures in his vision; they are very similar. It is just breathtaking. Ishtar is the same as the goddess Astarte, which you find in the Old Testament; it is a fertility feminism goddess. That is the famous Ishtar Gate.

There have been many Babylons in history. Where is Babylon today? Where has it been? Which cities have, as it were, taken over Babylon's role since it was destroyed? Well, undoubtedly, since the New Testament, Rome had taken over Babylon's role, and it is interesting that when Peter in his letter refers to Rome, he calls it Babylon. He is not the only New Testament writer to do that. It became the nickname of the cities that concentrated sin, greed, pride, lust, and anger.

In 1 Peter 5:13, it says that the church who is in Babylon sends greetings. Well, by that time, Babylon had been dust for centuries. There is no question that he is referring to Rome, and we know that Peter was in Rome. In Revelation 17:9, it says Babylon stands on seven hills. Well, if you know the city of Rome, it is built on seven hills. So that was the Babylon then; what is the Babylon now?

PHOTOGRAPH 7

Some time ago, I was in Nuremberg. Somehow, there is a fascination about Hitler and what he did, and I am old enough to remember. He was a prophet in Munich, and a king in Berlin, but he was a priest in Nuremberg. He combined the roles of prophet, priest, and king for the German nation in the 1930s. He built in Nuremberg the most fabulous areas where there could be mass demonstrations, which were virtually religious ceremonies, worshipping the state embodied in Hitler.

I stood on the very platform where he announced a millennium, a thousand-year German Reich or kingdom, but it was gone in less than 20 years. There is a picture of Hitler walking up the centre with massed crowds and the grandstands, and this temple at the end. That was Nuremberg before the war. It is deserted now; I walked all over that, and not a soul was there. These were his religious ceremonies; in the 1930s, Germany was Babylon.

You see, Babylon moves on. We could say it is Bangkok, or

Amsterdam, or Rio de Janeiro, or I think quite a good candidate would be Las Vegas. An article in *Time Magazine* about it just made me say, "Hey, that's Babylon." Actually, the original Babylon was being rebuilt by Saddam Hussein; he was actually rebuilding the walls. He likened himself to Nebuchadnezzar.

He had a laser beam light show at Babylon, projecting his own head and the head of Nebuchadnezzar onto the clouds in the sky. He dressed up his soldiers in the old Babylonian uniform. He rebuilt the Ishtar Gate, though he only built it half-size, but there are those rebuilt buildings of Babylon. People say, "Is that going to be the Babylon of the end of history?" I do not think so; I think the reconstructed buildings are largely just monuments.

So, where is the Babylon of today? You see, this is the picture in the book of Revelation: a woman riding on a beast. We know who the beast is. It is not the devil, actually; it is the devil's kingdom with the different rulers that he manages to bring together. That is the picture that you read about in the book of Revelation, the scarlet woman, Babylon. So, where and who is it?

Some say that by the time the end really comes, there will only be one city in the whole world. By the year 2050, all urban areas will be interlinked physically as well as by computer. This is the plan of the world city for 2050; it is a continuous urban belt stretching around the world with large areas of desert and land in between. Is that a possibility?

Bear in mind that it is a financial centre. Revelation 17 to 20 pictures a trading centre that seduces men by saying, "Come here and I'll give you pleasure, I'll give you money." That is why Babylon is painted as a prostitute, because she takes their money and gives them pleasure; that is the whole picture of it. But it is clearly a financial centre. Now, not long ago, I went to the financial centre of Europe; it is called Frankfurt am Main. That is where all the finance of the European Union seems to be centring. They built a gigantic new stock exchange, and outside it, they have erected a golden calf, would you believe it?

I went to their new bank, and when I went in through the main door, I was horrified. In the reception area, there is a two-metre-deep mural all around the area. It is a painting of hell; all the demons are there; all the sins of man are portrayed; there are greedy men up to their knees in Deutsche Mark notes. The whole thing is occultic, it is demonic.

Then, when you go through from the reception hall to where you get your money, you have to queue at the counter alongside life-sized statues in bronze of naked men and women in the utmost stage of decadence and degradation. Their faces are disgusting, their bodies are disgusting, and you have to queue with these statues to get your money.

When I tell people about this, they do not believe it, so I have to show them a photograph that I have in which you can see the money and the demons making love to humans. You can see all the things, and those are the horrid figures that you have to queue with to get money. The whole thing says, "Come in here and taste hell," and they treat it as a joke. It must have cost hundreds of thousands of Deutsche Marks to do all this, but this is the financial centre of Europe. I do not find it hard to apply the label "Babylon" Whether it is the last Babylon or not, I do not know, but you certainly get the same feel as you get from the picture in the book of Revelation.

But this is what Revelation means by Babylon. It is saying that one day there will be the last Babylon. It will be the world's centre of trade and commerce. Who knows, it might be in the Pacific area. We do not know. There was a time when many thought it would be a revived Roman Empire, and, as mentioned, when the European Community got up to ten nations, many Christians got excited. Now it has got many more than that, and they have cooled off a bit.

In other words, with all these things, until it actually happens, we do not actually know. But we can see foreshadowings of it in things that are happening all around us. So, Revelation does not give us the location or the size, but it is clearly a place that is visible from the sea, which Frankfurt am Main is not, so I do not think Frankfurt am Main will be it. It will be visible from the sea, which again perhaps points to the Pacific Rim—I do not know.

It does tell us about its nature. The nature of this city is to give people what they want for money, which is what a prostitute or a harlot does: pleasure without purity, materialism without morality, corrupting luxury and debauchery, the worship of mammon, the worship of wealth—the city. It mentions that music will play quite a large part in the life and culture of the city, and religion will. It mentions that the city will be the financial centre for seven and then ten heads of state, so clearly there will be a federation of countries that will be caught up in the city of Babylon.

The bulk of the world's business is in the hands of an ever-decreasing number of companies—probably fewer than 300 now. There was a time when you could find 300 companies in a small town in Britain. What a change! Now here comes the key: the woman sits on the beast. Let us look back at that.

That beast represents those ten heads of state caught up in her trade. What it means is that economics rules politics, that businessmen control politicians, and that business and economic interests control the government. Now, that is a very important point. It is saying, and it literally says that the queen rules the kings, which is always the reverse of God's order, all the way through God's Scripture. Here we have the queen ruling the kings.

You know that in the history of Israel, they never had a queen; they only had kings. God always promised sons to reign. While Sheba had a queen, Israel never did, except once a queen mother killed her own son in Israel, and indeed, all her family except one, which the high priest hid. She took over the throne, so at one point, a queen ruled Israel. You know, she was the daughter of Jezebel; that is the only time Israel ever had a queen. God's people are meant to have a king rather than a queen.

Here in Revelation, at the end of history, the queen, representing commerce, rules the kings of politics, and it says that they resent that and ultimately resolve to destroy her. Babylon will be destroyed not by God, but by the political rulers jealous of her power. Now, that is an incredible insight, and it is entirely credible when you look at politics today, which is ruled by economics, ruled by interest rates, ruled by the banks, the businesses. It is all heading up that way.

Hitler resented the fact that most of the banks were in Jewish hands, particularly the Rothschild family, who still owns one of the most prominent banks in Paris. He was jealous of the fact that the Jews controlled the money, and he got rid of them for that reason, although it impoverished Germany. It is very interesting that politicians resent control by business, and ultimately, the book of Revelation says that those ten political leaders will resent Babylon's power and will resolve to destroy her and raise it to the ground with fire. As old Babylon fell into ruin, so will that last Babylon, but it will be done by the political leaders jealous of her control of money.

It says God will put that purpose in their hearts, so in a sense God will destroy Babylon, but he will do it by putting into the hearts of political leaders jealousy and resentment against the economic city. They want the power and authority not from the city, but for themselves. So, after Babylon has fallen, you realise that no longer will power be in the hands of business or the economists, but instead in the hands of the military, and that will lead to the biggest battle at the end called Armageddon. You can see how these last events begin to shape up.

Now, the crucial question is, "What is the position of God's people in relation to the final Babylon?" Three things need to be said. The first thing is that the woman is drunk with the blood of the saints, those who have borne testimony to Jesus. Now, how can we think that Christians are being snatched out before all this happens when she will kill those who bear testimony to Jesus? Obviously, Christians are in there. But the first thing is that the

Christians will be martyred in Babylon, and that is mentioned all the way through. They will be seen as enemies of immorality and money-making, so they will be persecuted.

Secondly, therefore, the Christians are told in chapter 18, "Come out of her my people, so that you will not share in her sins, so that you will not receive any of her plagues, for her sins are piled up to heaven, and God has remembered her crimes." Now, that is the last city of Babylon and it says, "Christians, get out of it! Don't stay in it." Notice that God does not take them out; they have to come out. They have to make the decision.

They probably will lose their money as they do and lose their business, but they must come out of that last concentrated city of sin. Notice that God tells them to come out not so much for their safety as for their salvation, so that they are not sucked into her sins and lose their salvation. But notice, thirdly, that the martyrdom of the Church will not be total. Some will get out into the country.

So that is the second major thing. The first is that the woman is drunk with the blood of the saints; the second is that the Christians are told to come out. I have just made the three comments that they are not taken out, they have to come out, and it is not for their safety, but for their salvation, and it saves them all from being martyred. Thirdly, when Babylon finally falls, the Christians are commanded to rejoice. In other words, when the world stock exchange collapses and all the banks close and all the money markets of the world collapse, Christians are commanded to rejoice.

It says, "Rejoice over her, O heaven, and you holy apostles and prophets, for God has avenged you on her!" and they are told to shout out something similar to the Hallelujah Chorus. Now, have you heard Handel's *Messiah*? Well, you know that marvellous Hallelujah chorus, "Hallelujah, hallelujah, hallelujah, hallelujah, hallelujah!" Have you sung it? It is magnificent.

The King of England, when he heard it, stood up, and ever since everybody stands up when they hear the *Hallelujah Chorus*, but actually he was bored stiff and had stood up to leave. He thought this was the climax, the last song, and it was not. But that is a little bit of English tradition. How muddled we are in our traditions in England, so we all stand because the King once stood, but he thought it was all over.

People thrill to the sound of Handel's *Hallelujah Chorus*, which is taken from the beginning of Revelation 19, "For the Lord God omnipotent reigns." "For the Lord God Almighty reigneth." Do you know it? Now, when people hear that and get thrilled and say, "Isn't that Hallelujah Chorus wonderful?" I say, "Do you realise that it is a celebration of the collapse of the stock exchange and the world financial market and the closing of all the banks?" and that ruins it for them, of course. But Christians here and apostles and prophets and saints and the angels of heaven are commanded with an imperative: "Now rejoice, because Babylon has fallen, the harlot is dead!"

That is the first part of the good news, that Babylon, which is controlling the world through finance, will collapse, be finished. I guess the only people singing the *Hallelujah Chorus* that day will be God's people. I cannot imagine anybody else singing the Hallelujah Chorus. In Revelation 18:17–18, it says the merchants of the earth will mourn. It says that even the sailors on the ships at sea, seeing the smoke of Babylon rising on the land, will cry out, and there will be no music except something like the Hallelujah Chorus, God's people shouting out. For God will have dealt with her for what she did to God's people.

The prostitute is gone, and from now on, there is nothing more to happen but for the Bride to appear. Immediately after the Hallelujah Chorus at the fall of Babylon, it says, "Now the wedding has come, for the Bride has made herself ready. She is clothed in white linen, and that white linen represents the righteous deeds of the saints." You see, the Bible is a romance from beginning to end; it is the story of how a heavenly Father sought a Bride for his Son. Like every good romance, it finishes with a wedding and they get married and live happily ever after. That is how every good romance should finish, and the Bible finishes this way. The prostitute is finished and the Bride has come. Now we begin to look at the Bride.

The next part of Revelation is made up of visions, because if you have been reading carefully, you will have noticed that most of the chapters 17 to 20 have "I heard". "I heard an angel say"; "I heard a voice cry"; "I heard multitudes singing"; "I heard the sound of many waters"; I heard, I heard, I heard. Then, quite suddenly, half way through chapter 19, after we have been told that the Bride is ready, we have a series of "I saw, I saw, I saw, I saw, I saw, I saw, I saw." If you count them up there are seven visions and after them you go back to "I heard".

You see, unfortunately, the person who divided our Bible into chapters made a dreadful mistake many times. Often, those chapter divisions have put asunder what God has joined, and we miss the flow of Scripture and the continuity of the Word of God because of these chapter breaks, which God never put there, which he never wanted there. I hope one day you will get a Bible without chapter and verse numbers in it because God did not want that, and it has spoiled the Bible for us.

I have searched and searched commentaries on the book of Revelation—I cannot find one that has noticed we now have a series of seven visions. Of course, it makes a lot of sense because so much in the book of Revelation is in sevens. We had seven letters to seven churches; we had seven seals on the scroll that were broken one by one; we had seven trumpets; we had seven bowls of wrath, and now at the climax, we have seven visions, and this time they are all good ones. They balance out the bad sevens so that we have seven pictures which John now sees.

Like the other series of sevens, they divide into four, two and one. Every series of sevens from the seals onwards divides into four, two and one, as if you sort of focus in from four things, to

> ### SEVEN VISIONS ("and I saw")
>
> 1. **PAROUSIA** (19. 11-16) KING OF KINGS, LORD OF LORDS.
>   RETURN   'LOGOS' = WORD
>   WHITE HORSE, BLOODSTAINED ROBE
> 2. **SUPPER** (19. 17-18)   ANGELS INVITE BIRDS...
>   ...TO GORGE ON CORPSES.
> 3. **ARMAGEDDON** (19. 19-21) KINGS AND ARMIES DESTROYED
>   BY 'WORD' = LOGOS
>   BEAST AND FALSE PROPHET INTO LAKE OF FIRE.
> 4. **SATAN** (20. 1-3)   BOUND AND BANISHED TO 'ABYSS'
>   BUT FOR LIMITED TIME.
>   * * * * * * * * *
> 5. **MILLENNIUM** (20. 4-10) SAINTS AND MARTYRS REIGN
>   FIRST RESURRECTION
>   SATAN RELEASED, INTO LAKE OF FIRE.
> 6. **JUDGEMENT** (20. 11-15) RESURRECTION OF 'THE 'REST'
>   BOOKS AND 'BOOK OF LIFE' OPENED.
> 7. **RE-CREATION** (21. 1-2) NEW HEAVEN AND EARTH
>   NEW JERUSALEM.
>
> *DIAGRAM 8*

two things, to one thing. There is a kind of zoom lens in operation. So, let us look at the seven visions and what they are. The key to them is the phrase, "I saw". You notice that they stretch from the middle of chapter 19 right into chapter 21. But because they have been split into chapters, most Bible students have missed this, and they think that chapter 20 is a complete unit in itself. It is not.

In fact, the first three visions are in chapter 19, the next three are in chapter 20, and the last is in chapter 21. This has separated what God meant us to see together; it is a consecutive sequence of seven clear events in their correct chronological order.

The first vision is what we call the *parousia*, the coming of Christ, and John sees Jesus coming back to earth. The second vision is of an extraordinary supper for birds, for birds of the air. They are invited to the Lord's Supper—that is a strange vision. He sees an angel calling to vultures, "Come and gather together for the supper of the great God," and the supper is a ground covered with dead bodies. There are so many that they cannot be buried, and that is why the birds are called to come and clean it up. That is the result of the third thing; the birds are to get ready because the third thing is the Battle of Armageddon, the last battle of this age.

Then he sees Satan locked up, which is the fourth vision. Next, he sees what is going to be the subject of the next chapter in the present book, the controversial subject of the millennium. He sees Jesus and the saints reigning on earth for a thousand years, at the end of which Satan is released again. That is an extraordinary development, which we will look at in detail below. Number six is the Day of Judgment, and people begin to be thrown into hell in five, and six; they belong together.

The Antichrist and False Prophet are thrown into hell in vision three; the devil is thrown into hell in vision five, and all sinners are thrown into hell in vision six at the end of the Day of Judgment. Then comes number seven, which is completely different from the other six: "I saw a new heaven and a new earth". Now, these are seven things which John saw one after the other. When you put them together, you are seeing the seven last events of history— seven last things. Let us go through them in more detail.

The first one he sees is of a figure riding a white horse. Now, remember that a white horse is a symbol of military aggression. When Jesus was on earth the first time, he rode a donkey because he came in peace, but in his second visit, he is coming on a white horse, a symbol of war. Jesus did not come to kill anyone the first time, but to save them. But bear this in mind: the second time, he will kill millions. He personally will kill them. Now, that is a side of Jesus' character that you rarely hear preached. Let us see how it happens.

He has various names. On his thigh is written the name "King of kings and Lord of lords", and his garments are blood-stained. He comes now to shed blood, so he is on a white horse and has blood-stained robes with the name, "King of kings and Lord of lords". He is also called "the Word" or "the Logos" here. The only other place he is given that name is at the beginning of John's

Gospel, and it is the same John writing.

That is the first vision, and that is where Jesus' return changes the whole picture. We have already had one piece of good news (Babylon has fallen), but we have not yet seen the two beasts dealt with, the Antichrist and False Prophet, and we have not seen the devil dealt with yet. It is interesting that the order in which the four great enemies of men and women are introduced in the book of Revelation is: the devil, the Antichrist, the False Prophet, and Babylon. They are now each dealt with in the reverse order: Babylon falls, the False Prophet and the Antichrist are thrown into hell, and then, last of all, the devil is thrown in there too.

We have already had the fall of Babylon; now we must look at what happens to the others. As soon as Jesus gets back, the armies that are left after the fall of Babylon—remember, only military power is left—those armies march on the Middle East, determined to kill Jesus again. They know that he was killed once; now they come to kill him again.

Then why do they come with such a huge army? Because the first time it was easy to kill Jesus as nobody stood with him, and they just crucified him by himself. But when he comes back a second time, millions of his people, both dead and alive, will be with him in Jerusalem. Therefore, it will take a gigantic army to defeat them, and that is why this huge army gathers and marches on the Middle East to kill Jesus a second time, and all his followers who have gathered with him.

They get as far as a huge triangular plain in the north of the Promised Land. The Promised Land mainly consists of hills, but at one point the hills are broken by a vast triangular plain called the Plain of Esdraelon or the Plain of Jezreel, it has got various names. Have you ever been to Israel? If so, have you seen the Plain of Esdraelon? You must have done. Mount Carmel is on the west of it, and Mount Tabor is on the east of it; the hills of Galilee and Nazareth are on the north of it, and the hills of Samaria are on the south, and there is this vast triangular plain.

PHOTOGRAPH 8

This is a picture of it, or of part of it. It is a huge plain and at the west end there is one hill standing by itself called the hill of Megiddo. In Hebrew hill of Megiddo is *Har-Magedon* (Armageddon), and that is where the battle will be. Churchill called this plain "The cockpit of the Middle East". It is where Saul and Jonathan died; it is where the Egyptians were defeated; it is where Napoleon marched. It is the only open area in the Promised Land where armies can gather in any great number.

That is where they will gather to march on Jerusalem, but they will not get any further than there. It says Jesus will kill them all with one word. That is the same Jesus who commanded the storm to die—because that is what he commanded. It says literally, "He destroyed the storm with his words." That is the word that is used. And he will also destroy that army. That is the area that will be filled with dead bodies—too many to bury—but already the birds of the air will have gathered in the skies above to clean up the mess.

It is an amazing picture, isn't it? But it becomes entirely credible. When the world hears that Jesus is back with millions of his followers all in the same place, and they think, "Now we can deal with him once and for all," and they get no further than that. It says Jesus slays them with the sword of his mouth. He just says, "Be dead," and they are dead.

Well, that clears the decks, and it says the two beasts, the Antichrist and the False Prophet, will actually be with their armies; they will be there, but they will not die; they will be thrown alive into the lake of fire. They will be the first ever to experience hell. They will experience it by themselves for a long time. The first two into hell will be two human beings who have made the earth hell for so many, and they are the first to go.

That leaves on earth many people who were not in the army—all the Christians, Jesus, and the devil, because he is not destroyed in this battle. The next vision that John sees is of one angel chaining Satan—I mean this is the final insult to Satan that one angel deals with him. God does not deal with him, and Jesus does not bother with him. God just says to an angel, "Go and tie Satan up." I like it, don't you? Satan is bound and thrown into the lowest, darkest dungeon under the earth and locked in and sealed over.

There are six verbs there; it could not have been put more strongly. It means that Satan will now be able to do absolutely nothing on earth. He is seized, bound, thrown, chained, locked, sealed. That is him done. That is him out of the picture. We now have an earth, this old earth, still with many people living on it who did not march with the army. All the saints and Jesus and no devil, no Babylon, no False Prophet, and no Antichrist, so what is going to happen?

That leaves a huge political vacuum. Who is going to govern it? Who is going to run it? Then comes the most astonishing revelation, and this is the clearest passage about it, although there are many other references to it in the rest of the New Testament, and indeed the Old. For the next thousand years on this earth, Jesus and the saints together run the whole show. It will not be a democracy; there will be no elections, no votes. Jesus will appoint people. For example, he said in the parable of the talents in Luke 19:17, "'Well done, my good servant!' his master replied. 'Because you have been trustworthy in a very small matter, take charge of ten cities.'

Now, I wonder what responsibility he will give you. You see, the Christians will be looking after all the banks, after the courts, after all the counsels, after all entertainment, after industry. We'd better start getting ready for this job. We are going to be governing the world with Jesus. We shall reign with him. In this vision John sees a particular group, as well as the saints, but from among the saints he singles out all those whom governments martyred for Christ. They will now be the government. Isn't that exciting?

We will not go into much detail now, but here we have the saints and martyrs reigning with Christ on the old earth for a thousand years. This means, therefore, that there are going to be two resurrections. We know that sooner or later everybody is going to be raised from the dead, the righteous and the wicked. Daniel says that in Daniel 12:2, Jesus says it in John 5:29, and Paul says it in Acts 24:15 when he is on trial. He says that he is on trial because he believes "that there will be a resurrection of the dead, both of the just and the unjust".

The key is that they will not be raised together. There will be two resurrections, says Jesus, explaining it to John. First, there will be those who come to life at the beginning of the thousand years to reign with Christ: "Blessed and holy is he who has part in the first resurrection." The rest of the dead will not be raised until the end of the thousand years, immediately prior to the Day of Judgment.

Now, that is what, for example, Paul meant when he wrote in Philippians of his desire to "know him and the power of His resurrection, and the fellowship of His sufferings, being conformed to His death, if, by any means, I may attain to the resurrection out from among the dead". In fact, he uses the word "out" twice in Philippians 3. He says, "the out resurrection", "out from the dead", which is an unusual phrase and is used of Jesus' resurrection too because that was "out from among the dead"; in other words, a resurrection before the general resurrection of everybody else—"Out from among the dead".

Clearly, there are two resurrections: one of the righteous with Christ at his coming to help him run the world for a thousand years and the second for everybody else for the Day of Judgment. Now, in the next chapter, I will tell you that not all Christians agree with what I am telling you, but I believe this is the most straightforward understanding of what we see here.

Now comes the biggest surprise of all perhaps. It comes at the end of this thousand years of great blessing for everybody, a time of tremendous peace and prosperity, a time of much longer living, when somebody dying at a 100 will be regarded as a tragically premature death and the ages of people at the beginning of the Bible will be matched—remember Methuselah lived to be 969.

So, people will be healthier. There are promises in the Old Testament of a time on this earth when wild animals will become vegetarians, not carnivores, will not eat each other, and when a little child can play happily with lions. Lions and lambs will lie down together. It is astonishing that the whole of nature is going to be affected by Jesus' ruling on the earth, and certainly human nature will be affected.

Yet at the end, Satan is released to have one last go at deceiving the nations. Now, why should that happen? It is the most astonishing development that at the end of a thousand years of perfect world government of peace, prosperity, happiness, and health, Satan is allowed back in. I will tell you why I believe that is. We are not told here, so I am just guessing, but I believe it is for this reason: It is to prove that sin is not the result of our environment. It is to prove that people, after they have been given a lovely earth to live in and everything they could ask for still want to be free of God and his people and that the devil can still deceive them into thinking that if they could be free of God and his people, they would be happier—which is a lie, it is deception.

It seems to me that God is going to expose the utter contradiction in the humanist lie that if we got the environment right, everybody would behave correctly. It is just not true that we are products of our heredity or products of our environment. Too many people have risen above their background, and too many people have fallen below their background, to prove that we are determined by our background. It is not true. If you gave everybody a beautiful house to live in and enough money to live on, enough food, do you think they would all be good? No.

You see, during those 1,000 years, there is one-world government under Jesus, but it is imposed, it is not chosen. Even though it will bring such peace and such health people will still want to be free of the government and the devil will persuade them that they could be. That gives the lie to the humanist understanding that we are products of our environment. The communists believed that. They believed that if people shared out the wealth equally there would come into being a classless, crimeless society. It never worked; human nature is still sinful.

At the end of the millennium—and we call it the millennium because that is the Latin word for a thousand years—the devil, it says, is let back into the world, released from custody on parole. He then deceives the nations and it says he gathers people from all the four corners of the earth for a kind of second Armageddon.

This time, it is called Gog and Magog. Do not ask me what that means because I do not know. It picks up Ezekiel 38 and 39, because Ezekiel predicted in there that after the Son of David reigns on earth, Gog and Magog will still attack. That is what is picked up here. Now, I hope you do not get Gog and Magog and Armageddon confused. They are a thousand years apart. Armageddon is not the last battle of history; that is Gog and Magog. That is simply a phrase for the enemies of God marching again on the Middle East.

This time, God the Father himself deals with them by sending fire from heaven. Christ does not deal with them; God the Father himself sends fire from heaven, and they never even get near God's people. That is the fifth vision. Now he sees the sixth, and he sees everybody who is dead coming back to life.

Have you seen the paintings of a man called Stanley Spencer? He lived in Cookham up the River Thames. He painted Cookham churchyard, a huge, famous painting of Cookham church and the gravestones, the graveyard. But in the painting, all the stones have been pushed aside and the local villagers are climbing out of their graves. He has called it "The Resurrection". It is a fascinating painting, because people could recognise villagers they had known climbing out of their graves. It is a magnificent picture.

This is the reason, of course, why Christians prefer to be buried to being cremated—they always have. Now, God is able to raise up the dead from ashes as well as from dust, but somehow being buried allows you to think of resurrection, where cremation does not. It is purely psychological, but burial is like planting something in the earth from which you expect something to grow.

Paul uses this argument in 1 Corinthians 15: the resurrection is like putting a seed into the ground and that seed will die, but another seed like it will come out of the ground. So it will be with the resurrection. It is for that reason that although in the Roman Empire cremation was almost universal, Christians always chose burial. They buried them in the Catacombs below Rome. It was not that they did not believe God could raise a cremated person— far from it—but it was that it spoke of planting in the ground from which you expect something to emerge, and therefore the link could be made much more clearly.

Cremation speaks of something that has gone and that is it, whereas if you bury someone, you always think of them as there, and you think of the possibility of something new growing from the earth. You see, burial speaks of planting, whereas cremation does not. I certainly would choose to be buried, although I know that cemeteries clutter up and get very messy after a bit.

Nevertheless, I would want people to think that by planting me I will grow again.

In this he sees all the dead set free—even those who had been buried at sea. He mentions that particularly because, naturally, the fish have eaten them all up, and, of course, a body even buried in the ground goes back to dust. There is that famous debate about George Washington, I believe it was. An apple tree grew on his grave, and they found that the roots had gone down into his coffin and into George Washington. So, if you ate an apple, were you eating George Washington? That is the big debate that has gone on.

You may well have done; somebody could have been eating cells from George Washington. You see, God has no problem; he does not need to gather all the cells, or if a man lost a leg on the Normandy beaches, God does not have to go and collect the leg from Normandy. He is creating new bodies for us. Nevertheless, burial does speak more of resurrection; that is all I am saying.

The sea is going to give up the dead, and who could find any remains when they found the Titanic? There are no remains of the people who perished. They did not find even skeletons, did they? I have an interest in the Titanic. It is fascinating. What an achievement to find it, but no human remains. Yet every soul who perished on the Titanic will be raised from the sea on that day.

How many millions must be at the bottom of the ocean with all the shipwrecks that have been there? They will all be there at the general resurrection, the second resurrection. Blessed are those who have a part in the first resurrection, but it does not say blessed are those who come up the second time, because they only come up for judgment. Then he sees the books open. I think they will have red covers. That is only my idea, because I think the cover will have four words, "This is your life." It will not only be the nice bits either.

I often wonder what the researchers for the programme *This is Your Life* find and suppress. I know they find bad things, as I remember once a man came on and he was an employee of my grandparents and he was a rogue who had to be sacked and yet he was presented on *This is Your Life* as if he was a great hero, for things he had done in the Blitz and London in the fire service, but he was a rogue.

It says that on that Day of Judgment, books will be opened, and in those books will be everything we have ever done, or thought, or felt, or said—all our words, and all our deeds. I tell you, if that is the only book that is opened for me, then I am damned. I would have to praise God for sending me to hell and doing the right thing. But there is another book opened called the Book of Life and it is the book of Jesus' life.

It is not only the book of his life, but it has got in it the names of his relatives, and if your name is in that book, that makes all the difference. Bear in mind that earlier in the book of Revelation, Jesus said, "He who overcomes shall be clothed in white garments, and I will not blot out his name from the Book of Life". The Book of Life is mentioned in four books of the Bible. It is mentioned in Exodus, the Psalms, Philippians, and Revelation.

On three of those four occasions, it talks about names being blotted out from the Book of Life. That is the greatest tragedy that can happen to a Christian, to have their name blotted out from the Book of Life. You get it in through Christ, but to get it blotted out because you have not overcome, that would be tragic.

The first time in Exodus, Moses is told by God, "I have seen this people, and indeed it is a stiff-necked people! Now therefore, let me alone, that my wrath may burn hot against them and I may consume them." Moses said, "But now, please forgive their sin—but if not, then blot me out of the book you have written". God replied to Moses that he would not do that to him, but he would blot out of his book every one of his people who was sinning. Interestingly, that is the first mention of the Book of Life in the Bible. In Psalm 51, after David has sinned with Bathsheba and fallen into sin, he prays to God, asking him to "Hide your face from my sins, and blot out all my iniquities."

The Bible draws a very clear distinction between accidental sin and deliberate, continued wilful sin. It is the deliberate, continued, wilful sin that is the serious side. There is no sacrifice in Leviticus for intentional sin; there are only sacrifices for unintentional sin. Hebrews 10:26 says the same thing, that if we deliberately go on sinning after we have been forgiven, there remains no more sacrifice for sin, only a fearful expectation of judgment, for we have insulted the Spirit of Grace. It is a fearful thing to fall into the hands of the living God. So, your name is in the Book of Life now through Christ. Will it still be in there on the day the book is opened? That is the key thing.

The whole message of Revelation could be summed up like this: It is written to keep your name in the Book of Life until the day when it is opened. That is the Day of Judgment. And finally, there is the last vision. Oh, what a complete change, an entirely new universe. New space, new planet Earth, all new; the old has dissolved in fire and just gone back to the energy from which God created it. Every atom of this dust is packed with energy, and God packed it, and one day he will unpack it all.

So, the heavens and the earth will be dissolved in fire and out of the energy God will make a new heaven and a new earth, an entire new universe, but I am going to leave that until the next chapter. We leave that because it leads to the last two wonderful chapters, 21 and 22. The old heaven and earth pass away, replaced by the new heaven and the new earth, and the New Jerusalem comes down out of heaven, but we will look at that in the next chapter.

In the next chapter, I am going to describe something that you will not see until you get there, something of the New Jerusalem, a little bit of Revelation 21, that I have seen with my own eyes. I also want to look at this thing we call the millennium in much greater detail, because I am afraid there is huge division among Christians today about it.

Chapter 8

WILL CHRIST EVER REIGN ON EARTH?

The millennium, this thousand-year period, is a very controversial and divisive issue. Let me first of all go back to the seven visions. Read as a series of seven, they present seven consecutive events. Therefore, the millennium comes after Christ's return. Or, to put it another way, he returns, and that is followed by the millennium. Those who hold this belief are called *pre-millennialists*. "Pre" means Jesus returns before the millennium. A second view is called *post-millennialism*, because proponents of that view believe that Jesus will come again after a thousand years of peace and prosperity on earth, which frankly puts the Second Coming off for another thousand years.

This view, post-millennialism, is that the millennium comes before his return; therefore, they teach that chapter 20 actually comes before chapter 19, or is in fact a recapitulation, a throwback, a looking back. So that is the first huge division between pre-millennialists who believe Christ comes before the millennium and post-millennialists who believe that he comes after that thousand-year period.

Then there is a third view called *amillennialism* and "a" means "non". They should really call themselves non-millennial, but they do not like to be nons so they call themselves amillennial, as in atheist or amoral. It means non. So, the amillennialist says there is not going to be a thousand-year period at all. They therefore treat this as unconnected with any particular period of time; it is just a general picture of something else and not a time period.

So, let us now look at the varieties of the three views, because I am afraid that under each of the three views there are two, so that there are in fact six different positions on this one. It would be so much nicer if we just took Scripture as it stood, and that was it. But I am afraid that people do not.

So, let me look at the three views again, but this time bearing in mind that each has two different angles. Strictly speaking, the amillennialist or the non-millennial does not believe there ever will be a period of a thousand years of Christ's rule on earth, either before or after his coming. There are two groups there. The first I call the sceptical non-millennialists, and they just find the whole idea absurd. They dismiss this passage of Scripture altogether and just say that either John was suffering from indigestion or a bad headache or something at this point.

That is the sceptical view that the millennium is meaningless and that it has no message for us. You find a lot of liberal Bible scholars who take that view. They cannot make any sense of it at all. But then there are those, who do take the passage more seriously but treat it as a myth, as an allegory, as a story with a truth in it, but not history—just as people treat the beginning of the Bible as myth and say that you have to demythologise it to get the meaning, that you must not treat it as a real period of time. It is simply an allegory, a picture of what God would feel to be ideal—that Christ and the Christians ruling the earth would be ideal.

This links up with that view of interpreting the whole book as idealist that I mentioned earlier. The whole thing becomes an idea rather than an event. It is just a sort of embodied idea in a story. But they do take it a bit more seriously. The scepticals dismiss the whole passage; the mythological amillennialists treat it as an allegory. So, one treats it as an absurdity, the other as an allegory.

Now, at this point, I have to say something that will probably confuse you even further. Most Christians in this country call themselves amillennial, but when you scratch them, they are not. I mean, most evangelical Bible-believing Christians would call themselves amillennial. The London Bible College has a long tradition of amillennialism dating back to its founder, Ernest Kevan, who taught it very strongly. But, in fact, they are not amillennialists because if you ask them, "Don't you believe that chapter 20 refers to a period of time?" they say, "Oh, yes, we do." So, you reply, "Oh, which period of time does chapter 20 refer to then?" They all say, "Well, this church age." Now, to me, that makes them post-millennial.

They hide under the label amillennialist, but they are not amillennialists. There are very few evangelical amillennialists. They are actually post-millennial. They apply chapter 20 to the Church age before Jesus comes back. So, they do believe it is a period of time.

So, let us call a spade a spade. An amillennialist does not apply Revelation 20 to any period of time. A post-millennialist applies it to this period of time. A pre-millennialist applies it to the period of time after Christ's coming. The real amillennialists are usually in up to "a"—they are not in that at all. They are really spiritual post-millennialists.

Now, what do we mean by that? A spiritual post-millennialist believes that Christ and Christians are reigning now but only in a spiritual way, which means that we can cast out demons and march around cities and so on. But all we can do is reign over evil in a spiritual, not a political, way. We are not the government, but we are a spiritual government, meaning that Christ is already reigning in heaven, the dead saints are already reigning with Him in heaven, and in a sense, the Church has spiritual authority, so that the Church can reign over evil now. That is what most who call themselves amillennialist actually are. They believe we are in the millennium but that the only reigning that there will be, will be spiritual.

The other form of post-millennialism is the belief that the Church will take over the world and rule it for a thousand years. That in the name of Christ, the Church will rule the nations; not that everybody will be converted, but the majority will be. So, the nations will become "Christianised nations" and, therefore, the Church will take over the throne of this world before Christ comes back. Now, looking at the world today, we are a long way off that, and therefore we are at least a thousand years off the Second Coming. But it is amazing how many people currently believe this, and it is coming over from America under some unusual titles, such as "reconstructionism"—have you heard that word?

They believe that the Church is going to Christianise the world and take over and rule the world on behalf of Christ before he comes back. "Restoration" is another word for it. *Restoration Magazine,* before it went bust, had an editorial comment under the title of each issue, which said, "We believe that the Church will establish the kingdom worldwide before Christ comes." The restoration movement of some years ago believed that we were going to take over the world.

Many people left mainstream denominations and went over to house churches, believing that we were on the verge of taking over the world. Some young people still believe this. You know, "We're marching for Jesus. We're going to drive Satan through the Channel Tunnel into France, but we're going to clean England up in the name of Jesus." Do you know that kind of talk? I am caricaturing it, but there is a lot of this naïve optimism around that we are going to take over the world in the name of Jesus.

I think a bit of realism casts doubt on that. Another name that is coming over from America is Dominion Theology. Restorationists, reconstructionists, and those who follow dominion theology all believe that the Church will take over the world and that the last part of the Church age will be the millennium, after which Jesus will return. So, there is the spiritual post-millennialism, which says that spiritually we are in the millennium now, and there is the political version that says we will soon be taking over the world and running it.

Then, the pre-millennialist has two versions. One is our old friend dispensationalism, which I discussed in chapter six.

Will Christ Ever Reign on Earth?

You will recall that you find most of the dispensational pre-millennialists among the Brethren who have read the Scofield Bible and believe that the millennium is after Christ's coming, and that it is largely concerned with Israel and the Jews on earth. It is not at all clear whether Christians will be.

In contrast, the adherents of the classical pre-millennialism of the first five centuries of the Church believe that the Church will be ruling the earth with Christ, but the Jews will by then be part of the Church. Now, those are the six views—it is very complex, isn't it? Unfortunately, you will find all these views in books on Revelation. Now, I think you can guess which I am. I believe it is the most straightforward reading of Scripture.

Let us try to find out which one you are, if anything, and maybe all this is new to you, but let us try to find out with some simple questions. Question number one: "Will there be a period of a thousand years during which Christ rules on this earth?" You answer yes or no. Supposing you say no, then you are an amillennialist. If you do not believe there will be a millennium, you are a non-millennialist.

So, you then ask a further question: "Does this passage in Revelation 20 have any meaning or not?" If you say, "No, it has no meaning," you are a sceptical amillennialist. But if you say, "It has meaning, not for history, but it has a truth in it which can be applied at any time," then you are a mythological amillennialist. But supposing you said yes to the first question, "Yes, I believe there will be a period of a thousand years within the history of this earth." You then ask the question: "Well, do you believe it will be before or after Christ's return?" If you say after, then you are a pre-millennialist—Christ comes before the millennium, pre-millennium. If you say it is before he comes, then you are a post-millennialist.

Now, if you have found out that you are a pre-millennialist, then you ask a further question: Will this thousand-year kingdom on earth be a Jewish or a Christian kingdom? If you say, "Jewish," then you are a dispensational pre-millennialist. If you say, "Christian," then you are a classical pre-millennialist. But if, on the other hand, you say, "No, this thousand-year period will be before Christ comes," you then ask whether it refers to the whole of the Church age, even though it is now just less than 2,000 years. But you see a thousand years as a round term for the whole age. Therefore, the rule of Christ is not political, but it is spiritual; then you are a spiritual post-millennialist.

But if you believe the millennium will be the last part of the Church age when the Church politically takes over the world and establishes Christendom worldwide, then you are a political post-millennialist. Now, I have tried to put that as simply as I possibly can, although it is very complex when you find all these shades of opinions among Christians.

You may not have thought about it or been aware that there is such a division among Christians about all this. But anyway, that is the way to tell and if you meet somebody who says, "I'm an amillennialist," say, "Are you sure?" and check it out with this. I think you will find that most who call themselves amillennialists are, in fact, spiritual post-millennialists.

Well, those are the different views. I will just say a word about the history of those views. The early Church for the first 500 years, was solidly classical pre-millennial. That is why we call it classical. They looked forward to what they called "the bodily reign of Christ on earth", and about 30 or forty writers in the first 100 years all looked forward to a day when Christ would come and reign on this earth with the saints. The interesting thing is that for the first 500 years, there is no trace of any other view.

So, when did all these other views start? Well, the first change came with a man called Saint Augustine. I do not know why they call him a saint, because that man has done more damage to the Church than anybody else, because he reinterpreted the gospel in terms of Plato. He introduced Greek thought to Christian thinking, and we have been Greek ever since in our thinking. The Church needs to be de-Greeced and to go back from Greek thinking to Hebrew thinking.

But it was Augustine who converted the Church to Greek thinking. It was Augustine who really put the seal on baby baptism, for example. It was Augustine who wanted Christianity to be an established religion with the Church and state brought together. In fact, Augustine was a spiritual post-millennialist, and he took Revelation 20 from after Christ's return, and he put it before, and he said, "Christ is reigning now, and the saints are reigning with him spiritually." Of course, in his day, the Roman Empire had become Christian, and they really thought they were taking over the world. But you can imagine why they thought this way, as during the Middle Ages, the Church and the state became one kingdom called Christendom.

It moved through to this and became political post-millennialism, and they really thought they were in the millennium with the Holy Roman Emperor and the Pope running everything. They gave the pope the symbol of two keys, a silver key and a gold key, as the head of the Church and the head of state; political and religious power came together. So, by making the millennium a spiritual thing, this is what Augustine did with so much in the Bible. He spiritualised it, allegorised it, and he took away the reality of it, the Hebrew reality of so much. He spiritualised it all. He saw the Church as the New Jerusalem; he brought it all into the present. Read his book "The City of God". The next to appear was the dispensational view, which appeared in 1830.

Most people think all pre-millennialists are dispensationalists. That is the confusion I encounter all the time. People ask me, "What are you?" I reply, "I'm a pre-millennialist." They say, "Oh, you're a dispensationalist." I say, "No, I'm not. I'm a pre-millennialist as the early Church was." I believe the Church will be reigning with Christ on earth and that the Jews will by then have accepted Christ and be one with us; when they see him whom they pierced, they will be converted. So, we have established this historically. This, of course, came with liberal, critical scholarship at the end of the 19th century from Germany, and liberal interpretations of Scripture came sweeping in. You will find that most liberals today are one or the other of those two.

I am happy to tell you that there is a notable swing back today to classical pre-millennialism. I give you one or two names. Hal Lindsey, of course, but I give you one other name here: George Eldon Ladd, G E Ladd. Any books by him are tremendous books. He led the way back to this. Another name is Merrill Tenney. Any books by Ladd or Tenney are calling the Church back to classic pre-millennialism. I came to this view not through either of them, but just through sheer study of the Bible decades ago, and I have stayed with it ever since.

I find it very encouraging that there is such a swing now back to this to reconsider it, and classical pre-millennialism is now being preached in this country. You must make up your own mind. People say, "Well, why argue about all this?" It has very practical implications. But let me begin by showing you how the different views actually interpret Revelation 20, because that to me is the key, how they handle Revelation chapter 20. I am only going to look at the post-millennial and the pre-millennial because those are the only two views really held by evangelical, Bible-believing scholars.

If you put the millennium before Christ's return, how, then, do you interpret Revelation 20? I am really asking, "Which is fairer to Scripture: the post-millennial interpretation of Revelation or the pre-millennial?" And I am looking at both the spiritual and the political. In interpreting Revelation 20, both types of pre-millennialists are identical, whether they are dispensational or classical. So, I am going to compare the whole pre-millennialist view with those two. Regarding the thousand years, the spiritual post-millennialist says, "That's a symbolic figure." It simply means a long time. The fact that it has already been 2,000 years does not matter. The political is a little more definite. Sometimes the political proponents say it is symbolic, sometimes they say it is literal, but they all say it is the last period of the Church age before Christ comes. Pre-millennialists usually interpret it literally as a thousand years.

So, there is a difference of interpretation there. With the rider on the horse, the post-millennialists have a problem since the millennium comes after the rider on the horse. So, what do the post-millennialists make of that? Well, they say that if chapter 20 is in fact a sequel to chapter 19, then the rider on the white horse must be Christ at his first coming. The white horse is spiritual.

It was not a real horse at all. It was actually a donkey, but spiritually it was a white horse. Now, I mean, it begins to get ridiculous at this point. Those who accept that 20 is a sequel to 19, that it is part of the series of seven visions, apply that rider on the white horse to the first advent of Christ and therefore spiritualise it.

But more post-millennialists treat chapter 20 as a recapitulation; they say 19 is the Second Coming, but then the vision goes back 2,000 years to the millennium that began with his first coming. So, either way, I think they are messing up the Scripture. The pre-millennialists all apply it to the second advent, because if chapter 19, the rider on the white horse, is the first coming, then there is no mention of the Second Coming in the whole of the text of Revelation apart from the prologue and the epilogue. To cut the Second Coming out of the book of Revelation and to apply it to the first advent is just amazing, isn't it?

Now, let us take the binding of Satan. The pre-millennialist says he is bound in the future by an angel, and he is totally limited and can do nothing. You will remember those six verbs—seized, chained, thrown, imprisoned, sealed, and locked. The pre-millennialist takes that as meaning the devil, Satan, is banished altogether from the world for the thousand years. It is done by an angel. But you find that post-millennialists cannot cope with that because if you try to apply that to the present, then who is carrying on the business if Satan is no longer here? Do you see?

They have a problem, so how do they get around it? Well, they say that Jesus bound Satan when he was here the first time. It is not an angel binding Satan. They forget that. They say Jesus talked about how you have to bind a strong man before you can spoil his goods; therefore, Jesus bound Satan, but the binding was only partly effective. He is still quite active now. To me, that is just twisting it, though. How can Satan be seized, chained, thrown into a dungeon, sealed in, and locked up, and only be partly limited? That is the way they get around it.

The political post-millennialist would say that the binding of Satan was something to be done by the Church, and I am sure you have heard people binding Satan before a meeting. You never find that in the New Testament. It has become quite a common form of prayer. I am hearing it everywhere I go: "We bind Satan in the name of Jesus for this meeting." I wonder where we started that? It is all part of this post-millennial thing that came in.

So, Satan is bound by the Church in the present, and he can be severely limited by that and will be, but not entirely. So, which of these three is being truest to Scripture? It says an angel binds him totally. But here in the present, it is the Church binding severely or Christ binding him only partly in the past. Which is truer to Scripture? Let us take the first and the second resurrection—the pre-millennialist takes them both as physical. How can you have a first and a second if they are not the same thing? They are both bodily resurrections.

In fact, the same verb is used of both. They come to life, and the rest of the dead do not come to life until the end. Now, how do the post-millennialists handle that? Well, they make the first resurrection spiritual, saying that it happens at your conversion and the second resurrection physical at the end of history. You see, for the post-millennialist, there is only one resurrection of the body for everybody on the same day. Therefore, the first resurrection becomes a spiritual one, a resurrection of the soul rather than the body, when you are converted. They all get around it that way. Which is truer to Scripture? The pre-millennialist says that the loosing of Satan is at the end of the millennium; the post-millennialist says it is at the end of the Church age.

They also have a very different attitude to the restoration of Israel. The pre-millennialist usually believes that Israel will recover her own land. Post-millennialists do not believe that. They cannot believe that God has brought the Jews back to the Promised Land in our day. They only believe in a spiritual restoration of the people of Israel. In fact, one of the last issues of *Restoration* criticises very severely those who believe that God will bring the Jews back to their own land at the end. A number of my friends said that it will end the magazine *Restoration*. Sure enough, a few months later, it went bust. But on the issue of Israel, there is a big difference of belief. Post-millennialists do not have any understanding of modern Israel in the light of Scripture, whereas pre-millennialists do.

The pre-millennialist says that the reign of Christ will be on earth because the whole of chapter 20 is on earth, whereas the post-millennialist either says it is the reign of Christ and the dead saints in heaven or spiritually through the Church on earth. But it is not an earthly reign. Now here comes an interesting difference. Of these views, which has the strongest emphasis on the return of Christ? The answer is the pre-millennial. You will find that a pre-millennial view goes along with preaching the Second Coming strongly. The political post-millennialist preaches it quite weakly. They are the weakest on the Second Coming, because, after all, it must be at least a thousand years ahead.

The post-millennial spiritual proponents sometimes mention it, sometimes they do not. It has quite a direct effect. If you ask when a Christian prays every day, as Jesus taught us to pray every day, "Your kingdom come on earth as it is in heaven", whether they expect that to happen suddenly or gradually, what would they say? The answer would reveal which of these views they hold. The post-millennialist expects it to happen gradually over the centuries, whereas the pre-millennialist expects it to happen suddenly when Christ comes. Well, I only ask whether you can see in one particular view the twisting of Scripture. That is the real issue to me. Does the view deliberately squeeze Scripture into a previous decision that has been made to make it apply now and not in the future?

But let us face the question straight on. What does it matter? Now, there are many people today who say it does not matter which you are. I am sure you have heard a new label that people are now using in a tongue-in-cheek way. They are calling themselves pan-millennial, and if you ask them what a pan-millennialist is, they will say it is someone who believes everything will pan out all right in the end, whatever!

In other words, those who identify with that label are running away from the whole issue and will not think about it. They are just saying, "Oh, we'll wait and see. It'll all pan out." That to me is escapism. That is not eschatology, that is escapology. So, let us ask what difference does it actually make to our behaviour in this world which we believe in.

A friend of mine was asked, "Are you a-millennial, pre-millennial, or post-millennial?" My friend said, "That is a preposterous question," which I thought was one of the neatest responses I have heard. But actually, it is a very practical issue, and it has a profound effect on two areas: evangelism, winning the lost for Christ, and social action. By that, I mean whether you try to make this world a better place than it is. Now you see, it does have this effect, and this time I must show that the classical dispensational pre-millennialism has quite a different effect. Let us look first at evangelism.

Let us start with dispensationalism, which is one of the most common positions among evangelicals because of the Scofield Bible and Hal Lindsey and the Brethren influence. Dispensationalism, which, you will remember, believes that Jesus could come at any minute, produces a terribly high motivation for evangelism. We must save everybody we can now in case he comes tonight.

But it has just the opposite effect on social action, and you tend to think of the world as the Titanic going down, and all we have to do is try and get a few more souls into the lifeboat. Do you see what I mean? There is no point in painting the Titanic now. Dispensationalism produces very low motivation. What is the point of trying to make the world better if Jesus could come back tonight?

But what it does do is it makes you very keen to win everybody you can before Jesus gets back. So that is the pattern of dispensationalism—very high evangelism, very low social action. Classical pre-millennialism has quite a high motivation for evangelism, although not as high as the dispensationalist who says he might come back tonight. I must get my children saved before tonight.

Classical is high on evangelism, but medium on social action. It is average. Classical pre-millennialism gives some a reason for making this world a better place (I will come to that in a moment), but not nearly as low as the dispensational view. Now, post-millennialism of the spiritual kind, which believes that we are already in the millennium and are reigning spiritually, has a medium level of motivation for evangelism; it is neither high nor low. But it has a low motivation for social action because it spiritualises everything. You do not do anything political because the Church establishes a spiritual kingdom.

It would tend to concentrate more on personal welfare than on political reform. Do good to other people, but the post-millennial political view again is medium in its motivation for evangelism, but terribly high in motivation for social action, because if we are going to take over the world before Christ comes, we had better get on with it now. So, there is a terrific motivation to get into government, to engage in political protest, to get involved in political life and reform. The liberation theology of Latin America would fit very clearly into this.

It is the hope that the Church will liberate the poor and take over the world and even things up. You might even be low on this side in evangelism, but you can see that it is an oversimplification. However, it is my observation that the views you hold about the future do have a profound effect on your attitude to the present. It is not an academic issue.

That is where I would want to be, quite frankly. But that is what I have observed as I have talked to people, I have found the reconstructionist, the dominion theology, the restoration one, very, very high here on taking social action, and medium to low on evangelism. We have seen a swing in this country recently from evangelism to social action. Let me spell it out. There has been a huge swing of money from missions to relief. Charities like Tear Fund and Christian Aid have been attracting a large number of donations, whereas missions to evangelise are crying out for money and are often in real crisis. So, we have seen a very strong swing from evangelism to social action in this country. When you ask what lay behind that, I believe it was the loss of belief in pre-millennialism.

Now let me say why I believe that classical pre-millennialism provides a much greater motivation to social action than the dispensational view. The dispensational view sees the millennium in Jewish terms, with the kingdom of Israel being re-established and ruling the world, whereas classical pre-millennialism sees Christians involved in ruling the world for a thousand years. That gives you a very practical motivation for getting ready to do so.

If Christ is going to need magistrates and bank managers and others to handle the affairs of this world, then you have a motivation to be working towards that, of learning how to do it. Whereas if it is only going to be Jews on earth and we are going to be in heaven, then what is the point? So, a classical belief in the millennium after Christ comes involving Christians and the

Church, gives us a very sound motivation to be good at our current jobs in order to be ready to run the world with Jesus.

Whereas if he is coming to take us out of this world, as dispensationalism emphasises, then what is the point? Why try to make this world better? Now you see, a pre-millennialist does not hope to take over the world before Christ gets back, but is getting ready to take it over when he does. The post-millennialist, especially of the political variety, expects to take over the world before Christ gets back. But I think he will be disappointed. We do not seem any nearer to that now than we were 2,000 years ago in terms of proportion and government. I think Babylon is far more likely, an Antichrist is far more likely, in the near future, than the Church taking over the world. But the amillennialist has no hope of ever seeing Christ rule the world in any way.

The post-millennialist believes that he is ruling the world now spiritually, but many have hopes that he will also rule the world politically through the Church, but not in his physical presence, whereas I do have hope—more, I have the certainty—that Christ will reign on this earth and that I will be helping him to do it. That gives me hope for this world, a de-polluted present earth, even before the new earth. But what does Scripture have to say about all this? Because that is ultimately the test. Post-millennialists and amillennialists often tease pre-millennialists and say that since Revelation 20 is the only passage of Scripture that talks about the millennium, is that enough basis for such a big belief if it is the only passage?

Well, even if it was the only passage, it is still part of God's Word. My reply is, how often does God have to say something before we believe it? Within the passage itself, the thousand years is specifically emphasised six times. It is not as if it is only mentioned once. It keeps saying, thousand years, thousand years, thousand years, thousand years, thousand years, thousand years, six times. Furthermore, on two occasions, it talks about the thousand years with the definite article. Now that is pretty clear. You cannot just dismiss it so easily. Next, I would point out that the Church has built other doctrines on one verse, so why shouldn't we build this on one passage? May I give you two examples? There is only one verse in the whole of the New Testament that appears to apply the name "Israel" to the Church—that is in Galatians 6, and then it is ambiguous, it is not even clear.

Yet how often have you heard the Church described as the new Israel? There is only one possible verse in Scripture that does that. The word "Israel" is used 74 times in the New Testament, and only on one occasion could it possibly be applied to the Church. Yet the Church has built the doctrine of the Church as the new Israel on one ambiguous verse, so what is wrong with building it on Revelation 20?

Another example: the Church absolutely insists that you are baptised in the name of the Trinity, and without the Trinitarian formula, it is not a Christian baptism. Have you come across this? "I baptise you in the name of the Father, the Son, and the Holy Spirit." Every baptism in the book of Acts was only in the name of Jesus. They were baptised into the name of Jesus. There is only one verse in the whole New Testament that talks about baptism in the name of the Father, the Son, and the Holy Spirit, and that is in Matthew 28.

All the other verses—and there are many—only talk about being baptised in the name of Jesus, yet the whole Church has built on one verse a whole doctrine that baptism is not baptism if it has not been in the name of the Trinity, which I do not believe. In fact, there is a kind of movement among some Pentecostals called the "Jesus Only" movement. They believe you were not baptised properly if you were baptised in the name of the Father, the Son, and the Holy Spirit—it has to be Jesus.

So, I pleased everybody. I used to say, "In the name of the Father, the Son, and the Holy Spirit, I baptise you in the name of Jesus into his death, burial, and resurrection." That kept everybody happy, but I do not believe that it has got to be the "right formula" to make it work. That seems to me to be getting into legalism. But I am just giving you examples where the whole Church is building doctrine on one verse. Yet here is a whole passage which mentions the thousand years six times. Why can't we believe it?

Well, there can be two other objections to building a belief in the millennium on one passage. One argument is negative and the other is positive. The negative argument is the absence of confirmation—that there are no other Scriptures saying it. That is the negative. The positive argument is the presence of contradiction—that other Scriptures actually rule out the idea of a millennium. Now, those are the two further arguments. The first argument is that it is only in one passage, as if, therefore, you can ignore it. The second argument is that there are no other passages that mention it. The third argument is that there are other passages that contradict it. Are you with me so far?

So, this is why there have been all the arguments about it. Well, let us look first at the absence of confirmation. Certainly, Revelation 20 is the clearest passage, but it is not by any means the only passage that indicates there will be a reign of Christ on earth. What about the rest of Revelation? There are at least three places where the millennium is mentioned—the rest of Revelation, for a start. In chapter 2:26–27, Jesus says that overcomers will rule the nations.

My question is "When?" Overcomers will rule the nations, yet overcomers may be martyred. So, when will they rule the nations? It must be in the millennium after Christ has raised them from the dead. Revelation 5:9–10, the song to Christ, says, "because you were slain, / and with your blood you purchased for God / persons from every tribe and language and people and nation/ You have made them to be a kingdom and priests to serve our God, / **and** they will reign on the earth." Redeemed people will reign on the earth. They *shall*, not they *do*, they *shall*—when?

The only answer can be the millennium, or chapter 11:15.

John hears a song being sung: "Hallelujah! The kingdoms of the world have become the kingdom of our God and of his Christ." When? I do not believe that has happened yet, do you? It is going to happen, it is promised. So, in the rest of Revelation, there are plenty of indications about the millennium. It is not confined to Revelation 20.

Now, what about Paul's letters? Let us take 1 Corinthians, for example. In 1 Corinthians 6:1–4, Paul is saying to the believers of Corinth that he has heard that some of them have been going to a pagan court and suing other Christians there. He says, "If any of you has a dispute with another, do you dare to take it before the ungodly for judgment instead of before the Lord's people? Or do you not know that the Lord's people will judge the world? And if you are to judge the world, are you not competent to judge trivial cases? Do you not know that we will judge angels? How much more the things of this life!" Now, when will the saints judge the world?

Incidentally, when he says, "Do you not know that the saints will judge the world? He assumes they have been taught that it was part of his teaching when he first founded the Church that they are going to judge the world, and that that is the kingdom that is going to come. He is certainly not talking about the Day of Judgment, which will be in the hands of the Lord alone. In 1 Corinthians 15:23–25, the chapter on the resurrection, he says, "But each in turn: Christ, the firstfruits; *then*, when he comes, those who belong to him. *Then* the end will come, when he hands over the kingdom to God the Father…"

There are two "then"s; therefore, there are three stages of the resurrection. Christ, then at his coming, those who belong to him, then the end, the general resurrection, so that there are actually three resurrections. Christ's is the first, then there are two others (those at his coming who belong to him), and then the others. Again, it backs up Revelation 20.

Now, I have already mentioned this unusual phrase, "The out

resurrection, the out of the dead," which is used in Philippians 3:11. It is also used in 1 Peter 1:3, and it is talking about a resurrection of believers before the dead are raised out from among the dead. Here, we have clear recognition that there is not one day of resurrection for everyone, but two. Again, it backs up Revelation 20.

Let us come to the Gospels, mainly Matthew and then Luke. I could give you so many references here, but I will go fairly quickly through them. Luke 1:32–33 is a prophecy about Jesus before he was born: "He will be great and will be called the Son of the Most High. The Lord God will give him the throne of his father David, and he will reign over Jacob's descendants forever; his kingdom will never end." Has that happened? The throne of David is not in heaven. It is on earth. Has Jesus sat on the throne of David yet? Is he ruling the house of Jacob yet? So, when will he do that? There must be some time when the prophecy will be fulfilled. In Matthew 5:5, Jesus teaches that the meek will inherit the earth. The earth, when?

In Matthew 19:28, Jesus said to the disciples, "When the Son of Man sits on his glorious throne, you who have followed me will also sit on 12 thrones, judging the 12 tribes of Israel". Has that happened yet? When will it happen? In Matthew 20:21 the mother of James and John said, "Grant that these two sons of mine may sit, one at your right hand and the other on the left, in your kingdom." Now, Jesus told us to pray every day, "Your kingdom come, your will be done, on earth as it is in heaven." When will that prayer be answered? The dying thief said to Jesus, "Lord, remember me when you come into your kingdom." If you could ask the dying thief what kingdom he was talking about, he was talking about Jesus as the Messiah sitting on the throne of David. He was a Jew, and that was what he was asking.

In the parable of the talents in Matthew 24:21 and 23, the reward for faithful servants is, "I will put you in charge of many things." Luke's version of that in Luke 19:17 is, "have authority over ten cities". When? Luke 16:11–12: "So if you have not been trustworthy in handling worldly wealth, who will trust you with true riches? And if you have not been trustworthy with someone else's property, who will give you property of your own?". Now, when do we get these riches and this property if we have been faithful? There must come a time when these things are all fulfilled.

In Luke 20:35, he talks about "But those who are considered worthy of taking part in the age to come and in the resurrection from the dead....". In other words, there is a resurrection from the dead in which you can be worthy, whereas the general resurrection happens automatically. Similarly, in Luke 14:14, Jesus says, ".... you will be repaid at the resurrection of the righteous." Again, the resurrection of the righteous is different from the resurrection of the wicked. What about the book of Acts? Acts 1:6: "Lord, are you at this time going to restore the kingdom to Israel?"

That is one of the most misunderstood verses in the Bible, so let me go carefully into it. If ever I am asked a question, I often do not answer the question, but I unpack the question, because built into every question are certain assumptions, which we call premises.

For example, if you say, "David, have you stopped beating your wife?" I will not answer the question because you built into the question an assumption, so if I said yes, I would be admitting I had been beating my wife. If I said no, I would be admitting I was still beating her. You frame the question in such a way that I cannot answer it.

Now, behind this question, "Lord, will you at this time restore the kingdom to Israel?" are four assumptions. Number one: Israel once had a kingdom. You cannot restore a kingdom unless it was once there. Number two: Israel has lost the kingdom, or it would not need to be restored. Number three: Israel will recover the kingdom. They were confident it would be recovered. And number four: Jesus would be the one to do it.

The interesting thing is that Jesus does not challenge one of those assumptions. Based on those four assumptions, they only have to ask when—at this time or later—he is going to do this. Jesus did not say, "I'm not going to do it." He did not rebuke them for asking the wrong question. But every preacher I have heard refer to this verse has said they asked the wrong question. No, they did not. Jesus did not rebuke them. What he said was, "It is not for you to know the date that Father has fixed."

Now, what does that answer tell you? It tells you that it is going to happen. When? "Lord, will you at this time restore the kingdom to Israel?" "It is not for you to know times or seasons which the Father has put in his own authority." Now, supposing they had asked Jesus whether he would now kill Pilate and Herod? He would have said, "It is not for you to know the date Father has fixed." What does that answer tell you? It tells you that he is going to do it, right? Not that it is wrong to ask, but that he is going to do it. Do you see? The very answer that Jesus gave accepted the question as valid. That is a very important point and he is careful unpacking it, because most people assume they had asked a silly question and all Jesus said was I want you to be missionaries to the ends of the earth.

No, he did not say that. In Acts 1:7–8, he said, "It is not for you to know the times or dates the Father has set by his own authority. But you will receive power when the Holy Spirit comes on you; and you will be my witnesses in Jerusalem, and in all Judea and Samaria, and to the ends of the earth." The phrase "the resurrection out from among the dead" comes from Acts 4:2. So you see, all the way through the Bible there are many hints and indications that only fit into a future reign of Christ on earth. Are you with me so far? That is my answer to the absence of confirmation elsewhere in the New Testament; it is there if you look for it.

But secondly, we turn to the alleged presence of contradiction, and the main argument here is that there are texts that imply the simultaneous occurrence of events that Revelation 20 separates. In other words, there are events that in Revelation are separated by a thousand years, which in other parts of the New Testament appear to happen together with no thousand years in between.

There are two in particular. First of all, the resurrection of the righteous and the wicked is mentioned as if it all happens on the same day. Let us take one example. In John 5:28–29, Jesus said, "Do not be amazed at this, for a time is coming when all who are in their graves will hear his voice and come out—those who have done what is good will rise to live, and those who have done what is evil will rise to be condemned."

Now, that sounds as if the resurrection of the righteous and the resurrection of the wicked are the same event, whereas Revelation 20 puts them a thousand years apart. Or we can turn back to John 5:25: "Most assuredly, I say to you, the hour is coming, and now is, when the dead will hear the voice of the Son of God; and those who hear will live." I believe that that can be spiritualised, but it is also true that Lazarus and Jarius's daughter heard the voice of the Son of God and came back from the grave. I do not believe that verse is a reference to the End Times, but it is often quoted as that. But verse 29 is, and it looks as if the two resurrections are together.

The next two things that appear to come together elsewhere are Matthew 25:31 onwards—the sheep and the goats parable. It says, "When the Son of Man comes, he will separate the people, put the sheep on his right and the goats on his left," as if it all happens together at his coming. Here the coming and the last judgment have been put together, but when the Son of Man comes, he will judge separately.

There are other texts. For example, 2 Thessalonians 1:7, "God's vengeance against persecutors will happen when the Lord Jesus is revealed from heaven," which, again, sounds as if the judgment and the Second Coming happen together. Now, it is on the basis of those apparent contradictions that the postmillennialists say there is no millennium after Christ's coming.

The third thing that they point to is the phrase, "The day of the Lord," which covers the Second Coming and the Last Judgment and the same phrase is used for both, "The day of the Lord". If you take the word "day" with anything like a literal sense of 24 hours, it means that the coming, the Second Coming, and the Judgment happen on the same day. But I believe the word "day" in "day of the Lord" is being used far more generally in the sense that man has had his day and God will have his. The day of the Lord covers quite a period, actually. If you read the phrase, "The day of the Lord" in the Old Testament, it covers a lot of events. It is the day when God puts things right rather than the 24 hour period as many take it to be.

Now, what do we say about those others—the resurrection of the righteous and the wicked appearing to be together and the Second Coming and the Day of Judgment appearing to be together? We are here dealing with prophecy, predictions about the future. One of the characteristics of prophecy in the Bible is what we call "prophetic foreshortening", as if the prophets look through a telescope into the future and see events squeezed together through the telescope. It is as if you were looking at mountains from a long way away through a telescope, and you saw two peaks that looked to be together. But if you went to them, you would find a big valley in between. You find this telescoping happening constantly in all predictions about the future. They see things as so close that they cannot see the gaps in between them.

For example, the Old Testament only sees one coming of the Messiah. But we now know that between his first and his Second Coming is a huge gap of at least 2,000 years. But looking ahead through the centuries, they saw the two comings together. They spoke of only one coming, both to save and to judge. We now know that he was coming first to save as the suffering servant and the second time to reign as the King of kings. But they saw him coming as Saviour and King together. That is why, of course, they did not recognise Jesus as the Messiah, because he did not come to rule. But he will do it on his Second Coming.

Now, this foreshortening of future events is characteristic of prophetic vision. They see future events together, so they could see both resurrections as the resurrection of everybody, the first and Second Coming as the coming of the Lord. In fact, this happens with many other prophetic visions, that later in the Bible they get separated in time. Do you follow me? Things that are seen together actually take place at different times. I am sure that is what has been happening in both these cases. When you are looking forward through 2,000 years, it looks as if the Second Coming and the Day of Judgment are right together.

But later, it is explained that they are not together. It looks as if the dead rise all at the same time, righteous and wicked, but when you get closer to the events, as you do in Revelation, you see that, in fact, they are separated by some time. This explains Jesus' parable of the rich man who died, and it says he was in Hades suffering the fires of hell. Now, that is a contradiction, isn't it? Because Hades is where people go after they die, not hell. The fire follows the Day of Judgment, which is still in the future.

But Jesus telescoped the two to get across his point in a parable. He was not trying to teach a complete programme of future events. He wanted people to realise that the state of that rich man beyond death was much worse than here. So, he squeezed Hades and hell together and had the man suffering and tormented in the flames in Hades, which is an anachronism. But you see, to make his point, he squeezed the whole future into one picture.

That is what prophets were constantly doing, squeezing the future into one picture. But in fact, it is like seeing the distant mountains through a telescope, all crowded together, but then you walk towards them, and when you reach them, you find there is a great valley in between them, and they are quite a long way apart. I believe that is what happens as you go through prophecy in the Bible.

Go through prophecies in the Old Testament; they are squeezed together, but they gradually get spread out in the New Testament between the first and Second Comings of Christ and between the first resurrection and the second, and the whole thing becomes clearer, and the valleys in between the peaks become clearer.

Let me finish with the Old Testament. The Old Testament is full of prophecies about the future of a day on earth when the saints will reign on the earth, a day when the earth will be filled with the knowledge of God as the waters cover the sea. In particular, Daniel 7 repeatedly makes these predictions.

Let me just run through them. It says he saw "one like the Son of Man, coming with the clouds". It continues: "He was given authority, glory, and sovereign power; all peoples, nations, and men of every language worshipped him. His dominion is an everlasting dominion that will not pass away, and his kingdom is one that will never be destroyed." Then further on we read: "But the saints of the Most High will receive the kingdom". And some lines below: "the Ancient of Days came and pronounced judgment in favour of the saints of the Most High, and the time came when they possessed the kingdom". It is all on the earth. Then the sovereignty, power, and greatness of the kingdoms under the whole of heaven will be handed over to the saints, the people of the Most High.

My question is "When?" I believe Revelation 20 picks up all that from the Old Testament, as well as the hints in the New Testament, and gives us a crystal-clear picture that after Christ comes again, the kingdoms under heaven will be handed over to the saints of the Most High, and they will reign over the nations.

That means us. And, of course, if you really believe this, you realise that the job you will get on this earth in the millennial kingdom relates directly to how you do your work today, how faithful you are now, how reliable you can be looking after other people's property now. So, what a motivation this is. He is coming back to earth and, of course, many Christians I have talked to have not even realised that if Jesus is coming back, then so are we. It is here that we get our new bodies and when he comes back even all the dead Christians come back with him. Why back here? So that we can show this world what it can be like.

I finish with one promise in the New Testament. The New Testament promises that one day every knee will bow and every tongue confess that Jesus is Lord. They will not confess that Jesus is Saviour, but they will confess he is Lord. When? I believe that is in the millennium. Well, you must study the different views; you must come to your own conclusion and conviction. I can respect people who hold a different view, provided they have searched the Scriptures and they are not just passing on what they have been told.

I can respect someone who has a different conviction than mine, provided they have done as much work as I have in studying the Scripture and really come to their conclusion that way, and they are not mishandling or twisting the text to fit their ideas. Well, that is enough for this chapter. In the next chapter, we will look at Revelation 21 and 22, the happy ending. You must read that; otherwise, Revelation will leave you depressed, and I want to leave you rejoicing.

Chapter 9

HAPPILY EVER AFTER

We have reached the end of the book of Revelation and the end of history, the end of our world. It is the only book in the entire world that can tell you how the world will end. I want to begin by reminding you that we are in the good news section. We have left the bad news behind now. We are into the section to which I will give the title "Things will get much better after they have got worse." So, it is going to be good news, but we are not quite finished with the bad news yet. There is one last little bit of bad news that comes out in a most surprising way.

Let us go back to the seven visions with which this book closes. Very few people notice these seven divisions because the chapter divisions have cut them up into three parts. I am afraid the chapter divisions in the Bible are very naughty. They should never have been there, and they often put asunder what God has joined together. But we have these seven visions, all of which begin with these simple words: "I saw". On either side of the seven visions, it is a case of "I heard", "I heard", "I heard", You see, God brought some things to John's ears and some things to his eyes. Some things are verbal and some things are visual. Here we are in a series of seven visions—"I saw".

In the last chapter, we went through the first five. The first four belong together in every series of seven in the book of Revelation; then the next two go together, and the final one is something quite on its own. This series of seven follows that pattern of four, two, and one. The four visions that go together, which we looked at in the last chapter, are all concerned with Christ coming again to deal with the unholy trinity that controls the world at the end of our age; namely, the devil, the Antichrist, and the False Prophet.

He deals with them in a big battle, which we call Armageddon, after the Hill of Megiddo, where this final confrontation takes place. But there really is no battle; with a word, Jesus kills all the forces that have been gathered by those three awful beings to try to destroy Christ and the Christians. They have gathered a great army to deal with the millions of Christians who will have gathered in the Middle East with Christ.

So, the first vision is of Christ coming again, what we call the *parousia*, the arrival. The second is an angelic invitation to the vultures to come and clean up the mess after the battle because there will be too many bodies to bury. The third vision is the battle itself, which is not really a battle; the kings and their armies are destroyed, and the two human puppets of the devil, Antichrist and the False Prophet, are thrown into the lake of fire.

They are the very first two human beings to go to hell—nobody is in hell yet, not even the devil. Those will be the first two human beings to be sent there, thrown there as you throw rubbish away. People are always thrown into hell; they are not sent there; they are not told to go there. They are thrown there. That is the verb that is always used.

An interesting comment is made from which we get our understanding of what hell is like. It says, "They will be tormented without rest day and night forever and ever." That is where we get the doctrine, the belief, in eternal suffering, everlasting suffering. It is in this chapter and some other verses that are scattered through the New Testament.

Then, in the fourth vision, we see that Satan was not sent to hell or thrown into hell at that point, but he is clearly banished from the earth and totally isolated and prevented from engaging in any further activity that deceives the nations, so that he is out of the picture. With the departure of all the military forces, with the throwing into hell of the Antichrist and False Prophet, and with the complete isolation of Satan, that leaves this world in a political vacuum without a government.

It is the next, the fifth vision, which tells us what fills the vacuum; namely Christ and those who have been faithful to him now take over world government. With Satan out of it and Christ back in, and Christians running it, the world will be a very different place. This, of course, involves the resurrection of Christians at this point.

This is why chapter 20 makes it quite clear that there will be two resurrections—one at the beginning of this period of the saints reigning and the other at the end when the rest of mankind is raised. So, there are two major days of resurrection at the end of history. One is when Christ comes. Christ will raise all his followers, and in particular, John notices that those who have been killed for their faith are now taking the place of the authorities that condemned them to death.

Now comes the great surprise. It comes at the end of that period of a thousand years. Whether it means exactly a thousand or that is a round number for a very long time, I do not know. Every commentator agrees that it is a long period, and whether we take it literally or metaphorically, it is for a long period. But at the end of the period, Satan is released again. Now, that really is a shock.

Why on earth should God do that? We are not told the reason, and I can only speculate and guess, but to me it makes sense. You see, the humanist lie is that if only people lived in a perfect environment under a perfect government and justice and peace were everybody's experience, then people would be good and would love God, and they only do not love God because they suffer, or the world is in a mess or because there is injustice and immorality and inhumanity.

All that will change when Jesus takes over world government. Yet it says that when the devil is released it will be at the end of that period of peace, prosperity, justice for all, a time of greatly extended life, so that a person dying at 100 will be counted as a premature death, a time when even nature will be changed so that wild animals will live together without preying on one another, so that little children can go and play anywhere in the world, even with wild animals. It sounds like a dream, and yet that is what will happen.

Yet at the end of all that, Satan can still deceive enough people who want to be free of the government of Christ and Christians. Far from being content with a perfect environment, human nature is still sinful, still rebellious, and still willing to be talked into a revolution by Satan. It is at that point that Satan gathers people—it says, from "the four corners of the earth".

To that great company marching on the Middle East, this book gives the name Gog and Magog, which is a quotation from the book of Ezekiel chapter 39, where he predicts that even after the coming Son of David has perfectly ruled the world for a long period, people will want to rebel. Gog and Magog are the mysterious names given to the ruler and the people who will rebel—Gog being the ruler, Magog being the nation.

Now, we will not know the meaning of those two names until it happens. Where will they come from? Who will the company be led by? We do not know. What we are sure of is that they will not get very far. In fact, it says that this time God himself will deal with them by sending fire from heaven as he sent it down on the fire of Elijah on the top of Mount Carmel.

I have held a piece of stone in my hand from Elijah's altar, a piece of limestone that on one side has been turned into a green crystal by the sort of heat that you get in an atomic explosion, which is so intense that it can melt the stone, and after it has been melted, it forms crystals. I have held a piece of Elijah's altar in my hand from Mount Carmel, which has been melted by the fire of God on one side. It sends shivers up your spine to see what the fire from heaven can actually do; it can melt rock, that is fire, and that is what will happen to this great company.

It is at that point that the devil is thrown into hell and not before. It says he joins the Antichrist and the False Prophet, who are already there and have already been tormented for a thousand years. Now the stage is set for the great division of mankind, which will happen on the Day of Judgment. You see, at this point, it is absolutely clear that there are those who want to live under Christ's rule and those who do not. Nothing could be clearer. There are only two sorts of people in the world: those who want to live in the kingdom of God and those who do not. It is as simple as that.

So, having demonstrated that even when the perfect government of God is established on earth, when the kingdom has come on earth as it is in heaven, still, there are people who do not want it, there is nothing more for God to do except divide people into the two groups, and that is what the Day of Judgment is all about. It is to divide the human race into those who want to live by God's rules in his kingdom through Christ and those who do not. This is shown by the way people have lived on earth, by their deeds.

Now, let us be quite clear: We are justified by faith but we are judged by works. The basis of all judgment is what we have done while in the body. What we have done is the evidence of whether we want to live God's way or our own way. That evidence has all been recorded. Our words have been recorded because speaking is something we do. Our speech—Jesus said, "For every careless word we shall be brought into the Day of Judgment." Careless words reveal you more than carefully thought-out words, when you have prepared what you are going to say; things that slip out when you are off guard reveal you much more readily than prepared speeches do.

That is why we are surprised to hear famous people use swear words when they are caught off guard. It comes as a surprise because you never hear famous people, such as royalty, swear when they are making speeches. But when they are off guard, it slips out. That is the real self that comes out when you are careless about your words, and that is when people know what you are really like. So, our words and deeds have all been recorded.

It says that on that day, books will be opened. I have a feeling they might have a red cover and that the title might be, "This is Your Life." Frankly, if everything I have ever done and said is recorded in a book, "This is Your Life, David Pawson," then I would have to say, "I'm damned," and I would have to say, "God, you are justified in sending me to hell." It says that all the dead reappear for that day—this is the second resurrection, the rest of mankind. Even those who drowned at sea, whose bodies are nowhere to be found, they also reappear. So, as we were saying in the last chapter, all the victims of the Titanic, the Lusitania and the rest will all be there so that the dead reappear.

But at the same time, it says, "the first earth had passed away. Also, there was no more sea". So, there is a reappearance of human beings and a disappearance of everything else on that day. Therefore, God does not have an earth in front of him or a sea, he just has the people who lived on earth and drowned at sea. Then the books are opened—one book for each person.

But there is another book that is also opened. It is called the Book of Life. In a sense, it is the book of another person's life called Jesus, and, of course, his life was perfect. But that book of his life also includes those who have had faith in him and remained faithful to him. Now, that is very important. It is not just a book of faith people, it is a book of faithful people; people whose lives have been full of faith since they came to Jesus Christ. That is the emphasis of the whole book of Revelation: "He who overcomes shall be clothed in white garments, and I will not blot out his name from the Book of Life".

The Book of Life is mentioned in four books of the Bible. It is mentioned in Exodus, Psalms, Philippians, and Revelation. The interesting thing is that in three of those books, the talk is of names being rubbed out of the Book of Life. As I mentioned briefly in chapter 7 of this book, Moses had an argument with God one day. God was fed up with the children of Israel because, having rescued them from slavery, he saw that they just got right back into their bad ways. Moses tried to "twist God's arm".

We read in Exodus 32:32–33 how very boldly he said to God, "But now, please forgive their sin—but if not, then blot me out of the book you have written". God's response was, "Whoever has sinned against me, I will blot him out of my book." The first mention of the Book of Life in the Bible concerns blotting out God's people who went back into their old ways.

In Psalm 51, David through his sin with Bathsheba, broke five out of ten commandments: he coveted his neighbour's wife, bore false witness against the husband, stole the wife, committed adultery with her, and murdered the husband. That is five out of ten commandments broken in one day. But when David was confronted with his sin by Nathan the prophet, he was so overcome with shame that he begged this of God: "Hide your face from my sins, and blot out all my iniquities." He knew that he deserved to have his name blotted out, but he pleaded that it should not be.

Here again, in the book of Revelation, we have this warning that a name once in that book can be rubbed out. As mentioned in chapter 2 of the present book, the literal phrasal verb there is "scraped off", because in the days of writing in ink on parchment or papyrus, the way they rubbed out was to take a penknife and scrape the ink off it. They did not have rubbers; they scraped the ink off so that they would be able to use the paper again. That is the verb used here: "The one who is victorious will, like them, be dressed in white. I will never blot out the name of that person from the book of life."

So, it is for those who have faith in Jesus and remain faithful to Jesus even to the point of martyrdom. One little proof of what I am telling you is that the word "faith" and the word "faithfulness" are exactly the same word in both the Hebrew and the Greek languages, and can be translated either way, so that faith and faithfulness are the same thing.

You really cannot say that you have faith in Jesus if you are not faithful to him. You see, if you believed in me today but did not believe in me tomorrow that would not be real faith, would it? It is not one moment of faith that saves us; it is a life of faith. It is the faith we finish with, not the faith we start with, that opens the kingdom of heaven to us.

One other little point, do you notice that it does not say who is sitting on the Great White Throne on the Day of Judgment? It just says, "and him who sat on it". It is not God the Father. That is the great surprise that people are going to get. It is not God the Father who sits on the Great White Throne on the Day of Judgment and divides people into two groups. It is the Son of Man who will separate the sheep from the goats. It is Jesus who will sit on that Great White Throne, because God the Father has appointed a man to have this responsibility.

And I am sure you have heard of that monologue called "The Great Silence". I cannot remember it all, but I can summarise it. It says something like this: "On the Day of Judgment a great company of people stood before the throne and said, 'You don't know what it's like to be human; you don't know what it's like to be tempted more than you can bear; you don't know what it's like to be born illegitimate; you don't know what it's like to be arrested by the police for a crime you never committed; you don't know what it's like to be put to death before your time; you don't understand.' Then they looked at the one on the throne, and they realised he did know all that, and there was a great silence."

Now, it is a very telling monologue, but that is the clear teaching of Scripture, of Jesus and of Paul, that it is not God the Father who will judge us on that day. It is Jesus who will separate one from another, and divide us into two groups and say to the one, "Come you blessed of my Father," and to the other, "Depart from me, you cursed, into the punishment prepared for the devil and all his angels." There is never any hint whatsoever in the whole New Testament that hell will be different for human beings than it is for the devil and the angels. It is the same place, the same punishment, the same destiny, and it is almost too horrible to contemplate, but the Bible tells us the truth.

So now we have got to the seventh vision, and, as we have seen, with every series of seven there are four, then two, and then one that is quite different and stands on its own. The last of the visions in this last series of visions is of a new heaven and a new earth. Now, let us get very clearly in our minds that we are not talking about *heaven*. We are talking about new *heavens*, plural. That is the word that the Bible uses for what we call space, where the stars are, the whirling planets—new heavens. You see, it is the phrase at the beginning of the Bible: "God created the heavens and the earth". The earth is this planet, and the heavens refer to everything else in our physical universe.

Now, we do not say, "Our Father who art in the heavens," we say, "Our Father who art in heaven." That is different; that is higher still; that is beyond the universe, as it were. But the heavens, from the beginning to the end of the Bible, are where the stars are, where the sun is, where the planets are, where the moon is—everything outside earth. Therefore, the new heavens and the new earth mean a new physical universe because the entire universe is to be recycled; never mind this earth, the whole universe is to be recycled. When Peter tells us in his second letter that it is to be dissolved in fire, I personally think it is going to be like this: every element of a wooden lectern that I use to teach a congregation is made up of atoms, each one of which is packed with fire, with energy, and we have now learned how to release that fire in some of the elements of the earth like plutonium.

We have not learned how to release them from wood yet. But God could; he packed them all in there, and the energy packed into this universe is enormous, and all that God would need to do to dissolve the whole universe in fire would be to release what holds those atoms together. I believe what he will do is release all the energy he has packed into the universe and then pack it again into a brand-new recycled space and planet Earth. That is as I see it.

The proof that he will do that is, I believe, that he has done it already to the body of his Son. For that is what happened to the body of Jesus; the old body that was buried in the tomb dissolved, passed away, which is why the grave clothes simply collapsed, and he came out of the tomb with a new body. If he had come out with the old body, he would be dead now, because the old body was subject to the old laws, and it would have grown older and died again of old age if Jesus had not been crucified. But Jesus is still alive because he now has that new immortal body, which we are going to get and which the entire universe is going to get. God is going to create an immortal universe. This one is full of death and decay; it is winding down.

The two laws of thermodynamics tell us that. The first law of thermodynamics is that the amount of energy in this universe remains constant, the same. But the second law of thermodynamics is that it is becoming increasingly useless, which means that for practical purposes it is running down. For example, once it is burned, the energy that I use running petrol in my car, is almost impossible to get back again, although the same amount of energy is still in the universe after I have driven somewhere. Nevertheless, I cannot get that energy back; it has become useless.

So, for all practical purposes, this world is running down, and the scientists tell us how many millions and millions of years it will be before the sun runs out of fuel and the earth cools down. It will not be millions and millions of years. God is going to do it long before that and dissolve this universe into its energy and from that create a new earth and space that will have the same characteristics as our new bodies.

What a concept. It is almost beyond your imagination to think of an immortal universe and us having immortal bodies in it, and you will not sing the line in the hymn "Abide with Me" "Change and decay in all around I see" in heaven or in the new earth. But your car begins to rust almost as soon as you have got it out of the garage. Everything is decaying. My teeth are decaying, my hair is decaying, everything is decaying, but that will not be true about my new body. It is not true about Jesus' glorious body. It will not be true even about the earth on which we live. The whole thing is going to be recycled.

But very quickly after the vision of a new universe, the attention shifts from the creation to the Creator, to the one who does it. Here we have an astonishing exclamation of the angels and they say, "Behold". Now, because that word in the Bible is not a word that we use today, it lacks punch, except for the Welsh. If you are Welsh, "Look you!" would be a good translation of it but in English it means, "Just look at that—hey, quick look!" Or you say, "Quick, come and look at this!" Well, sometimes I have seen Concord taking off and I have said to my wife, "Quick, quick, Concord's just flying over," and she dashes out.

Now, when you say to somebody, "Quick, come and look," then that is what the word "behold" means in Scripture, but unfortunately, we read it in a good Oxbridge accent, and it loses all its impact. But here in Revelation 21:3, the angel says, "Behold, the tabernacle of God is with men, and he will dwell with them, and they shall be his people." Now, that is the exact opposite of what most people think will happen at the end. Most people think we will go to heaven to be with God forever. Actually, the Bible finishes by telling us, "God is coming to earth to live with us forever." It is the exact opposite of what most people think. He is moving house, not us, and we are going to live on the new earth, and he is going to live on the new earth with us, and the new earth will be the very focus and centre of the new universe. That is what it is all about.

Now, the Son of God has been here on earth, and the Spirit of God is here on earth, but the Father has not been on earth since the very beginning; but he was then. Do you remember when Adam heard footsteps in the Garden of Eden, and they were

God's footsteps? God was taking an afternoon stroll on earth. You never hear of that happening again until the last page of the Bible. There are so many things that crop up again in the last pages of the Bible that you have not heard about since the first pages. The Tree of Life pops up again for the first time since the first pages of the Bible.

It is as if you have come full circle and you are back at the beginning again, and yet you are not back where you were; a whole lot has happened in between, and it is different. It is not going to be quite the same. For one thing, we shall all wear clothes in the future. There is no return to nudity in paradise; it has been dangerous for us ever since. So, there will be some differences.

There will be no sun. In fact, I was preaching in Sydney, Australia, about the new earth, and I said to them, "In the new earth, there will be no sun, no sea, and no sex." There was a dead silence, and nobody shouted "Hallelujah," and they all looked as if they wanted to get out of there quickly and get down to Bondi Beach, which was only five miles away, and that is where they worship all three. But then I said, "Listen, the new earth will be so wonderful that you won't even miss any of those three things." That tells you how amazing it is going to be, and we shall all be married, incidentally, to Christ.

So, it is going to be different, yet there is a sense of déjà vu; there is a sense of second time around; there is a sense of going right back to the beginning. That is why the beginning and the ending of the Bible are so important. That is why if the devil can possibly keep you out of the early chapters of Genesis, he will; or if you do get into them, he will tell you that it is myth. He wants to keep you out of the last bit of the Bible as well because he hates you to know how it began and how it will end. He wants to keep you in present-day existentialism and not think about the past or the future too much. But it is from the past and the future that we get our bearings and understand where we are in the present.

Then there is quoted a formula which runs right through the

Bible: "They will be his people and he will be their God." If you underline those words, you will find that they run all through the Bible. In every rope used in the Royal Navy, there is a red thread running through it. Did you know that? In every rope in the Royal Navy, and the whole way through the Bible this thread is running: "I will be their God and they will be my people"; "I will be their God and they will be my people"; "I will be their God and they will be my people." That is what the whole story of the Bible is about: God wanting a people for himself to bear his name, to love him, to be his larger family. So, we get that lovely refrain coming right here in Genesis 21.

Then he makes the statement, "Behold, I make all things new," or in modern terms, I am recycling every single thing I ever made. That is a statement. It is not just a promise; it is a statement of what he is even then engaged in. He is going to renew, recycle, not just us, but every single part of this physical universe in which we live—all things new. It is a wonderful statement.

Then he tells John to write. Time and time again, God has to remind John, who is so awestruck with what he is seeing that his pen stays in his hand and the paper is blank, that he needs to write. All the way through the book of Revelation, John is told to write. Here in chapter 21, he is told to "Write, for these words are true and faithful." Poor John in prison gets his pen again. I do not know where he got a pen—perhaps somebody smuggled it in to him—and he is writing it down again. Write it down, you're not writing. Every time he is commanded to write, you can assume he has stopped writing, that he is so absorbed in what he is seeing and hearing that his mouth is open, his eyes are out on stalks, and he is just lost. Write it down, John.

Then he begins to talk about a new city, a city built out in space. That is what the Americans and Russians would have loved to have done, but I do not think it is much nearer than it was. But God is going to build a city out in space. Now, this holy city is the place where Jesus promised to go and prepare for us.

Did you know that Jesus has gone back to being a carpenter, or at least back to making things with his hands again? He said, "I go to prepare a place for you." He talked as if he would take the people to that place, but now it is revealed that, in fact, the place will come to the people.

He sees this city coming down out of heaven like a bride adorned for her husband. Now, let us underline that he does not say that this city is the bride. The bride is the people. The bride has made herself ready. It only says the city is like a bride adorned for her husband coming down out of heaven.

Now, I remember my daughter's wedding. We held it in a hotel, and I took the ceremony, and she walked down the main staircase by herself into this lovely setting of a baronial hall, where we had it, and she was just beautiful, she really was. I had never seen anything like it. I had seen her in all sorts of conditions, mind you. I had seen her right after she had just washed her hair and all the rest, but she came down looking like a queen, in the most beautiful white gown, and her hair was carefully done, her complexion was looked after. That is the image I have in my mind when reading this: "Coming down out of heaven from God, prepared as a bride adorned for her husband". In other words, everything is just perfect, just beautiful.

Now, one of my hobbies is architecture. I design church buildings on the side. I remember going to look at one for a fellowship in Southampton that was almost complete. It was very satisfying to see what began as a sketch on my dining room table up in bricks and mortar. But you have to live with your mistakes—that is one snag. But I am fascinated with architecture, especially the architecture of new cities.

I have studied Canberra in Australia and Brasilia in Brazil. Both these cities dammed up a stream to create water down the middle of the city, which is an interesting exercise because that is exactly what the New Jerusalem will have: water running down the middle of the city. It seems as if water in the middle of a city makes the city. I thought of that when I walked along a bridge over the Thames.

But the thing that interests me is this: How do you create a large city that feels like it is on a human scale and feels homely for people? That is the architect's biggest problem. You see, high-rise buildings are not homely; huge blocks of apartments, such as you have in Brasilia, are not home. How do you create a huge city so that when people see it, they say, "Oh, this feels just like home. I want to live here." It is an awful problem, and we are told that this city is about 1,500 miles across in length and height. It is a cube, which has, of course, the exact proportions of the Holy of Holies in the temple—exactly the same dimensions three ways.

I am just waiting to see the architecture that God uses to solve the problem of a city that size, which, if the moon were hollow, would only just fit inside the moon. That is the size of it. It would stretch from Warsaw to Paris. Now, how do you have a city that big while ensuring that people feel at home there and do not feel lost in it? Well, God will have solved the problem because he is the architect as well as the builder.

Abraham lived in a very nice brick house, two storeys with central heating and running water in the house, in Ur of the Chaldees. We know that from archaeology. He left at the age of 80 and lived in a tent for the rest of his life. At 80! I do not know many people who would do that at 80! If he had not done it, you would not be reading this book. But you know, Abraham did it, and in Hebrews 11:9–10 it says, " By faith he made his home in the promised land like a stranger in a foreign country; he lived in tents, as did Isaac and Jacob, who were heirs with him of the same promise. For he was looking forward to the city with foundations, whose architect and builder is God." He was content to live in a tent because he believed in the city whose architect and constructor was God. He saw that city.

Now, if you can keep that city in your mind, you will be more content with where you live here. That is the truth. There is an old hymn that Christians used to sing years ago: "A tent or a cottage, what do I care? He's building a mansion for me over there." Well, it is a little naïve, but they had the right idea. They did not try to get everything into the ideal home here because they were looking forward to living in a much better place. So, this is the city that Abraham believed in.

Its size: 1,500 miles three ways. Its shape: a cube, the Holy of Holies. Its beauty is breathtaking—I shall come to that in a moment. Its openness: the city gates are never shut. You can come and go. You can go and have a holiday on Mars and come back, come back home. The whole universe is open, and the gates are open. We will look at the beauty of it in a moment.

Before that, let me describe the lake of fire. I was in Sicily some time ago, and as we took off in the British Airways plane, I was hoping we would fly over Mount Etna so that I would be able to see the volcano because I wanted to climb it. You can actually climb it and look down into it, but there were two reasons why

PHOTOGRAPH 9

we could not: the snow was too thick on it, and it was erupting; there was red-hot lava running down, destroying villages.

So, the British Airways pilot flew right over it and right over it, he tipped the plane right up on one wing, so we looked out of the window straight down into the boiling cauldron. I tell you, I was not only fascinated, I hoped he would move on fairly quickly. I thought, "If that thing blows again now, we've had it." But I looked down into that red-hot, boiling rock; it is fearsome, and yet it is probably the nearest thing on earth you can get to a picture of the lake of fire, or literally the sea of fire, a sea of flames.

Now, let us look at something quite fascinating. You know that the city is going to be constructed in materials that are rare in this world, so rare that they are called precious stones, and we pay a fortune for some of them, and women wear them as jewellery. Engagement rings usually have a precious stone in them.

Now, here is the fascinating thing that has only been discovered in the last few decades, because in the last few decades, we have been able to make pure light, straight light. You have heard of laser beams—very straight light. Normally, the light we are used to is coming at us from all angles; it is bounced. Light is being bounced off the walls, it is being bounced off the white paper that I hold up to my face, and light is normally bounced, so it is coming at it from all directions.

Now, if you have some Polaroid sunglasses, that is a kind of filter that only allows straight light to come in, and it cuts out all the bounced light from other directions. So, if you are at the seaside and you look at the sea, you cannot see the waves flashing because that is bounced light. You can only see the straight light so it is much easier to look at a bright scene with Polaroid sunglasses.

Now, if you take the two lenses out of Polaroid sunglasses and you put them on top of each other and turn them, one of them to 90 degrees, that becomes a much finer filter, and purer light comes through. I am simplifying it, but when you shine light onto a jewel through cross-polarised filters, as they are called—two

Polaroid lenses turned at right angles—then you are getting a very pure light through them.

With every jewel, one of two things will happen. Either it will lose all its colour and go black like coal or it will suddenly have all the colours of the rainbow, whatever colour it was to start with. It may have been red like a ruby, blue, or green like an emerald. Whatever colour it was, it either loses all its colour or it gains all the other colours. All precious jewels do one thing or the other. To give you the scientific term, the ones that gain all the colours are called anisotropic, and the ones that lose all their colour are called isotropic, and all precious jewels are in two groups, one of two groups.

Now, here is the fascinating thing. The 12 precious stones that God is going to use as material for the New Jerusalem are all anisotropic; they all become all the colours of the rainbow, and we pay a fortune for a precious jewel—Elizabeth Taylor, $500,000 for a diamond—yet in pure light it looks like a piece of coal dust. Let us look at those 12 stones *(see page 229)*.

These 12 stones are the ones that God is going to use in the New Jerusalem. God is not going to use the other ones (diamond, ruby, garnet) because in pure light, they would not look any better than a lump of coal. Now, here is the amazing thing: this was only discovered in the last few decades. How did John the Apostle know which stones unless God told him?

In this fact alone, you have got the proof that the Bible is the Word of God because the only person who knew about this in those days was God himself. We did not know, and people were paying a fortune for these jewels despite not knowing that they relied on bounced light. That is why you cut a diamond into anything up to 72 faces or facets so that it catches every bit of bounced light. But in pure light, a diamond has no colour at all. So, this is proof that the Bible is the Word of God, but there is more to it than that.

I have a little piece of jasper. That is one of the favourite stones

Happily Ever After

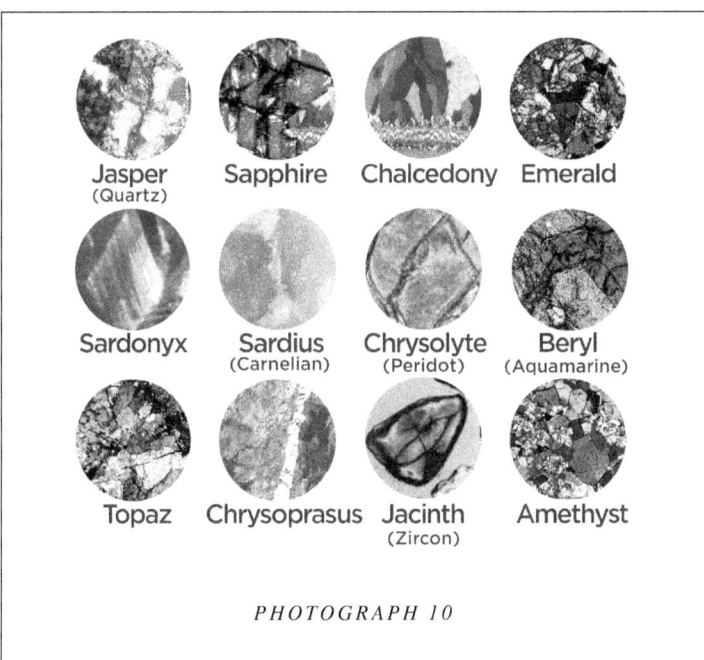

PHOTOGRAPH 10

of God, a speck of dust seven thousandths of an inch in size. Can you imagine how small that is? You can see the New Jerusalem in a speck of dust. That is what the dust will look like in Jerusalem. The colouring is absolutely fabulous.

But it is not just the colour, it is the shape. I am sure you know that it is much easier to build with angular stones than round

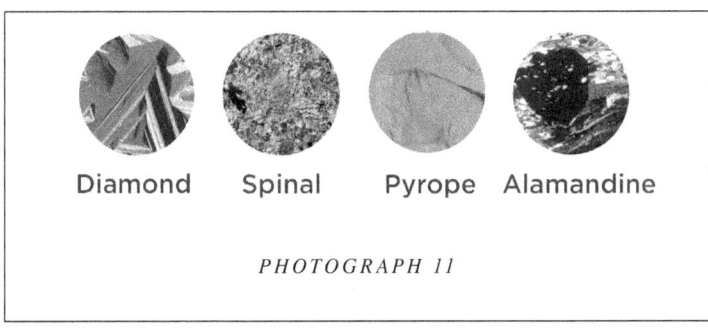

PHOTOGRAPH 11

stones. You try to build with round stones! I was in the Lake District, where they built a lot of stone walls, and they have nice angular slate stones to build those stone walls with. But I saw one wall in the Wastwater area up at Wasdale Head built of round stones. How the thing stayed up, I do not know, but what skill would be needed to build a wall of round stones?

Now here, again, there are two sorts of precious stones. There are angular stones and there are round stones. Which do you think are the stones of the New Jerusalem? Those are the stones that God is going to use. He is not going to use any of these precious stones because they are not much use for building, they are too round in their crystal form. So, God knew which precious stones to choose, and those are the stones that John has revealed in chapter 21.

Well, we could go on. The river of the water of life runs through it. The Tree of Life is back again, and we shall live on a diet of fruit, and the fruit trees will bear crops once a month. Do you like fruit? Well, you had better, but I will tell you, it will be the most wonderful fruit you have tasted. The leaves are for the healing of the nations. And above all, we shall see God. We shall actually see his face. I wonder what it will look like. He is going to reveal himself in a face to us and for the very first time human beings will see God's face. I will tell you what I think it will look like. I think it will look like the face of Jesus; we shall see the family resemblance. But how wonderful it will be to see God's face, and we shall serve him, and serve him gladly.

There are two misconceptions that I find Christians tend to have. The first one is that it will be an eternal holiday camp, and that is not good for anybody. There will be work to do; satisfying, creative, fulfilling work to do. But the other misconception that I find very common is that it will be an eternal Sunday morning service. You know, singing every chorus 17 million times. Have you had that misconception? I think of a little boy who turned to his mother in the middle of a sermon and said, "Mommy, is it still Sunday?" Do you ever get that feeling? Well, it is not going to be like that either. We shall be serving God; we shall be doing the most interesting, creative, fulfilling, satisfying things.

There will be no darkness there; there will be no cathedral or churches there. That will save quite a bit of money. It will be a truly international city with all the different nations represented, and the throne of God and of the Lamb will be in the city. Above all, the two peoples of God on earth will become one because the names of the 12 tribes of Israel and the names of the 12 apostles of the Church are engraved on that city, which tells us that Jew and Christian will be together as one people of God in the city.

But who will get into it? We are told two things in chapter 21. First, he who overcomes will inherit all this. Again, we have this tremendous emphasis in the book of Revelation on the overcomers, those who stay faithful and obedient to Jesus, whatever happens, those who overcome all the pressures outside them and all the pressures inside them to be faithless and disobedient; it is those who overcome who will inherit all of this.

But it then says, "The cowardly and the faithless and the immoral and the deceitful will be thrown into the lake of fire." Now, I want you to realise that that little list is addressed to believers, and the whole book is addressed to believers. It is not written to unbelievers. It is written for the seven churches of Asia, and the cowardly and the faithless and the immoral and the deceitful are, in fact, believers who have gone back into their pre-Christian life. That is the worrying thing, and we need to hear that.

A little later on in the chapter it says, "Nothing impure will ever enter it, nor will anyone who does what is shameful or deceitful, but only those whose names are written in the Lamb's Book of Life," and, of course, the present tense there, "are written", means, "are still written", "are now written"; only those whose names are now written in the Book of Life. The lake of fire, you see, is mentioned right up to the very end of the book. Note the order: before the Day of Judgment, Antichrist and the False Prophet go to hell; they are human beings. Later, the devil himself goes there. It says that after the Day of Judgment, all those whose names are not in the Book of Life will go there. Of course, Jesus always used the Valley of Hinnom as a picture of hell (Gehenna), and it was the rubbish dump of Jerusalem, and you do not place rubbish, you throw it. That is why that verb is always used of hell because it is God's rubbish dump.

What happens to those who are thrown into it? The great debate that is going on at the moment, and for which I wrote my book, "The Road To Hell", is between believers in annihilationism and believers in eternal torment. Are people incinerated or incarcerated in the lake of fire? That is the big question. Chapter 20:10 seems to me to be the total answer to it: "they will be tormented day and night forever and ever", or literally "till the ages of the ages". There is no stronger term in the Greek than that.

I do not think annihilation will ever be feared or contemplated with horror, yet Jesus talked of hell in terms of the utmost horror. Weeping and gnashing of teeth does not sound to me like annihilation. So, it is a common assumption, I am afraid, that Christians are certain to go to heaven and non-Christians to hell. It is not quite as simple as that. It is those who are faithful to Jesus and who overcome who will inherit the new heaven and the new earth and the New Jerusalem. So, it is a fundamental misunderstanding here that we are once saved, always saved.

The bad deeds which qualify people, including believers, for the lake of fire, are listed twice at the end of the Bible. You have that list, to which I have already referred, in chapter 21:8, and in chapter 22:15, there is a similar list. Here the people who continually persist in these ways are called "dogs", and there will be no dogs in the city; it says they will be outside, outside the whole new universe.

There is an addition in that second list of practising magic, occultism, astrology, playing with Ouija boards, tarot cards—all that is included. Believers must avoid superstition. Remember, this book is addressed to Christians. Sin is always sin; whether it is an unbeliever or a believer, sin is sin. The believers know what to do with it. If we go on confessing our sins, he is faithful and just to go on forgiving our sins, and the blood of Jesus goes on cleansing us from all sin. Therefore, says the letter to the Hebrews, "Make every effort after that holiness, without which no one will see the Lord." You see, if we went to this place as we are now, we would pollute it. It is so important to press on, to be clean, to be pure, ready for the city.

We have now reached the epilogue of the book of Revelation. Chapter 22:7–21 is an epilogue. But now with the unholy trinity having been dealt with, we now have the holy Trinity emphasised: God, the Lamb, and the Spirit. So, the Holy Trinity is now in the forefront. There is a strong emphasis on timing in this epilogue: "The time is near," "I am coming soon". Indeed, the word "soon" occurs four times in the epilogue: verses 6, 7, 12 and 20. Well, 19 centuries have passed. What do we make of the word "soon"? It is a relative term from heaven's viewpoint; it is soon for God. For God, a thousand years is as a day, and therefore it has only been a couple of days, the last 2,000 years. But what we can say is all this must be even sooner for us than it was for the original reader 19 centuries ago.

So, this epilogue says that a choice must be made now. In this epilogue, it says, "The day of opportunity is still open." The thirsty may still come and drink freely of the water of life, so the day of opportunity is still open. Yet there is a warning that a day is coming when destiny will be irrevocably fixed and unchangeable. Verse 11 has the sentence, "He who is unjust, let him be unjust still; he who is filthy, let him be filthy still; he who is righteous, let him be righteous still; he who is holy, let him be holy still." In other words, there will come a time when it is impossible for the dirty to be cleaned, but the day of opportunity is still open.

The thirsty may still come, and on the very last page of the Bible, there is the invitation, "And the Spirit and the bride say,

'Come!' And let him who hears say, 'Come!' And let him who thirsts come. Whoever desires, let him take the water of life freely." The believer must take this water of life now while they have the opportunity and before the day comes when they will be fixed morally in the condition in which they are. So, for all of us, death fixes that destiny. Your character is fixed the day you die. That is the end of the opportunity to come freely and there is an emphasis here: "It's free, come and take it. It's a free gift." You do not have to earn it; you do not have to work for it, just come and take it, but then remain faithful to Jesus.

At the very end of the book, there is a section all about the book itself and its significance. It is called a prophecy four times—in verses 7, 10, 18, and 19. This is a prophecy and, therefore, it is a word from the Lord and therefore it is to be treated as sacred. It is a word from God; it is a word to man. The things in this book were not discovered by human beings, by human reason. They were declared by divine revelation; they were shown to John. John could never have thought up all this himself, nor could any other human being have written this book. God showed it through prophecy to man.

It was delivered through an angel. Angels are only God's postmen. They are only his messengers. John himself made the mistake of worshipping the angel who brought him all of this, and the angel said, "Get up off your knees, I'm just God's servant like you are." We must not worship angels, or demons for that matter; only God is to be worshipped.

It has come directly from Jesus, who is given two new titles in this epilogue. He is the Root and Offspring of David. Now, how strange, the Root and the Shoot of David. David came from him, and he came from David. Isn't that interesting? The Root and Offspring of David. He is also called the Bright Morning Star. I wonder if you have ever been up early enough to see the bright morning star; when all the other stars have gone, there is always one left shining, and it is down low near the horizon. It is a wonderful title. It means here that when all the pop stars and film stars and stars of the human race have all disappeared, there will be one Bright Morning Star. The Bible also promises that we shall shine like stars, but there will be one Bright Morning Star.

When I read that, I think of The Beatles. I think of John Lennon's infamous claim that the Beatles were more famous than Jesus. What incredible impudence. Well, he came to a sad end, and when John Lennon and The Beatles are long forgotten, the Bright Morning Star will still shine. That is what it means. It is for the churches. By the way, look at all the titles of Jesus in this epilogue: The "Root and the Offspring of David, the Bright and Morning Star", and earlier in verse 13, "the Alpha and the Omega, the Beginning and the End, the First and the Last"—all these titles just piled up to put the attention on Jesus, for that is where it belongs at the end of this wonderful book.

It finishes by saying that you must be very careful how you treat this book. There is a curse attached to this book; it is the only book of the Bible that has a curse attached to the book itself. This curse does not refer to the whole Bible; it refers only to this prophecy. Revelation 22:18–19 says, "I warn everyone who hears the words of the prophecy of this scroll: If anyone adds anything to them, God will add to that person the plagues described in this scroll. And if anyone takes words away from this scroll of prophecy, God will take away from that person any share in the tree of life and in the Holy City, which are described in this scroll."

That is a solemn warning to Christians not to meddle with this book. Yet I have to say it with tears that Christians all over this country are tampering with this book and changing it to fit their own ideas. That is why it is urgent that it must be clearly and properly taught. Even if you find it difficult to accept, do not change it. Do not add your own thoughts to it, and do not take anything out of this book. You can take things away from this book simply by ignoring things that are in it.

Well, it finishes very positively, including the words: "Amen.

Even so, come Lord Jesus!" The earliest prayer in the Church is on this scroll, and we have it still in its original language, which the early Christians prayed: "Maranatha! Maranatha!" And it means: "Come Lord Jesus! Come Lord!" One of the definitions of a Christian in the New Testament is someone who is waiting for God's Son from heaven. I think that is a lovely definition of a Christian. A Christian is someone who is waiting for God's Son from heaven.

Do you know that the coming of the Lord Jesus is, in fact, mentioned 318 times in the New Testament? Do you know that the Cross is mentioned about the same number of times? The two most important things for the Christian to remember are the Cross of Jesus and the Second Coming of Jesus. We live between the two; we look back with gratitude for one, and we look forward with expectancy to the other. We look back in faith for what God has done for us; we look forward in hope for what he is going to do for us, and meanwhile, we seek to live in love as he intended us to do. That is why faith, hope, and love are the most important things in a Christian's life.

We want these seven final visions to happen as soon as they possibly can. If you want those seven things to happen soon, then "the Spirit and the Bride say, 'Come,'" and the Holy Spirit within the members of the Bride focuses them on the Second Coming. It has always been a mark of any move of the Holy Spirit of God among his people that there comes a much greater emphasis on the return of the Lord Jesus Christ. It is one of the tests of revival. There are others like repentance and conviction of sin, but the eager hope of the second coming always surfaces again when the Holy Spirit of God moves in a fresh way.

Well, we will stop there, and in the final chapter, we shall look first at one of the areas of controversy that we have raised and finally at some of the positive reasons why the Church of Christ today needs to be studying the book of Revelation.

Chapter 10

CAN BELIEVERS LOSE THEIR INHERITANCE?

In this book, we have tried to look at some of the controversies—questions over which Christians disagree. There is one big one that I must face before the end of this book. We have touched on it a number of times. It is the question of once saved, always saved, and whether our salvation can be lost, whether having begun the Christian life, we are on an escalator that will land us at the top sooner or later or whether it is a walk that we may or may not finish. In other words, it is one thing to start; it is another thing to finish. Two and a half million people came out of Egypt, but only two got into Canaan. That is held before believers in the New Testament as a warning to us by three different writers: by Paul, by Jude, and by the person who wrote the letter to the Hebrews. All of them say many left Egypt, but only a few got into Canaan, and Christians need to remember that.

The question is acutely raised in the book of Revelation, which, as I have tried to show you, is throughout addressed to believers. It is written to all the saints. It is written to the Lord's servants. It is written to the seven churches. It is the most unsuitable book to give to unbelievers. I would never give this book to an unbeliever to read. It is addressed to believers to help them to endure and overcome so that they may inherit the future and keep their names in that vital Book of Life.

Now, this is not the only book to raise the issue. Two other books in the New Testament raise it acutely. The letter to the Hebrews is well known for raising this question because it has some of the most severe warnings concerning those who drift away or neglect their salvation or stop meeting together or deliberately go on sinning after they have been forgiven. Hebrews is full of warnings.

The other book in the New Testament that is very strong on this is the Gospel of Matthew. It is in this Gospel that we find almost all of our Lord's teaching about hell. When you study the context in which he spoke of hell, you find that almost all of his warnings are given to believers, not unbelievers, not sinners. For example, one of the clearest things he ever said was, "Don't be afraid of those who can kill your body and after that do nothing more. Rather fear him who can throw body and soul into hell."

Now, who is he talking to? He is not talking to sinners at all. He is talking to his own disciples just before he sent them out as missionaries. He did not say, "Teach others to fear hell," he said, "You fear it. As you preach to others and demonstrate the kingdom, if you fear him who could throw you into hell, you will not fear martyrdom," because the greater fear swallows up the lesser fear. But, in fact, as we shall see, every writer in the New Testament warns believers to keep on believing and points out what will happen if they do not.

So, the phrase itself, "once saved, always saved," is not in the Bible, although it is so often quoted as if it were the Word of God. But it is not in the Bible, and I am not even sure that I know what it means. What does the first half mean? Once saved—once saved from what? If you say once saved from sins, then I am not once saved yet. It is still going on. I am not perfect yet. I am going to be. My wife finds that difficult to believe. It takes her faith to the brink of doubt. But she relies on God's Word that one day her husband will be perfect, and I keep assuring her of that. It is the promise of God—that he ain't done with me yet.

But nevertheless, people usually mean once saved from hell, and they usually mean once safe from hell. But is that so? Salvation is a process. It begins when we first believe in Jesus. It will be finished when he comes back, and we shall be like him, for we shall see him as he is. So, from one point of view, I am not saved yet.

In fact, the verb "saved" occurs in the New Testament in three tenses. The New Testament says we have been saved, we are being saved, and we will be saved. Now, which of those three tenses is most common, do you think? The answer is the future. Salvation is something the New Testament teaches us to look forward to. It says in Hebrews 9:28, for example, that he will appear from heaven a second time to bring salvation to those who are waiting for him.

Peter, in his first letter, says that we are waiting for a salvation, ready to be revealed, and we are looking forward to the process being completed, with even our bodies saved. So, I do not even understand the first part of this little phrase, once saved. I do not think I will be able to say even that until Jesus returns. Then I will say, "I am now totally saved. I really am. The process is complete."

Unfortunately, it is Church history and tradition that has confused this issue, in particular, through the man I have mentioned before, who really has done more damage to the Church than any other man, I believe. Yet he has been sainted and we call him Saint Augustine. He emphasised predestination and taught that God's power is such that he cannot be resisted and once he has elected you and once he has predestined you, that is it, and there is nothing you can do to alter that. His emphasis went through to the Protestant reformers and was picked up by Luther very strongly. Luther wrote a book, *The Bondage of the Will*. Neither Augustine nor the Protestant reformers could cope with the fact that God has given us the freedom to resist his will.

Actually, Calvin is usually quoted or blamed for the belief that you cannot be lost. Those who believe you cannot be lost once you have been "saved" or born again are usually called Calvinists. I am sure you have heard this. Those who do not believe that are usually called Armenians after a man called Arminius, who denied Calvinism. Actually, if this does not confuse you too much, it was not Calvin himself who taught this so strongly, but rather his successor, a man called Beza. It is Beza who is really responsible for the phrase "once saved, always saved". Arminius argued with Beza, not with Calvin. But since Beza's name is not known, Calvinism is usually the label that people apply.

But Calvin himself said this. He wrote a very famous summary of the Christian faith called "The Institutes of the Christian Religion". Calvin's *Institutes* are world famous. This is what he says at one point in that book: "Still, our redemption would be imperfect if he did not lead us ever onward to the final goal of our salvation. Accordingly, the moment we turn away, even slightly, from Christ our salvation, which rests firmly in him, gradually disappears. And as a result, all those who do not repose in Christ voluntarily deprive themselves of all grace." Now, that is Calvin. I agree wholeheartedly with that.

In other words, you do not have salvation apart from Christ. You are not given eternal life like a package that is now yours apart from Christ. The Bible says that this life is in his Son, and as long as you stay in the Son, you have that life. That is why, in John 15:1, Jesus said, "I am the true vine," and in verse 5: "I am the vine; you are the branches. If you remain in me and I in you, you will bear much fruit; apart from me you can do nothing. Then, in verse 6, Jesus says, "If you do not remain in me, you are like a branch that is thrown away and withers; such branches are picked up, thrown into the fire and burned." It separates from the vine, it goes dead, and it is cut off and burned, said Jesus, so we are to abide in him. It is the same context.

There is nothing that we have outside of Christ. We have not been given anything to have by ourselves without him. Everything we have we have in him. There is no condemnation for those who are in him—not those who were once in him, but those who stay in him and are in him. Do you see? This emphasis on continuing in Christ, on staying in Christ, on going on believing in Christ runs all the way through the New Testament.

Now, this is not salvation by works. I am afraid that many Calvinists say that this is teaching salvation by works. No. It is not by works, lest any man should boast. We are saved by the grace of God. Regeneration is God's creative work in us. Salvation is God's work in us from beginning to end. There is no reason why any believer should lose their life in Christ, because once you have begun, all heaven's resources are available to you. God the Father is on your side. It is his will that you should be completely saved. He is able to do it, and he is able to keep you from falling, and he is faithful to his promises.

God the Son is on your side, and he ever lives to make intercession for us. He is praying for us. God, the Holy Spirit, is on your side, and he wants to be with you forever. He is earnest about our inheritance, the foretaste of what we will acquire one day in Christ. So, the Father, the Son, and the Holy Spirit are all on your side to give you the grace to complete what has been started. So, there are many texts of encouragement and comfort. John 6: "This is the will of him who sent me, that I should lose nothing of all that he has given me, but raise it up at the last day." John 10: "I give my sheep eternal life and they shall never perish. No one can snatch them out of my hand." Romans 8: "For I am convinced that neither death nor life, nor angels nor demons, neither the present nor the future, nor any power, neither height nor depth or anything else in all creation will be able to separate us from the love of God that is in Christ Jesus our Lord."

Here are the other relevant verses: John 6:39, 10:28; Romans 8:38–39. Philippians 1:6: "being confident of this very thing, that he who has begun a good work in you will complete it until the day of Jesus Christ". 2 Timothy 1:12: "I know whom I have believed, and am convinced that he is able to guard what I have entrusted to him until that day". 1 Peter 1:5: "who through faith are shielded by God's power until the coming of the salvation that is ready to be revealed in the last time". Jude verse 24: "To him who is able to keep you from stumbling and to present you before his glorious presence without fault and with great joy."

Now, many have taken those few verses out of context and built upon them a doctrine called "The Perseverance of the Saints". That is a strange word to use because I thought perseverance was keeping at it. But the doctrine is called "The Perseverance of the Saints", and means that saints will persevere, and not the saints must persevere. Now, the normal meaning of the word "persevere" is that we must persevere. But the doctrine of once saved, always saved states that the saints will persevere, whatever happens and whatever they do, they will get there, they will make it.

Now, is this the whole picture? I want to say that I do not believe it is. You can find about a dozen texts like that scattered through the New Testament, which taken in isolation might seem to suggest that once you have got on the escalator, you will get off at the top whatever happens. But the real issue behind all this is a really simple one: Is grace irresistible? That is the very heart of this controversy.

Can the grace of God be resisted, or is it an irresistible force that you cannot stop? The so-called Calvinist—I wish we could call them Beza-ists or something—will say you cannot stop the grace of God. Once God, who is all mighty, all powerful, has decided, nothing can stop what he has decided from coming to pass. Therefore, if he has chosen you as one of the elect, then nothing can stop you from arriving in the new heaven and new earth.

Now, there are two aspects to this question—is grace irresistible before your conversion? In other words, once God has pulled your number out of a hat or your name out of the hat, that is it, and you will be converted. There is nothing you can do about it. Or is it true to say that God calls a person and they can resist that call, resist for a long time, resist all their life and say no? That is the root question: can we say no to God? Can we resist his grace? Or there are some who believe you can resist it before you are converted, but once you have been converted, you cannot resist it, and from then on it is inevitable, and God will force you to come back to him if you slip away.

The creed that has had the most influence on Christians in this country is called the Westminster Confession of Faith and was written out in Westminster Abbey. The Westminster Confession of Faith says this: "The perseverance of the saints depends not upon their free will but on the immutability of the decree of election." Now, again, that has had more influence in this country than perhaps any other creed or confession. I want you to notice that there is not a word about faith in there. In other words, your salvation is entirely the decision of God. It is not your decision; it is his, and once he has decided, that settles it forever. Most evangelicals in England would disagree with what I am teaching you here. They would say there is no risk of your name being blotted out from the Book of Life, none at all. Once it is there, it is there to stay because it was written there from the foundation of the world, and that is it.

So, this has become a doctrine called "The Perseverance of the Saints". That is an ambiguous word. I think they should re-label it "The Preservation of the Saints", because perseverance, as they define it, is divine preservation rather than human persistence. I read it as human persistence, but they would read it as divine preservation. The word "perseverance" is ambiguous.

I believe we are saved by grace. It is God's work, not ours. But we get there through faith, and that is what we need to do. Faith is in the imperative and not the indicative mood. Faith is commanded of us. It is not something that God does; it is something that we do—we believe in Christ. They asked Jesus once, "What must we do to do the works of God?" He said, "Believe in the one whom he has sent." That is what we do. Grace is what God does. Faith is what we do.

Unfortunately, there is one verse that has been badly translated and interpreted. It is Ephesians 2:8. It says, "For it is by grace you have been saved, through faith—and this is not from yourselves, it is the gift of God, not by works, so that no one can boast." Many have assumed, when reading this in English, that the gift of God is faith. But in fact, the gender of "that not of yourselves, it is the gift of God" does not agree with the gender of the word "faith". It agrees with the gender of "saved". It is by grace that we are saved through faith, and salvation is not of ourselves. It is the gift of God. It is not the faith that is the gift. It is the salvation that is the gift.

But unfortunately, that verse has been assumed to mean that your faith itself is something that God brings about and not you. But it is very clear when you read the New Testament that faith is always a human act in response to God's grace offering salvation. But it is not something God does in you. It is something you do in response to that.

I could put it this way. If you were drowning in the River Thames and someone threw a rope to you and said, "Grab hold of this and keep hold of it until I get you pulled in," then your grabbing hold of the rope and keeping hold of it would be faith. But the person pulling you is the person who saves you. You have not saved yourself. If you went around boasting afterwards, "I saved myself from drowning by grabbing hold of the rope," that would be ridiculous. But you had to keep hold of that rope until you got safely to shore.

That is the clearest picture I can give you. Salvation is not of yourself; grabbing hold of a rope does not save you. It is the person pulling the rope who saves you. But you need to grab hold and keep hold of it until you are safe on shore. That is how we are to see it.

I was given an article on the middle voice that is so common in the New Testament. Now, we do not use the middle voice in most of our normal speech. We use either the active or the passive voice. The active voice is when I do something—I walk. The passive voice is when somebody does something to me—I am carried.

But the middle voice is where I agree to somebody doing something for me, and I have to take the initiative so that he can do it for me. "Grab this rope so I can pull you to safety," would in Scripture be in the middle voice. You see, you are not saving yourself. But you have to do something so that somebody else can save you.

The word "baptised" in the New Testament is in the middle voice. You do not baptise yourself, or it would be in the active voice. It is not just something done to you, although it is to a baby. The baptising of a baby would have to be passive because the baby is doing nothing about it except yelling its head off. But in Scripture, it is in the middle voice. In Acts 22:16, Ananias says to Paul, "And now why are you waiting? Arise and be baptised". That is the middle voice. It is not something he could do for himself, but it is something for which he had to take the initiative before it could be done. Then the rest of the sentence goes, "and wash away your sins, calling on the name of the Lord".

In other words: Nobody will force you, Paul, to be baptised. You have to ask for it. You have to rise and be baptised. But somebody will do it for you. Do you see what I mean? That middle voice perfectly combines this idea: I am saved by the grace of God, but I need to believe in him and grab hold of it. There is a beautiful balance there. Now, in the same way, this is where Scripture is so careful. It says we are saved by going on believing, by continued faith, by abiding in the vine, by continued trust and obedience.

The verb "believe"—and here is another bit of Greek for you—is often in the present continuous tense, which means to go on doing something. Jesus did not say, "Ask, and it will be given to you; seek, and you will find; knock, and it will be opened to you." What he did say was, "Go on asking and you will receive; go on seeking and you will find; go on knocking and it will be opened."

Now listen to the famous verse John 3:16 properly translated: "For God so loved the world that he gave his only begotten Son that whoever goes on believing in him will never perish but go on having eternal life." Now, does that alter the sense of the verse for you a little? It is not whoever believes once. It is whoever goes on believing. It is not that everlasting life is suddenly given to you like a package, but you go on having it by going on believing. You must stay in touch with the source of eternal life, Jesus, to go on enjoying it.

Having said that, I just want to run through the New Testament very quickly and show you what the whole New Testament really does say. The first three Gospels, what we call the synoptic Gospels—Matthew, Mark, and Luke—all quote Jesus' words, "He who endures to the end shall be saved." That is future salvation, the completed work, and it is he who endures to the end.

I have already said that in Matthew there are warnings about hell given to born-again believers who have believed in Jesus' name and been born of God, especially in the Sermon on the Mount, which is addressed to sons of the kingdom. The parables of the bridesmaids and their lamps and the talents show that the bridesmaids whose lamps are not burning when the bridegroom comes are not included. The man who has buried his talent and has not used it—and this is said to the 12 disciples—is the man who finishes up in outer darkness.

One parable in Matthew chapter 22, the parable of the wedding feast, finishes up with the story of a man who accepts the invitation to come to the feast, to come to the wedding of the king's son, and then turns up without having changed his clothes. That is as big an insult to the king and his son as it is to refuse the invitation. He is bound hand and foot and turned out.

In Luke's Gospel, Jesus says, "No one who puts his hand to the plow and looks back is fit for service in the kingdom of God." In the same Gospel, Jesus also taught that the salt can lose its saltiness and can never get it back again. These are serious warnings. John, I have already mentioned: "If anyone does not abide in me, he is cast out as a branch and is withered; and they gather them and throw them into the fire, and they are burned." In other words, if you do not stay in Christ, the life of the vine will not be in your branch.

Romans 11:22 is very clear: "provided that you continue in his kindness. Otherwise, you also will be cut off." What could be clearer than "Provided that you continue"? In Galatians 5:21, after listing the works of the flesh, Paul says, "of which I tell you", and "you" refers to believers, saints. He says, "I warn you, as I did before, that those who live like this will not inherit the kingdom of God". He says the same thing in 1 Corinthians 6:10.

In Philippians 3:11, Paul says, "I have not arrived. I press on. I want to know Jesus and to share his sufferings, and so, somehow, to attain the resurrection out from among the dead." That is a reference to the first resurrection in Revelation 20. In Colossians 1:21 23 we read: "Once you were alienated from God and were enemies in your minds because of your evil behaviour. But now he has reconciled you by Christ's physical body through death to present you holy in his sight, without blemish and free from accusation—if you continue in your faith, established and firm, and do not move from the hope held out in the gospel."

Once again, it is *if* you continue—it is terribly clear. In 1 Timothy 4:16, Paul urges Timothy to go on preaching and teaching the Word of God. He says, "Watch your life and doctrine closely. Persevere in them, because if you do, you will save both yourself and your hearers." If you continue teaching them the way of salvation and living it, Paul said that you will save both yourself and your hearers. Then in 2 Timothy 2:12 it says: "If we endure, we will also reign with him. If we disown him, he will also disown us." Jesus himself said that in Luke 12:9.

Hebrews is packed. I will give you the references. Hebrews 2:3: "How shall we escape if we neglect so great a salvation?" That is addressed to believers. Here are some references: 6:4–8, 10:26–31, 10:38–39 and 12:14—there are five major warnings to Christians, to saints, to believers in Jesus. Do not go back on it, do not drift away, do not neglect, and above all, do not deliberately continue to sin.

Then, 2 Peter 1:10 says this: "Therefore, my brothers and sisters, make every effort to confirm your calling and election." That is something that you do; to make your calling and election sure, you have got to do something. So, what have you got to do? He says, "to add to your faith goodness; and to goodness, knowledge; and to knowledge, self-control; and to self-control, perseverance; and to perseverance [that is something you do], to perseverance godliness, and to godliness, mutual affection; and to mutual affection, love. For if you possess these qualities in increasing measure, they will keep you from being ineffective and unproductive in your knowledge of our Lord Jesus Christ." That is clear, isn't it?

But it is 2 Peter 2:20–22 that completely settles it for me. It is so important to reference: "If they have escaped the corruption of the world by knowing our Lord and Saviour Jesus Christ and are again entangled in it and are overcome, they are worse off at the end than they were at the beginning. It would have been better for them not to have known the way of righteousness, than to have known it and then to turn their backs on the sacred command that was passed on to them. Of them the proverbs are true: "A dog returns to its vomit," and, "A sow that is washed returns to her wallowing in the mud." Now, note this carefully: if a person who has escaped the corruption of the world through knowing Christ goes back into it, they are worse off than if they had never known Christ. How that can be so if they are still going to heaven, I do not know. If they are worse off, it means that there is a worse judgment for them than if they had never come to faith, never known Christ. That is clear. The little letter of Jude finishes with that wonderful statement, "Now to him who is able to keep you from stumbling". It does not say that he is certain to, but he is able to. But just above that is verse 21, which says, "keep yourselves in the love of God, looking for the mercy of our Lord Jesus Christ unto eternal life".

It is very clear in the New Testament that grace can be resisted. This is stated many times. You can resist grace (Acts 7:51; Matthew 23:37). You can receive the grace of God in vain. That means you can receive grace and then waste it—2 Corinthians 6:1, Hebrews 12:15. You can insult the Spirit of grace (Hebrews 10:29). You can fall out of grace (Galatians 5:4). Now, all these statements need to be put into the whole mix. It is one thing just to quote half a dozen verses, but you have got to balance them with many other verses—even those verses I quoted to you above that the Calvinists love to quote. Let us look at one or two of them more carefully.

Let us take the one in John 10: "My sheep hear my voice, and I know them, and they follow me, and I give them eternal life, and they shall never perish; neither shall anyone snatch them out of my hand." But that statement has a context. The context is "My sheep go on following me, and none shall pluck them out of my hand." You see, there is a condition in there. Go on following Christ and no one can snatch you out of his hand. He does not say about you jumping out of his hand, he says, "No one else can take you from me when you're following me."

Or let us take another one—Romans 8:38–39: For I am convinced that neither death nor life, neither angels nor demons, neither the present nor the future, nor any powers, neither height nor depth, nor anything else in all creation, will be able to separate us from the love of God that is in Christ Jesus our Lord.

There is one thing that is missing from that list. Do you notice what it is? Yourself. It says nothing else can, but it does not say you cannot.

Look at Philippians 1:6: "being confident of this very thing, that he who has begun a good work in you will complete it until the day of Jesus Christ". That word, "confident", is not the word "certain". It is the word "optimistic", because on the same page Peter, writing from prison facing trial for his life, said, "I am confident that I will be released." But he does not say he is certain. He is ready to die if that happens, but he is optimistic that he will be released. He is optimistic here that the Philippians will go on being faithful to Jesus and have the good work completed in them. Wherever you get a statement in Scripture of God keeping us, somewhere on the same page there is a statement that gives you the condition that you keep in him.

Paul says, "I am not ashamed, for I know whom I have believed and am persuaded that he is able to keep what I have committed to him until that day". By the way, he is speaking there at the very end of his life. Paul is speaking about how he (God) is able to keep him from death until the great Day of Judgment. That is what he means. But in the context, he says, "I have kept the faith". You must relate those two things together: I have kept the faith and now I'm about to die, so I'm persuaded that he is able to keep me from now on until the day. Do you see? So, there are always two sides to perseverance; God is able to keep us, provided we keep trusting him. That is the balance of Scripture, I believe. But you must look into this very carefully for yourself.

I have quoted a lot of verses that question the so-called Calvinist once saved, always saved position. So, what do they do with all these verses? How do they fit them in? The answer, I am afraid, is only too simple. They put them all in one big bag and label it, "Never really born again". In other words, they question whether they ever believed—that if they go back into their old way of life, they cannot really have been converted. I just think that is a cop out, because it is very clear that these verses are about those who are branches in the vine, who are salt of the earth, who are partakers of the Spirit, and who have known our Lord and Saviour Jesus Christ. I cannot possibly apply those to the unconverted.

I have found that people who believe once saved, always saved did not find that in the Bible. They heard it preached by someone. I have discovered that those who know nothing about this controversy and who simply come to their Bible with an open mind, as a new Christian, come to the conclusion that they could lose their salvation if they do not go on believing. But I am afraid it is because the Westminster Confession, the Augustine-Luther line, has been so preached in this country that people think it is in the Bible. I would only ask you to search the Scriptures for yourself and come to your own conclusion. Do not say, "I agree with David Pawson." I do not want you to agree with me. I want you to search your Bible and find out your answer by yourself with an open mind. Look up all the verses.

One man I talked to, a new Christian, had become aware of this question among Christians. So, he just took his Bible, and he took two sheets of paper, and he wrote every verse that pointed one way and every verse that pointed the other way, taking verses out of context by themselves. He came up with about a dozen verses on the side of once saved, always saved. He came up with three dozen verses on the other side. So, then he went back and looked at those in their context and found that in context, they also were on this side. That is what settled it for him. Unfortunately, his pastor told him he was now a heretic because he was in a very Calvinist church.

I am afraid that this division was also seen in the 18th-century revival. A man called George Whitefield preached Calvinism, and John and Charles Wesley preached Arminianism. It was John and Charles Wesley who had the lasting fruit into the 19th century. Alas, the Methodist Church, which was that fruit, has now got into a real pickle. But nevertheless, Whitefield saw little permanent fruit into the next century, whereas the Wesleys did.

But Charles Wesley wrote a little two-verse hymn for people to sing to themselves to remind themselves. This is the hymn by Charles Wesley. We love to sing his hymns, don't we? "And Can It Be That I Should Gain" and "O for a Thousand Tongues to Sing". I wish we sang them all. Well, mind you, he wrote six thousand. So, you can understand why many have gotten lost.

But I have got all of them at home. I love reading them.
Here is this little one:

> Ah Lord, with trembling I confess,
> A gracious soul may fall from grace,
> The salt may lose its seasoning power,
> And never, never find it more!
>
> Lest this my fearful case should be,
> Each moment knit my soul to thee,
> And lead me to thy mount above
> Through the low veil of humble love.

That is a lovely little song, isn't it? I believe he was summing up the message of the New Testament. Well, that is the big controversy. I would simply finish by quoting 1 Corinthians 10:12: "So, if you think you are standing firm, be careful that you don't fall!" Well, what does all this have to do with the book of Revelation? I have tried to show you that the book of Revelation is written precisely to keep your name in the Book of Life, so that you may not fall. So, what did Calvin make of the book of Revelation? He could not handle it. He wrote a commentary on every book in the New Testament except the book of Revelation. Luther said the book of Revelation ought not to be in the Bible. The main Protestant reformer was Ulrich Zwingli in Basel, Switzerland. He said the book of Revelation ought not to be in the Bible. It is interesting that those who believe once saved, always saved find the book of Revelation difficult to fit in. That is significant.

Well, I finish on a positive note. Why read the book of Revelation? We have looked at the curse at the end of it. But it is the only book with a blessing attached to the beginning of it. It says, "Blessed is the one who reads aloud the words of this prophecy and blessed are those who hear it and take to heart what is written in it because the time is near." Other books encourage faith in God's past work and love in his present work. But this book produces hope in his future work. This book encourages ten necessary elements in authentic Christian living. In closing, I just give you these ten things.

WHY STUDY "REVELATION"?
1. COMPLETION of BIBLE
2. DEFENCE AGAINST HERESY
3. INTERPRETATION of HISTORY
4. GROUND for HOPE
5. MOTIVE for EVANGELISM
6. STIMULUS to WORSHIP
7. ANTIDOTE to WORLDLINESS
8. INCENTIVE to GODLINESS
9. PREPARATION for PERSECUTION
10. UNDERSTANDING of CHRIST

DIAGRAM 9

Number one: it is the completion of the Bible, the happy ending to God's story, to God's history. It has a striking resemblance to Genesis. It completes the circle. It is a romance—the Father looking for a Bride for his Son. In fact, the Bible begins and ends with a wedding of God's arrangement. God found a Bride for the first Adam and for the last Adam called Christ, and they get married and live happily ever after. Without the book of Revelation, I believe we would have to call the Bible the Amputated Version of Scripture. It is the completion of the Bible.

Secondly, it is a defence against heresy to know the book of Revelation. If you do not know this book well, you are vulnerable to sects and cults calling at your door. So often the Jehovah's Witnesses get hold of people, church people, who do not know the book of Revelation. They teach their own interpretation of it, which I believe is a twisted one, and because the church member does not know it, they fall for the Jehovah's Witness teaching. Christadelphians and Mormons both have their own teaching on this book. It is a sad thing that the average church member in this country has not been taught this book. Therefore, when somebody calls at the door offering to explain it to them, they fall for it. These callers know it better than most churchgoers.

Thirdly, this book gives us an interpretation of history. Future events cast their shadows before them. If there is going to be one Antichrist, there are now many antichrists in the world. There is going to be one False Prophet, but there are now many false prophets. There is going to be one-world government and one-world economy—we are moving towards that very rapidly in our world. It gives us insight into current affairs and an understanding of our daily newspaper.

There was a cartoon in the *New York Herald*. A little boy was saying to his grandfather in 1948, "Now that Israel is back home, what will happen next?" His grandfather replied, "Hold on, son, while I get my Bible." Now, the Bible does tell us about the future. We can interpret history. The apocalyptic pattern of history fits best. That is the view of history that it will get much worse and then suddenly better. It will get suddenly better when Jesus returns.

Fourthly, it gives us a ground for hope. "Jesus wins" was that American janitor's summary of the book—Jesus wins. There is no doubt about the outcome. God is not surprised. He has not lost control. He is still on the throne. Everything is going according to plan, his plan. Christ will defeat Satan. The saints will inherit the earth and rule it. No human empire will survive, but the Church will be eternal. We are the people of tomorrow.

Although today paganism, secularism, and godlessness seem to triumph, we know that that is part of God's plan. It is the world getting worse before it gets better. We are the real new agers. I am happy to use that term. I belong to the real new age, not the one that people think they belong to. We are the coming people of tomorrow.

Fifthly, the book of Revelation gives us a very clear motive for evangelism. There is no clearer presentation of the alternatives. Either we finish up in the new heaven and the new earth with God on earth with us, or we finish up in the lake of fire. There is to be a day of judgment, after which it will be too late for anyone to change their mind. The day of salvation is still here. Whoever wishes may drink of the water of life. What a motivation for taking every opportunity we can to tell others about God's plan to recycle the earth and put in it everybody who is willing to be recycled now.

Sixthly, the book of Revelation is a great stimulus to worship. It is full of worship, full of singing and shouting. There are 11 major songs in this book, which have inspired many others, from Handel's *Messiah* to the *Battle Hymn of the Republic*. Do you know the *Battle Hymn of the Republic*? "Mine eyes have seen the glory of the coming of the Lord, he is trampling out the vintage where the grapes of wrath are stored." Where does that come from? Straight out of the book of Revelation. "Glory, glory, hallelujah!". where does that come from? Out of this book. The sight of God and the Lamb on the throne, surrounded by angels worshipping, is enough to start you worshipping. "Therefore with angels and archangels, and with all the company of heaven, we laud and magnify thy glorious name; evermore praising thee, and saying, Holy, holy, holy, Lord God of hosts, heaven and earth are full of thy glory".

Seventhly, it is the antidote to worldliness. The problem is that if we are not careful, then from Monday to Saturday, we hardly think of the next world at all. People around us are so preoccupied with this world that the words of the poet Wordsworth come true: "Getting and spending we lay waste our powers." What a description of the world in which we live, "Getting and spending we lay waste our powers."

You see, most of the people around us do not believe there is any other world but this one; they are living 100 per cent for this world. The book of Revelation brings you up with a jerk and says, "Which world are you living for—this one now or that one then?" Colossians 3 talks about those who are earthly-minded and those who are heavenly-minded. Mind you, people tease us, they ridicule us. They use such phrases as "Pie in the sky when you die," and I say, "That's better than pain in the pit when you flit." But nevertheless, they tease us because we are heavenly-minded. But I believe it is right to be heavenly-minded. Paul says in Colossians 3:2, "Set your mind on things above, not on things on earth."

Eighthly, it is an incentive to godliness. It shakes us out of our complacency, slackness, and indifference. It tells us that holiness is essential if we are going to survive the troubles. It calls us to overcome pressures outside and temptations inside. It says blessed and holy are those who rise in the first resurrection. God is always praised in this book as holy, holy, holy. The emphasis on holiness here is an incentive to godliness.

Ninthly, it is a preparation for persecution. Jesus predicted that his followers would be hated by all the nations before the end of history. That has not happened yet. There have always been some nations where Christians are not hated. The number is quite small now. But before the end, we shall be hated everywhere. This is the main reason for this book being written, so that it speaks loud and clear to Christians who are suffering and who are facing suffering. There are a number of voices now, prophetic voices, being raised in this country, saying that we have less than ten years to get ready for persecution here. So, it is important for us to read this book.

Tenthly, above all, it gives us a balanced view of Christ and an understanding of Christ. Without Revelation, you have a distorted picture. This book is called "The Revelation of Jesus Christ". That has a double meaning; it can mean it is a revelation from him, or it can mean it is a revelation about him. I think it probably means both. But here we do not have the pale Galilean or the gentle Jesus, meek and mild. Here we have him riding on a horse with blazing, angry eyes, coming to deal with evil by force. Here we have the Lion and the Ram.

In the Gospels, we have Christ the Prophet. In the epistles, we have Christ the Priest, who ever lives to make intercession for us. But in the book of Revelation, we have Christ the King, the King of kings and the Lord of lords, the Christ with a throne and a crown. The world has never seen him like this, but will one day, and then every knee will bow and every tongue confess. This is the Jesus the world will see. No longer a baby in the manger, no longer a "victim" on a cross; the world will see Jesus on a throne, a great white throne wearing a crown—the carpenter from Nazareth.

My own reaction is that after reading this book, you can never be quite the same again. You can never quite forget about it. It becomes part of your thinking, part of your outlook. Indeed, we need to keep reading it. It says, "Blessed are those who read it and take it to heart." That means you need to let it find a resting place in your inmost being so that it becomes part of you. I have not taken you through this book just to prepare you for an exam or so that you might qualify and get a certificate from a Bible college. I have written these words because you are a Christian, and you need this book, and you are going to be teaching others, and they need it too. And because of all the confusion that has surrounded it. I hope I have clarified it a bit for you and at least brought you to the point where you feel, "I'm beginning to get hold of it and I feel I can begin to teach others what this book is saying." So, God bless you as you do so.

www.ingramcontent.com/pod-product-compliance
Lightning Source LLC
Chambersburg PA
CBHW052018070526
44584CB00016B/1806